J C:

Also by John Ciardi

JOHN CIARDI: Dialogue
with an Audience

J. B. LIPPINCOTT COMPANY
Philadelphia and New York

FIRST EDITION
Manufactured in the United States of America by H. Wolff, New York
Library of Congress Catalog Card Number 63–15440
Design: Marshall Lee

PN
1064
.C5

FOR NORMAN COUSINS

—in that corner, wearing the purple trunks.

ACKNOWLEDGMENTS

All but two of the pieces here collected appeared in *The Saturday Review* and the old *Saturday Review of Literature*.

Acknowledgment is due to Norman Cousins and *The Saturday Review* for permission to reprint Mr. Cousins's editorial titled "John Ciardi and the Readers," which appeared in *The Saturday Review* for February 16, 1957. And certainly special thanks must be given to *The Saturday Review* for granting permission to reprint many letters from its Letters to the Editor page as necessary documentation to some parts of this collection.

"The Act of Language" is here reprinted from *The Saturday Evening Post*, copyright 1960 by the Curtis Publishing Company. "Poetry Is for Pleasure" is reprinted from *Glamour*, copyright 1960 by The Condé Nast Publications. Grateful acknowledgment is hereby made to both.

Acknowledgment is also due to Blanche C. Gregory and *The Saturday Review* for permission to reprint Lord Dunsany's article, "The Poets Fail in Their Duty."

CONTENTS

THE SITUATION OF POETRY

PREFACE

This selection of magazine pieces is gathered, with four exceptions, from those I have written for *The Saturday Review* in my seven years as Poetry Editor. Two of the present pieces appeared in the old *Saturday Review of Literature* thirteen years ago, and two of them, written while I was *SR*'s Poetry Editor and originally intended for *SR*, appeared in other magazines that happened to ask for an article and that happened to offer payment at rates *SR* could not match nor my greed resist. My sins noted, it is still accurate to say that all but these two *SRL* pieces were written from an editorial sense of *SR*'s particular and particularly vocal readership. They are part of a dialogue I have been having with an audience.

The most characteristic thing I know about that audience is that to write for it is precisely to engage in a dialogue.

The "Letters to the Editor" page is *SR*'s family rumpus room and anyone may join in the free-for-all. Let me say that I have refused to take any part in selecting the letters to be printed on that page. Three or four times in the last seven years, Norman Cousins has sent me letters he thought involved *SR* policy and has asked me to reply. With those exceptions, I read the letters to the editor when the readers do— after they have appeared in print.

I do read them, to be sure, as I read the thousands of letters addressed directly to me. I have, moreover, crisscrossed the country on free-swinging lecture tours in the course of which I have talked to many thousands of *SR* readers face to face. By now I think I know this audience.

It is no monolithic thing: how could it be? But certainly its central characteristic is its profession of faith in the life of the arts, and its central merit resides in the fact that large parts of this audience not only profess that faith but live in it. If there is such a thing as a "general audience" for the arts in America, SR speaks weekly to several hundred thousand members of that audience in the cities, in the suburbs, and in the far reaches.

The idea of a general audience is not one that is received in universal good standing. The *avant-garde* is fond of mocking such an idea as middle-class and middlebrow. And it is true, I think, that this audience, at its lowest levels, falls into "the suburban vague" of those willfully hopeful souls who chatter what should be spoken, and who play at what should be lived by. Yet, at its center—and above its center, at its best—this audience is most of what there is for the arts to speak to today.

Poetry is the least engaged art in any modern society. It is the habit of our cultural pretensions to invite it to the wedding, but only as an attendant. At dark times, I am half ready to think it does no good to address a general audience for poetry; that poetry is, finally, for none but the passionate marriage, and, like all that is passionate, is necessarily more than an attendant grace (which is to say, a part-time venture).

Perhaps what is wrong with all our lives is that none of us is born with enough experience to qualify as a specialist, while the forces of our comfortable, conforming (and yet, let it be noted, uneasy) society too readily persuade us to remain unspecialized in our own perceptions. We are all—all but the best and rarest of men—given to more emotions than passions. To the extent that only psyches of special intensity can achieve a passionate and liberating involvement in their own lives, the art of enlarging one's own awarenesses may be only for the specialist. It is not easy to endure a change of imagination. That man is mad who thinks he may, by mere "general interest," achieve the special perceptivity for which a Dante must prepare himself by rigorous (and joyfully rigorous) disciplines. Since poetry is passionate or nothing, it is pointless to try to bring it to those who dabble in amateur easiness. If the general audience offers no more than that amateur easiness, there can be no hope of bringing art to such an audience.

But if that hope is foregone, we may as well tear down our liberal arts colleges and leave only the technical schools standing. For what justifies the liberal arts curriculum except its central effort to bring the passionate excellences of the arts—poetry among them—to a general audience of undergraduates who are not much different from *SR's* general audience except in being younger, and many of whom are a part of the *SR* audience?

When I came to *SR* I was still a professor of English at Rutgers. I gave up teaching later because I found my own papers more interesting to work on than those of my students, and because I found a tax problem to be more interesting than planned poverty. I have already confessed that greed is among my sins. But as best a sinful man might, I had been trying for years to bring poetry to that general audience of undergraduates, and my heart was pure in that effort. I could not believe then, nor can I now, that poetry has no place among them, that there is no such thing as a nonspecialized audience for poetry, nor that the effort to discuss poetry with such a general audience is in a lost cause. Karl Shapiro has made the point that any piece of literature must finally be judged by nothing less than the total of those who speak its language, and if I may first underline the word *finally*, I must agree with Shapiro. My own notion of the "vertical" as opposed to the "horizontal" audience (see the last fourteen paragraphs of the first piece in this collection) is close to Shapiro's point. The hope for poetry does not lie in the immediate popular reaction of the horizontal audience but in an increasing accumulation of the vertical. The good of any dialogue on poetry is that it may lead some parts of the total audience to a more "vertical" view.

For the attempt to popularize poetry too often succeeds only in prostituting it. The audience must be brought up to the life of the poem, not the life of the poem down to the audience. Nor can everyone be raised to the height of good poetry. It takes attention, and the labor and joy of shaping one's attention are beyond the conversation of most minds.

Yet I cannot believe that only the specialist can talk to the specialist. That dialogue of specialist to specialist already exists in academic circles, nor am I inclined to argue for its suppression, though I believe it has developed a needlessly intramural language.

Significantly, as I believe, that language is more generally written than spoken. When I was teaching at Harvard I found myself in regular weekly talks over coffee cups with a good friend, a professor of philosophy and a specialist in aesthetics. Our talks, I think I may say, were a love feast. We seemed to bring light to one another's thoughts and the more deeply we shone the light the more deeply we seemed to agree. Those were glorious talky hours, and one day my friend capped my pleasure by leaving with me a batch of monographs he had written for philosophical journals on the very subjects we had been discussing so long and so happily. I raced off to my cubbyhole in Warren House ready for joyous reading. And I was in despair by the end of the first paragraph. I simply could not understand what was being said. I tried. I gathered together an unabridged dictionary, and several textbooks in aesthetics whose glossaries or whose indices might explain the special language of the monographs, and I asked for help from friends who had majored in philosophy. I had to end by confessing defeat and I had to return the monographs with the embarrassing confession that I did not know how to read them. Their language was unknown to me.

Monographs for a professional journal may be a special case. But even the critics of the literary quarterlies lean needlessly toward jargon. Among them, none has produced a more specialized language than has Kenneth Burke. Burke's is not an unsolvable language, and the reader who will develop a tolerance for it will be rewarded. Yet, to note again the difference between the written and the spoken language of many critics, I must report that I have found Burke a greatly rewarding man to talk to and that his conversation conveys lively insights without requiring a glossary.

Praise all that makes visible. Yet I continue to sense in Burke's written language the—to me—appalling premise that the English language urbanely and sensitively used is not capable of describing its own poetic achievements and possibilities. Burke's written language moves in distrust of the very English whose poetry he discusses, and I am left no choice but to distrust that distrust.

The fit dialogue on poetry will take place in the mother tongue. It will phrase itself in what Dante called "the language of the court" and Matthew Arnold "the language of the center." For myself, I think of it not as the language of the man on the street, but as the language that would be spoken on the street if every man on it spoke his mother tongue in love and pride.

The pieces in the present collection have been written, as fallibly as must be, toward the dream of such a dialogue. They are not exactly continuous. Yet to the extent that they were written out of my developing editorial sense of *SR*'s particular audience (including those few published elsewhere), they are all parts of one dialogue.

Since that dialogue has been interrupted by controversial exchanges, and since the controversies, in the nature of things, have received more attention than has been paid to the continuity of the dialogue, I hope the present gathering may help set the controversies to scale. My aim has been to establish a responsible dialogue, not to squabble. My notions of poetry may be shallow or they may be badly presented. Such as they are, they are an effort at an honest exchange: what motive could there be for any other effort? For such reward as it is (and it is one I value), I know from the mailbag and from the various editors who have anthologized many of these pieces for use in high schools and colleges that my notions have seemed useful to some readers. It still seems appropriate to add a note on (if not necessarily to) those I seem to have offended.

The mask of innocence has never looked plausible on me and I shall not try to draw it on. I have yet to find much merit in innocence as a human condition and must prefer even imperfect knowledge to perfect innocence. Yet I must enter as a confession of ignorance, if not of innocence, that I simply did not foresee such hot and lengthy controversy as my views on poetry have called forth. (Though I think I recognized all the patterns of thought of these controversies as they unfolded. Which is to say, I suppose, that I knew such views existed, but that it had never occurred to me to take them seriously, except as I had had to chide students for them from time to time.)

The hottest controversy, as *SR* readers know, raged around my review of *The Unicorn*, a review some readers took to be a calculated bid for attention—as if I could have dreamed that bad poetry could have become a two weeks' wonder as a national issue. I confess that I had not realized when I wrote that review how deeply many *SR* readers, particularly women in their fifties and beyond, had identified with Mrs. Lindbergh in what she had suffered, and, thence, in what she wrote. I did, however, labor carefully to make the opening point that I was not discussing Mrs. Lindbergh, but only that character-invented that every author must be within the role of his pen name. That distinction remains intellectually valid, I submit, and it will so remain after all of us are invalidly dead.

There is no point, however, in explaining here what is fully, and perhaps fulsomely, parsed out in the pages that follow. Any reader may review and interpret the exchange for himself. Let me hope that such a review, removed in time from the journalism that rode with the original exchange, will make my intent clear. To assist such a review, I have dated the various parts of the controversy and reprinted them in their original sequence. (For the rest of this collection, I see no point in attaching to each article its quota of letters in blame or praise, or in dating the articles, or in presenting them in strict chronological order, and I have not done so.) I cannot, however, pass over these controversies without adding a note or two on some of their less visible background.

In gathering these pieces from the back-copies file, I have even discovered an earlier, though lesser, controversy I had not known about at the time it occurred. Let me begin with it.

In 1950–51 I was on a half-year leave from Harvard and my wife and I were church-mousing it into a full year in Europe. We were in London when SRL cabled that Edna St. Vincent Millay had died; would I write a summary of her poetic career? I was a bit surprised by that request from across the water, for I had had only one earlier article in SRL ("What Does It Take to Enjoy a Poem?," SRL, December 10, 1949). Once, however, I had read Millay with real passion, and I welcomed the idea of thinking back to that passion. The cable reached me late one Friday afternoon and copy had to be off by airmail on Monday morning. I began to make notes that Friday night but I had few books by me and none of Miss Millay's poetry. My head was still full of her lines, however, and I quoted from memory as I went. I spent most of Saturday prowling London bookstores for copies of her books in which I might check my quotations and reread her poems, but though I tried for eight full hours, I could not turn up a single copy.

I returned to my desk to scribble and revise, still quoting from

memory, scribbled and revised again all Sunday morning and afternoon, and finally two-fingered the piece through the typewriter on
Sunday night. I could scarcely pretend that the passion of my adolescence was still with me as I said the poems over to myself, but I
found myself writing with the sort of nostalgia one might feel for a
lost love. So passed Sunday. Monday morning I was at the American
Embassy Library when the doors opened. There I found two volumes
of the poems and managed to check three or four of my quotations.
And by then time was up. I added a note to *SRL* explaining the state
of the quotations and underlined the need to check all but the three
or four I had marked with an asterisk. Adding another sentence asking
that the check be sent to my sister for deposit to our skinny account,
I dropped the whole thing in the mail and forgot about it.

We were in Paris when the article appeared (November 11, 1950). I
did not see it, nor did I know the quotations had not been checked (I
have here left them exactly as they were first published). We were in
Germany and then in Austria in December, January, and early February. I did not see *SRL* and I did not know that angry letters had
been written to the editor. I first learned of those letters when I began
to search the back files in preparing the present collection. I was immediately struck by the fact that the early letters were identical in
their terms, tone, and preconceptions with the letters of protest I later
received.

The central preconception of all these letters of protest, early and
late, involves an idea of poetry. Defenders of that idea like to say that
poetry should be *simple, sensuous,* and *passionate,* but they never add
what is also of the essence, that it must be disciplined and learned. (By
"learned," let me say, I do not mean footnote-learned but, rather, responsive to millions of passionately registered details of the art of
writing. Perhaps, most simply, I mean that the writer must come to
his writing informed by the hundreds of wastebaskets he has filled with
despairingly shredded manuscript.)

Most of the readers who have been outraged on critical (as distinct
from personal) grounds favor *simplicity, directness, sense, beauty, inspiration,* and *message*—these are their chosen terms. They tend to
hate—again their own terms—*difficulty, obscurity, unintelligibility,
this modern stuff, analysis* (more often called *dissection* or *carping*

criticism), and anything smacking of technical attention, which they tend to call *mere technical detail*. They want a poem to sit squarely on the page, each line to begin with a capital letter, and the whole thing to move to a mellifluous diction and a regular meter. Any departure from these norms is likely to strike them as *typographical absurdity, gibberish,* and *ugliness*. They have a predilection for what they call *beautiful images, the eternal verities,* and *elevation*.

Behind all these honorable terms, as I see it, they want poetry to be traditional, easy, and rather in the grand manner. They have a nearly endless tolerance for stereotypes—of phrase, image, rhythm, and attitude. And though they proclaim *the beautiful*, they are generally ready to settle for mere prettiness. Above all, they seem prepared to be offended by any poet whose work goes beyond what they studied in their two years of college literature courses, or who demands of them a mortal and venturesome mental effort.

Poetry, I must believe, is a deeper engagement than the shriller lovers of beauty conceive it to be. Beauty and truth are no irrelevancies. Neither can they exist except as they are specified in the given form of a given work. The good poet makes beauty, but what he seeks is reality. It is on his way to reality that he captures specific instances of beauty. He knows, moreover, that the beautiful and the pretty are never the same thing. He does not write differently from the Romantic and Victorian poets because he hates them, but because he has to find the language, images, rhythms, and forms of a world the Romantics and Victorians did not know—a world in which serenity is not easily come by; of which discords and discontinuities seem to be a native idiom; in which a pretense to the grand manner is likely to feel like a lie (compare Frost's "Anything more than the truth would have seemed too weak"); in which ambivalence is a basic human condition and the claim to unmixed emotions is a denial of reality; and toward which doubt and self-doubt are measures of simple honesty.

If I have stated this difference in terms too heavily weighted in my own favor, any man may adjust the terms to his own taste and balance. Whatever the terms, I believe the core of all the controversies I have touched off at *SR* is in some such difference between a disciplined and an undisciplined aesthetic.

The one series of hot letters to the editor not grouped in the section headed "Controversies" followed the article "Robert Frost: The Way to the Poem." I have preferred to group it with my other pieces on Mr. Frost. Another reason for separating this "controversy" from the others is that it differs from them. In the others, though I could not have foreseen the vehemence of the disagreement, I could have foreseen at least some of it had I stopped to put on my foreseeing-cap. In this case, I had no least thought that anyone would be moved to object. I recall passing in the typescript to Peter Ritner, then *SR's* feature editor, with some remark to the effect that "even *our* readers can't find a fight in this one."

I was wrong, but what they found to fight about that time was not even the everlasting *ad hominem*. To be sure, my character, or the lack of it, is touched upon in passing. But what emerges as the enemy is the very act of attempted analysis.

In my "Letter to Letter-Writers" (page 162) I tried to reply to those readers who fear all technical discussion as a "desecration of beauty." There is one anecdote I wish I might have included in that reply but could not because the incident described had not yet taken place. Let me offer it here as a postscript years after the fact. Appropriately, the anecdote offers a reply from Robert Frost himself.

One evening at Bread Loaf Mr. Frost was reading his poems and talking about them. He was often a sort of horse trader in ideas. He seemed to pull out a conceptual stick to whittle while he talked *around* the idea he was trading for, rambling off in what seemed to be indirection, only to turn and surprise the idea from behind. It could be a great performance, and that night's was one of his greatest.

His conceptual stick for the occasion was "technical tricks": he wanted to tell us about some of his. He read a poem, paused to ask the audience in what meter it was written, and then had fun scolding those who did not know it was in hendecasyllabics. A bit later he interrupted a reading to say he was "a synecdochist by profession," and went on to have his fun with those who did not know which trope a synecdoche is, or even that it is a trope. So he went on. He pointed out rhyme pairings in which he took special pleasure. He paused to underline some of what he called his "bright ideas" for the management of the poem. He had things to say about "the tune" of this poem and that. He was well cast in the role of the master craftsman and he was having a good time.

I had been watching a sweet elderly lady in the second row. She had been giving signs of increasing agitation as the talk went on. The applause had hardly died down when she was on her feet, waving her arm furiously for attention, and spilling out the question she had been repressing (if it could be called a question) even as she called for attention. "But, Mr. Frost," she cried, "*surely* when you are writing one of your *beautiful poems, surely* you can't be thinking about"—and here her voice slurred the dirty words—"about *technical tricks!*"

Mr. Frost put his hands together, the spread fingers touching tip to tip, looked owlish for a moment, and then leaned forward into the microphone and said in a playfully gravelly bass: "I *revel* in 'em!"

As I say, I wish I might have had that anecdote available at the time for the benefit of those readers who seem to think that technique is an affront to "beauty," that the piano plays itself without the need for painful learning, that arias sing themselves without scholarship, and that poems are the product of mindless effusion untouched by the disciplines of technique.

It is just the ubiquity of such mindlessness that makes so many good poets and good critics despair of anything like "a general audience." Perhaps it is as a confession of failure that I must add I am not yet desperate. As the sermonizer in residence, I have no choice but to preach against the sinfulness of such persons, and to remain unmoved by their protests. There may be no such heaven as I dream of preaching. In the dream of it, however, though heaven must not be forbidden any man, it simply will not do to offer encouragement to the vacuous.

Of this particular controversy, I can say I did not know the gun was loaded. In hindsight, of course, I can see both that it was, and why. Of this and other controversies, moreover, I can also see in hindsight —and in ways the general reader could not know—that the gun was to some extent pre-cocked.

I came to SR in January of 1956 after the death of Amy Loveman. Miss Loveman, a gentle and sympathetic lady whom I scarcely knew but who seems to have been loved by all who did know her, did not pretend to be a poetry editor. She was an associate editor who handled

SR's poetry (among many other duties) because no one else on the staff would take it on. Because she was a loyal and gracious friend, and because she had spent most of her life in New York literary circles, she accepted many poems out of loyalty to old friends. Or perhaps Miss Loveman was right in her taste and I have been wrong, but in any case our tastes were not alike. So it was that I found myself with an uncomfortable legacy on my hands.

My first act at SR, after I had told Norman Cousins that I would look things over, was to read through the poetry files. One of the fattest was labeled "Accepted Poems Not in Type." (Perhaps I should explain that SR uses poems primarily as "filler." Accepted poems are set in type and held in the make-up department. When a "hole" appears in the paste-up of a forthcoming issue, the girls in make-up go through the file of "Poems in Type" and pick out one that will fit the "hole.")

There were 181 poems in the first file. I read through them in dismay, and turned to the thinner file of poems in type. There I read 32 more with the same sensations. When I had finished, I had to conclude that barring one or two borderline cases (about which I could generate no enthusiasm) there was not a poem in either file I should myself have accepted for publication. Two hundred and thirteen poems, moreover, add up to, roughly, a two-year supply at SR's rate of publication. The question before me was simple enough: "How can I hope to establish an editorial policy of my own with the first two years of my selections already set by a taste so different from mine?" The obvious answer was that I could not.

Back I went to Norman Cousins to tell him I could see no way of taking on the job as things stood. He had asked me to set a poetry policy for SR, and unless I could start with a clean slate, there was too little I could do: the poems had to go back. I could see that to return them would call lions howling from their dens and I offered to step aside and let someone else try it, but if it was my job to do, it had to be on my terms.

NC (to fall back on the standard office-memo designation) was understandably reluctant, but he granted my point and agreed to let me return the poems.

Let me say, as office history, that I have at times fought with NC. At the time of his editorial on the controversy over *The Unicorn*

("John Ciardi and the Readers," p. 84) I was furious at his Monday-morning quarterbacking and quit cold, though my letter (from Rome, as it happened) was hot enough. We patched that one up with a careful treaty. I have since squabbled with him a few times over SR policy. But you fight this man with respect. Leaving that editorial rift between us to healing time, I have learned comfortably but gratefully that he will stand to principle, and that he will back the principles he has stood to. The greater pleasure, therefore, in dedicating this book to him (and though I mention fighting in my dedication, let me stress the fact that it is the champion who enters the ring in the purple tights).

NC backed me then, and with his reluctant approval, I returned the poems—all but a few of those in type, which had to be held for the first few issues. A bit over two hundred of them went back to their authors with a covering letter in which I made it clear that the decision was mine, and that NC had yielded only upon my insistence that I could not establish a poetry policy for SR unless I could start unencumbered.

Back to me came the outraged letters. Two hundred or so offended poets, moreover, can turn out to be the wives, husbands, parents, relatives, and social and emotional collaborators of an astonishing number of people. Before I had published a word as SR's Poetry Editor, within two weeks of the return of the poems, I had a cardboard carton full of letters written between rage and anguish.

Nor was it coincidence that many of those letters bore signatures I was to find again and again attached to angry letters to the editor. I am happy to say that by now many of those first furious ones have made good their repeated threats to drop their subscription. SR's circulation manager will perhaps be alarmed by my pleasure in the fact. But I must take every such cancellation as a hope that the dialogue may continue in reason rather than in heat, and that it will become increasingly possible in SR to discuss poetry as a passionate, disciplined, and venturesome form of human awareness.

For my faith—my perturbed faith—in this audience remains, and not as an article of employment, but as one of faith in the communicability of human perceptions. Poetry needs its *avant-garde*, it needs its specialists; it even needs its jargonauts and its lunatic fringe. But with no thought of bowing to the general audience as an ideal one, I shall still believe that poetry may be served by such a body of general readers. Some among them can certainly be brought to a more than merely general interest in poetry. And what point can there be in lumping those hopeful ones with the sweet but hopeless lovers of vague beauty? The dear lady who asked Mr. Frost her dear question looked suspiciously like an SR reader, but I must insist on thinking of her as the bottom of the barrel. I know that above her, on whatever scale does measure, there are those in the audience who have minds that may be spoken to and perceptions capable of enlargement.

Because the three pieces specifically titled "Dialogues" were some sort of deliberate effort at evolving a tone for the dialogue, I have placed them first. I doubt that it is the final and best tone for the discussion, and I do not mean to return to it; but let me hope it will serve as a beginning.

Let me add my thanks to the good friends with whom I have worked at SR these past seven years. To list them by name would be to make too long a directory, but certainly what I value most at SR is the fact that so many of the people I work with there are truly good friends. They know it, I believe, and I certainly do, and bless the happy fact. But let me say thanks for it, too, lest blessing seem to be taken for granted in a world that offers such blessings rarely.

J. C.

Metuchen, N. J.
January, 1963

DIALOGUES

DIALOGUE WITH THE AUDIENCE

"I'm not exactly illiterate," says the Citizen. "I'm a pretty fair historian. I can read Freud—at least some of him—without being entirely in the dark. But I get nowhere with this modern poetry. I've given up trying."

The Poet has heard it all before, but the Citizen obviously wants to talk about it. The Poet, as a matter of fact, rather likes the Citizen. Maybe, the Poet thinks, if I can peg the talk to something specific it won't just ramble on aimlessly and forever. Aloud he says: "Just for the fun of it—who is the last particular poet you gave up on?"

"It was Wallace Stevens," says the Citizen. "I read your review of the Collected Poems and I shelled out $7.50 for it on your say-so." He reaches up to a shelf and hauls down the book. "Here it is," he says, tossing it on the table, "a big fat collection of unintelligibility."

"Sorry," says the Poet, "no refunds, if that's what you're getting at. But do me a favor: show me a specific poem that you take to be unintelligible."

The Citizen stares. "Do you mean to say you understand every poem in this book?"

The Poet shakes his head. "Far from it. I don't even understand White House news releases. But I like Stevens better."

"Without knowing what it is you like?"

"Let's keep the talk as specific as we can. I've asked you to cite a poem: turn around is fair play—find a poem called 'Asides on the Oboe.' Here, take this passage":

The obsolete fiction of the wide river in
An empty land; the Gods that Boucher killed;
And the metal heroes that time granulates—
The philosophers' man alone still walks in dew,
Still by the sea-side mutters milky lines
Concerning an immaculate imagery.
If you say on the hautboy man is not enough,
Can never stand as god, is ever wrong
In the end, however naked, tall, there is still
The impossible possible philosophers' man,
The man who has had the time to think enough,
The central man, the human globe, responsive
As a mirror with a voice, the man of glass,
Who in a million diamonds sums us up.

"Let me get it straight," says the Citizen. "Is this an example of a passage you do understand, or of one you don't?"

"As a matter of fact, it's an example of both," says the Poet. "Suppose I were to say I found it elusive, yet clear—would that make any sense? I can't unravel it detail by detail. I encounter areas of obscurity in it. Yet the total force of the passage is both unmistakable and moving, and just beyond every momentary obscurity I keep emerging into areas of immediate clarity."

"No, in a word. It makes no sense to me."

"Well, what do you mean by sense? Stevens does not write for factual-information sense. Why should he? He picks up a theme and orchestrates it. His 'sense' is a structure. The reader must keep that total structure in mind in order to grasp Stevens's kind of sense. He does not, moreover, 'mean' any one thing, but rather all the possibilities of all the relationships he is orchestrating."

"Clear as navy coffee," says the Citizen. "Am I supposed to swallow it?"

"You do in music," says the Poet, glancing at the Citizen's collection of recordings, "why not in poetry?"

"Because, among other things, words have meanings."

"They have," says the Poet, "but far more meanings than anyone thinks about in reading factual prose. A word is not a meaning but a complex of meanings consisting of all its possibilities: its ability to identify something, the image it releases in making that identification, its sound, its history, its association-in-context with the other words of the passage. Good poets use *more* of the word than most readers are used to."

"Yes," says the Citizen, who is proud of being a fair-minded person, "I suppose that *is* true."

"But not only is the individual word a complex. It is used in a phrase that is itself a complex of complexes. And the phrase is in turn used in the complex of the total poem's structure."

"So a poem is a complex of complexes of complexes," says the Citizen, half indignant now. "I'm beginning to get a complex myself."

"No," says the Poet, "that's a complex you've always had. You are used to words basically as denotations in statements intended or purporting to intend to convey facts. You have the 'practicality complex' and your basic symptom is 'why doesn't he say it straight?'"

"Well, why doesn't he?"

"As a matter of fact he does at times—even in your terms. Take the line 'The man who has had the time to think enough.' How much 'straighter' could he make the praise of that line?"

"I can agree there," says the Citizen. "But what about 'milky lines'? Why does he have to say it on 'the hautboy'? And what's all that about 'a mirror with a voice'?"

"One at a time," says the Poet. "The 'milky lines' is one of those details I remain unsure of. I suspect that Stevens was thinking of the sea as a kind of mother-of-life and that he used 'milky' in that connection. If my guess is right that makes 'milky lines' mean something like 'lines fed by the essential life fluid of all-mothering nature.' But that is only a guess and I have no way of verifying it. In fact, some of what follows in the poem—not in this passage—troubles my guess. That is one of the obscurities I feel in the passage. One I feel and *welcome*, may I say.

"The hautboy, on the other hand, is a straightforward Stevens signature, a part of his personal idiom, like his blue guitar. The hautboy is the kind of detail that reveals itself immediately as you get to know more about the way the poet writes. For the time being I can only suggest that you take the hautboy to be one of the instruments of art.

On that instrument of artifice, Stevens must make the 'fiction' (always a special term in his writing) that can replace the 'obsolete fiction' of the gods. In Stevens, the rituals of art constantly take the place of the rituals of religion—themselves richly obscure.

"As for the 'mirror with a voice'—there I have to charge you with petulant misreading. Stevens has established the context of his statement clearly enough for any willing reader, and it is no reading at all to ignore the context. What he is saying is roughly that 'it is *as if* the responsive man were a mirror with a voice reflecting all of us in a heightened way, *as if* summing us up in the million-diamond-reflection of his artifice.' I am satisfied that the gist of it is about that, though I confess I am uncertain about it later when the poem becomes unmistakably Leibnizian. At that later point, I conclude I don't know Leibniz well enough to guess out Stevens's sense of him. I am left puzzled. But I am also left considerably richer. Certainly, I should be willing to read a much longer and much more obscure poem than this if only to meet that man 'who has had the time to think enough.' I want him in my mind."

"Yes," says the Citizen, "I can go along with some of that. Even with most of it. But why must he be so elusive about it?"

The Poet smiles. "We're back to the business of 'saying it straight' again. I suggest, first, that the thought itself is elusive. And, second, that it's a kind of thinking you're not used to, partly because you have not read enough Stevens to catch the flavor of his thinking, and partly because you're not really a reader of poetry and never have been."

The Citizen draws himself up. "Now I don't know about that," he says. "I took quite a lot of English courses in school and . . ."

"And you haven't read as many as three books of new poems a year since then."

"Well," says the Citizen slowly, "I guess you have me there. Maybe if I were a more practiced reader I'd see more. But isn't some of it the poets' fault? Why do they make it so hard for a man to read them? I'm no genius, but I'm reasonably intelligent."

"And rational," suggests the Poet.

"Certainly. What's wrong with rationality?"

"Ask yourself that question as you read through an issue of the *Reader's Digest* sometime," says the Poet. "Or let me ask you how rationally you got married? Or by what sequence of syllogisms you begot your children? Or what Certified Public Accountant writes the scripts of your dream-life?"

The Poet is talking fast now, warming to his most fundamental sermon. "We all contain elements of rationality, but we're all much more than those elements. A poet thinks with his senses, his nerve endings, his whole body. He hooks at his thought physically, and he hooks from many directions at once. He *feels* what he thinks, and he feels it most in the act of making a poetic structure of it. Just as a composer feels himself into his musical structure. There is no auditing of rationalities in that process; there is, rather, the accomplishment into form of some part of a whole life."

The Citizen is being fair-minded again. "I can't grasp entirely your way of putting things," he says after a while, "but I can get a glimpse of what I think you're saying—especially when I try to feel it in terms of what a composer does inside his music." He rubs his jaw. "I don't know. There are too many ideas in it that are new to me. I suppose if you say so . . ."

"The last time you started supposing on my say-so it cost you $7.50," says the Poet. "Suppose me nothing on my say-so: I refuse to be trusted by any man who can trust himself, and I doubly refuse to be trusted by a man who can't trust himself. Make up your own mind on the basis of what makes sense in itself."

"That's just the trouble," says the Citizen. "You make it sound sensible enough, but then I turn to a poem and I just can't get my hooks into it."

"That's just what I started to ask you in the beginning. There's the book: give me a for-instance."

"I remember one queer thing called 'Bantams in Pine-Woods,' " says the Citizen, thumbing the pages. "I swear I spent a day trying to make sense of the first two lines. Here they are":

> Chieftain Iffucan of Azcan in caftan
> Of tan with henna hackles, halt!

"What's the problem?" says the Poet.

"No problem," says the Citizen. "Just gibberish. What the devil is all this henna-hackled Iffucan of Azcan trashcan stuff?"

"Ah!" says the Poet, "I see. To tell you the truth I hadn't ever thought of those lines as a difficulty: they're having such fun with themselves—all those lovely exaggerated sound-sequences and that big spoofing tone."

"Is all that—whatever it is—enough excuse for writing nonsense syllables?"

"Ask Lewis Carroll," says the Poet. "But the fact is they're not nonsense syllables. Note the title. A bantam may certainly be taken as a pretentious and pompous bird strutting around in his half-pint ego as if he owned the world, and refusing to be dwarfed even by pine woods . . ."

"I'm still lost in the Azcan ashcan. And at this point I've had enough of your symbol-threading."

"But the Azcan business is a fact from the world," says the Poet. "Have you ever looked into a pedigree book? I assume this to be a pure-bred bantam and that he is registered as Chieftain Iffucan of Azcan. Stevens begins by reporting the fact, obviously relishing its pretentiousness. 'Caftan' is his first 'poetic' addition. But note this: a caftan is a garment that hangs down just about the way the leg feathers of a bantam do. The detail is physically right. And the sound of the word itself is exactly right for the sound-sequence Stevens builds. That's always a sign of the poet—the ability to do more than one thing at once and to have his choices come out equally right on all levels."

The Citizen sits thoughtfully, turning it over in his mind. The Poet, watching the Citizen, once more has the impression of a painful fair-mindedness at work. Somehow that sense depresses him. He has a vision of the Citizen forever laboring to be open-minded and forever lost to the real life of the poem.

"I have to conclude that you're right," says the Citizen. "But I also know I could never have seen it that way. And I still don't understand the poem."

"Nor do I, completely," confesses the Poet. "But what of it? I don't understand 'Kubla Khan,' nor 'Tiger, Tiger.' Not in detail. But I can certainly experience them as poems. I can, to put it metaphorically, identify their emotional frequencies and the areas into which they transmit."

The Citizen is not satisfied. "I'm still thinking of this Iffucan of Azcan business. There I bogged down on a detail I did not recognize. And perhaps I'll never be any better at identifying odd details. But what about the poem that comes right after it? This one—'Anecdote of the Jar.' Now there is a poem I spent a lot of time on and although I understand every word and every sentence, I'm blessed if I know what Stevens is talking about." He reads it over:

> I placed a jar in Tennessee,
> And round it was upon a hill.
> It made the slovenly wilderness
> Surround that hill.
>
> The wilderness rose up to it,
> And sprawled around, no longer wild.
> The jar was round upon the ground
> And tall and of a port in air.
>
> It took dominion everywhere.
> The jar was gray and bare.
> It did not give of bird or bush,
> Like nothing else in Tennessee.

The Citizen finishes reading and looks up. "I was bothered at first by 'port,'" he says, "but I checked the word in the dictionary and I think I see what he's doing with it. But how am I supposed to understand 'It made the slovenly wilderness surround that hill'? How can a jar make a wilderness surround a hill? The wilderness was already surrounding the hill, and long before Stevens and his jar came along."

"In a sense, yes," says the Poet, "but only in the most usual prose-sense. Poetry constantly makes over that usual sense of things. The jar is a made-form; as such it stands for all artifice. The wilderness is nature as-it-happens, the opposite of made-form. But to 'surround' is 'to take position around a center.' And what is formless has no center. It is human artifice, the assertion of human artifice, that puts a center to the wilderness. Because the wilderness is formless it still 'sprawls' but now it sprawls 'up to' the jar. It approaches form, that is, and therefore it 'is no longer wild.' "

"Wait a minute," says the Citizen, "aren't you the one who is doing the paraphrasing now?"

"Yes, surely. I have no quarrel with paraphrase: only with paraphrase as a substitute for the poem. I am not trying to say, 'This is what the poem comes to.' Far from it. I am trying to point out the symbolic areas in which the poem moves. The two poles of Stevens's thought seem clearly enough to be 'artifice' and 'formless nature.' Why shouldn't those poles be identified? But the poles are not the poem. The poem is much better seen as those poles plus the force-field they create."

"That does it!" says the Citizen and slams the book shut, "symbolic areas, force-fields, artifice versus formless-nature—what is all this jargon? Didn't you write once that a poem is an emotion or nothing?"

"I certainly did."

"Then tell me how on earth I am supposed to get an emotion from this sort of haywire theorizing?"

The Poet smiles sadly. "I'm about ready to grant you that all criticism is in fact haywire, but would you grant me that criticism is not the poem? At that, one can still rig a weathervane out of haywire, and that vane can point to the weather. The poem is not the vane, nor is it the haywire from which the vane is improvised: the poem is the weather that is pointed to.

"Stevens, as it happens, had very strong feelings about form versus the formless. Those feelings crowd all his poems. They are fundamental to his very sense of reality. His emotions, to be sure, are intellectual things. If you refuse to think a sense of aesthetic-reality, as opposed to some other more common ideas of reality, is worth an emotion, you are breaking no law, but Stevens is obviously not for you. And that, I find myself thinking, is your loss rather than his."

"Maybe so," says the Citizen, but now he is sitting up as if squared for battle. "I'll even say he is obviously not for me. Who *is* he for? I'm the one who brought up Stevens, and I'll grant he may be a special case. But Stevens is not the only one who is obviously not for me.

Who *are* you modern poets for? Is there no such thing as an audience?"

This charge, too, is a familiar one to the Poet. "You've fired a lot of questions," he says, "and a full answer would call for a long sermon. Let me try the short form.

"What is the idea of 'the audience'? Is it enough to argue, 'I have bought this book of poems and therefore I have certain audience-rights'? I think, first, one must distinguish between two ideas of 'the audience.'

"One idea may be called the horizontal audience and the other the vertical audience. The horizontal audience consists of everybody who is alive at this moment. The vertical audience consists of everyone, vertically through time, who will ever read a given poem.

"Isn't it immediately obvious that Stevens can only 'be for' a tiny percentage of the horizontal audience? Even Frost, who is the most seemingly clear and the most widely loved of our good poets, certainly does not reach more than a small percentage of the total population, or even of that part of the population that thinks of itself as literate—as at least literate enough to buy a best seller. The fact is that no horizontal audience since the age of folk poetry has been much interested in good poetry. And you may be sure that a few spokesmen sounding off in the name of that horizontal audience are not going to persuade the poets.

"All good poets write for the vertical audience. The vertical audience for Dante, for example, is now six centuries old. And it is growing. If the human race has any luck at all, part of Dante's audience is still thousands of years short of being born.

"Now try a flight of fancy. Imagine that you held an election tomorrow and asked the horizontal audience to vote for Dante as opposed to Eddie Guest. Guest would certainly swamp Dante in such an election. More people in the horizontal audience have read Guest and even, God save the mark, been moved by him—if only to their own inanition. But moved, nevertheless. And we're a democracy, aren't we? The majority rules: bless the majority?

"Not in art. Not horizontally at least. The verdict in art is vertical. Take the idea of majority vote a step further. Imagine that you held the same election on Judgment Day, calling for a total vote of the human race down through time. Can you fail to believe that Dante would then swamp Eddie Guest plus all the horizontalists from Robert Service to Carl Sandburg?

"The point is that the horizontal audience always outnumbers the vertical at any one moment, but that the vertical audience for good poetry always outnumbers the horizontal in time-enough. And not only for the greatest poets. Andrew Marvell is certainly a minor poet, but given time enough, more people certainly will have read 'To His Coy Mistress' than will ever have subscribed to *Time, Life,* and *Fortune.* Compared to what a good poem can do, Luce is a piker at getting circulation."

"Impressive, if true," says the Citizen, "but how does any given poet get his divine sense of this vertical audience?"

"By his own ideal projection of his own best sense of himself. It's as simple as that," says the Poet. "He may be wrong, but he has nothing else to go by. And there is one thing more—all good poets are difficult when their work is new. And their work always becomes less difficult as their total shape becomes more and more visible. As that shape impresses itself upon time, one begins to know how to relate the parts to their total. Even Keats and Shelley confounded their contemporary critics as 'too difficult' and 'not for me.' "

The Citizen throws his hands up. "All right, all right: I've been out-talked. But who *does* write for me?"

The Poet spreads his hands palms out. "Keats and Shelley—now that they have lost their first difficulty."

"And are dead enough?" says the Citizen. "Well, maybe. But why is it so impossible for *you* to think about writing for me? I'm willing to give it a try."

The Poet shrugs. "The sort of try you gave Stevens? But no matter. The point is, why *should* I write for you?—you're going to be dead the next time anyone looks. We all are, for that matter. But not the poem. Not if it's made right. If I make it for you I have to take the chance that it will die with you. I'm not sure you're that good an investment. Besides which, I have to invest in myself. If we happen to share some of the same sense of poetry, it may work out that I do happen to write for you. But that would be a happy bonus at best. I still cannot think of you as a main investment—not till you show a better 'vertical-sense.' "

"We who are about to die," says the Citizen, "salute the poems we cannot grasp. Is that it?"

"Like nothing else in Tennessee," says the Poet, bowing.

THE ENVIRONMENT OF POETRY

"Tell me," says the Citizen, "what do you do when you write a poem? What sort of human behavior goes into it? Do you have a firm idea when you sit down to the writing? Or do you wait for some sort of inspiration to tell you what to say?"

The Poet is always uneasy at this sort of questioning, especially when "inspiration" creeps into it. "What do you do for a living?" he asks the Citizen.

"I don't know what that has to do with my questions," says the Citizen, "but I'm a chemical engineer."

The Poet brightens. "That's better than I had hoped," he says.

But the Citizen looks wary. "Are you being condescending?" he says. "What's better than you had hoped?"

"I certainly am not being condescending. Why should I be?" says the Poet. "And what it has to do with your question is—in one word—*simultaneity*. As a chemical engineer you have to involve yourself in some very multiple and complicated calculations, calculations that require you to keep many things in mind *at the same time*.

"Now suppose I were to ask you to explain such a calculation to me. You obviously couldn't. You could probably explain it to another chemical engineer, but I lack the training that will allow me to join your thoughts both multiply and simultaneously."

"I half understand," says the Citizen, "but I'm still a bit lost in words."

"Let me try it in terms of music," says the Poet. "I am no expert in such matters, but join me in a guess. Let's say a composer has been wanting to write a symphony, and suddenly finds a first theme going in his head. He knows instantly that the theme is right for his purposes. It fills him with excitement. *This* is the theme he needs!

"He may be right or wrong as it works out later, but what are the sources of his excitement? I should guess that his thoughts must certainly include very complicated awarenesses of hundreds of very technical matters. Among other things, he must be reacting to some sense of the harmonic, contrapuntal, and orchestral possibilities of that theme. Note, too, that it must certainly be the *possibilities* he feels: there are no actualities as yet.

"How could that composer hope to explain his excited sense of right possibility to a person who has not studied harmony, orchestration, and counterpoint? And one must not only have studied those subjects, but he must have mastered them so thoroughly that he need not parse them out. Rather, he must *feel* the total impact of many complicated thoughts at once.

"Obviously, he must not stop to ask himself these questions any more than a pole vaulter must stop in mid-leap to count the muscles he is using. His business now is to act, to perform his sense of possibility in all its excitement."

"And that's the way the poet does it?" says the Citizen.

"At the first moment of the writing, yes. Or so I believe. Later, in the sweating hours of revision, he must work in a more plodding way. He must still account for all his multiplicities, but he is not under the same compulsion to keep the mood going. His first capture, I think, must be the rhythm, and the rhythm requires that he go with it. Once the rhythm is caught on paper, he can leave it and return to it. One writes from the inside and revises from the outside.

"But in that first urgent inside moment, the poet has no choice but to trust himself. The poem, in one sure sense, is written out of all the wastebaskets the poet has previously filled. In writing thousands of previous poems, he has, to whatever extent, made the medium his."

"I see that," says the Citizen. "I've had something of that same sense in finding the solution to a tough problem: you work yourself into the blind staggers, give up in despair, and then suddenly, while you're shaving or mowing the lawn, the whole answer pops into your head in one lovely shape."

The Poet smiles. "Who's the poet now?"

"One more remark like that," says the Citizen, "and I'll know you're condescending."

"No," says the Poet, "I must insist that I wasn't and am not. I only mean to endorse whatever it is that pops lovely shapes into the heads of men."

"I'll grant you," says the Citizen, ignoring him, "that I might have trouble explaining my way of working to a non-chemist. Or even, for that matter, to a chemist who happens to be working in another field. But there's still one thing I want to ask your poet on his pyramid of wastebaskets—can he explain it to himself?"

"But why on earth should he?" says the Poet. "Or let me ask you the same thing. When you're out mowing the lawn, or mowing your chin, and that answer pops into your head in one lovely shape—can you explain that to yourself?"

"We're talking about poetry," says the Citizen. "I've heard you say that the subject matter of poetry is, finally, how the human nervous system works. I have a human nervous system to work in myself, but my business is formulae and equations. The question is yours. Can you explain to yourself how you work?"

The Poet does not answer at once. "I hear your question," he says after a while, "and I also hear some strange assumptions lurking behind it. Let's whistle those assumptions out of the bushes and have a look at them before they trip up the whole discussion. Aren't you assuming, first, that it is the poet's duty to explain how he works, and to do so in something like the terms a clinical psychologist might use? Second, that if he cannot so explain himself, he will somehow be guilty of mystification? Whereby, third, he will be writing unintelligible poetry that you may feel free to dismiss as 'not making sense'?"

"Well, shouldn't a poet be able to explain what he does in writing a poem?"

"No more than a hen needs to explain what it does when it lays an egg—so long as it knows how to lay one, and so long as the egg is a good one. *Knowing* how to and *explaining* how are two very different terms. I have to insist that explanation is not the poet's function. I happen, *ex officio*, to be interested in theorizing how it might go, but the theorizing is to one side of my function as a poet. Can we discuss it in those terms?"

"I don't see why not," says the Citizen. "Use your own terms: you distinguished between explaining and knowing. Whether he can explain it or not, does a poet know how he does it?"

"Always. The good ones always know."

"Very well, then, how do you know they know?"

"Because," says the Poet, "—and here you may want to jump down my throat—because form and rhythm are ways of knowing. I don't know how to put it into clinical terms. I don't even know how to say it, except by analogy. But form and rhythm are languages—speakable, understandable, known languages."

"No throat-jumping," says the Citizen. "I'm ready to listen. I don't know what you're talking about, and you tell me you can't say it except by analogy. What sort of languages?"

"You'll grant me that there are many sorts of languages aside from language? I'm thinking of music, mathematics, spatial relationships, formulae, maps—these are all communications a man may send and receive."

"Yes. I'm willing to grant that."

"I like to think there is also something I want to call the *language of environment*."

"That I don't get."

"Put it this way. Assume the two of us are vacationing in the mountains and decide to take a flashlight and explore an old mine shaft. Assume, too, that neither of us has been in a mine before."

"Assumed."

"We get a few hundred yards into the shaft and you stop. You announce that there is something funny about the place and you want us to get out of there. I have noticed nothing funny, and on the assumption that my senses are as good as yours, I can be rather smug and brave about the whole thing. You may get out if you want to, but I am going on."

"What's your point?"

"Now repeat the same situation, but assume this time that the man I go into the shaft with is an experienced miner, and *he* says there is something funny about it and urges me to get out. When he says it, I get out—fast."

"Go on," says the Citizen. "I think I see what you're getting at, but I want to hear you say it."

"The point," says the Poet, "is that a man who has spent his life in the mines is sensitive to mine conditions: he speaks the language of that environment. He may not know he speaks it—which is to say, he may know it better than he knows he knows it. But he does know it; he feels it."

"But what about my uneasiness when I went down the mine shaft with you?"

"Not relevant. The assumption was that you had never before been in a mine. You do not speak the language of that environment."

"But all you're talking about is hunches."

"Precisely, but the hunches of trained men are worth something—at least when there is no more definite evidence to go on."

"And," adds the Citizen, "they may be wrong."

"Certainly."

"That doesn't answer the question," says the Citizen. "All you've said so far is that a) you have to feel your way; and b) you could be wrong."

"*At the moment of the writing*," says the Poet, "a man has no choice but to trust his sense of the environment of the poem. If it turns out later that he is wrong, he must throw away what he has done."

"Suppose I did that with a trainload of expensive alloys. Who would buy them if I turned out to be wrong?"

"The junkman, I suppose. But the difference between us is one I mean to treasure," says the Poet. "A poem is not offered for sale: it ventures into itself and hopes to find the language of itself. It may lose its way and find nothing and hear nothing, but whatever happens must happen *as it goes.*"

"Is it really as random as that?"

"There is no random to it. The poet may be wrong. He *will* be wrong at times. But he has no other way of being right. And when the environment of the poem is really speaking to him, he may very well know what he does better than he knows he knows it."

"Now I *am* ready for a little throat-jumping," says the Citizen. "You literary types are fast with words, but your ideas bounce around like Brownian particles. 'He knows better than he knows he knows.' Does that make sense? In science, at least, a man stays clear about knowing what he knows he knows. His results have to check."

The Poet smiles. "Have you checked your fantasy life, or your relations with your mother and father, or your own death recently? No, never mind. That's another discussion.

"What you must realize is that a poet's results have to check, too. Not immediately, perhaps, but always in time. Shakespeare certainly did not apply scientific controls to the writing of *Hamlet,* nor did Mozart in writing a symphony. They could only *feel* their ways in the kind of multiple and simultaneous engagement I have been trying to describe. But their results have checked exactly with the feelings of the human race. So exactly that the race can no longer do without their works."

"If it is that exact," says the Citizen, "why can't you say it in words that make sense?"

The Poet shrugs. "Everything I have said makes sense to me. Even mortal sense," he says. "And for that matter why do your chemical formulae pile up such queer symbols, and why does your calculus have to use all those queer squiggles? I refuse to believe that human experience is less complicated than a fancy molecule, or than the motion of a particle moving along the radius of a circle relative to another particle moving on the circumference of the circle—or whatever you solve for."

"Ah," says the Citizen, and he points his finger with his whole arm extended, "but chemistry and calculus are for specialists! And you yourself have said that poetry is about human emotions. What about your duty to state emotions I can perceive?"

"That," says the Poet, "is a number of questions. Let's begin by rephrasing the last one. Instead of 'stating emotions I can perceive,' will you let it read 'shaping experiences I can relive'?"

"Fair enough," says the Citizen with a shrug. "What's the difference?"

"Enormous," says the Poet, "but let that go. You say all men have emotions. They certainly do. But not by a long shot do they have the developed emotions of a Shakespeare or a Dante. Great artists are specialists in the same way that a great mathematician or a great botanist is a specialist—by the quality of the talent and of the attention they bring to their perceptions. Everyone is human, as the category goes, but not everyone is humanly perceptive to the same degree. I believe that to be a developed human being is the ultimate specialty. As Yeats put it, 'We must labor to be beautiful.' "

"And," says the Citizen, "does that give you the human right to look down on everybody who fails to be Shakespeare or Dante?"

"Those are your terms," says the Poet. "I can only reject them. My duty is to capture into form and rhythm experiences that are true of you, whether or not you are capable of engaging them."

"Because I'm stupid, I suppose?"

"Not at all. You may be profoundly human in your response to other media, and simply be insensitive (or untrained, or both) to the forms and rhythms of words in poetry."

"And what if no one manages to engage the experiences you put into form and rhythm?"

"Then I have written badly. Like the miner in the shaft, I can be wrong. But I repeat: I have no other way of being right. There is no other way in which the poet can work. And when he works well, the whole race wins. Polonius need never know that Shakespeare has drawn him as a sententious old fool. But in him, Shakespeare has imaged forth the human truth of a Polonius-strand in all of us. That human truth is there forever, for any man capable of perceiving it.

"And one more thing—there is *exactness* in the delineation of Polonius. He is in no sense a random product. By whatever means Shakespeare conceived him, the delineation has a correspondence to life, and even a life of its own, that seems exactly right to our understanding."

"I grant that sense of exactness," says the Citizen. "But can you really believe that Shakespeare could have drawn such a character without a very firm starting notion of what he meant to do?"

"I have to believe that the idea for Polonius came to Shakespeare as a possibility to explore, and that he worked it out as it came, by feel. The idea came to him as seed and left him as a fruit.

"As a matter of fact, one may locate pretty much the source of the seed. A Danish chronicler named Saxo Grammaticus wrote *Historia Danica,* and that chronicle—along with a lost play by an earlier sixteenth-century playwright—was certainly the seed of Shakespeare's

Hamlet. The *Historia Danica* even contains a suggestion of the character of Polonius as Shakespeare developed it. But only a suggestion.

"Shakespeare, I must believe, *felt the possibilities* inherent in that suggestion and went on to develop them. He was, after all, a collector of characters. He had spent his life creating characters, and he had certainly developed a sense of how a character could and should be developed. But I simply do not see how he could have known what to do with the suggestion *until he did it*.

"Shakespeare seems to have written without much revision. Another man might have had to try a development, cancel it out, and start over again. It seems to have been a quality of Shakespeare's enormous genius that he could foresee blind alleys before he started down them. But he still had to work it out as it came.

"For in any aesthetic form all the elements must serve a purpose. As Chekhov said, 'If you bring a cannon onstage—fire it.' It is also true of aesthetic form that as soon as you bring in an element for one purpose, it starts to serve another. You bring in that cannon in Act One in order to use it for firing a shot in Act Five, and by the time you get to Act Four, you find you have used it as a place for hiding a letter, as the place for two conspirators to meet, and as a device for proving that your hero knows something about soldiering. The fact of art is that everything tends to turn double and triple, and that not only must everything work with everything else, but that it must do so on all levels.

"Shakespeare brings Polonius onstage as a rather pompous counselor to the king, as suggested by Grammaticus. There is also a girl in Grammaticus's account, but Shakespeare decides to make her the daughter of Polonius. For good measure he throws in a son, Laertes. But he does not give Polonius a living wife. It might well have seemed logical to give Polonius a whole family while he was at it. Shakespeare—whatever his reasons—decided not to. The point is that decisions are constantly being made in a good work of art, and that each one opens a new possibility.

"Polonius's speeches to the king make it possible to show one side of his character. Once Shakespeare has given him a family, he finds it possible to show the private as well as the public Polonius. Shakespeare then makes a marriage between Ophelia and Hamlet seem quite possible—an enormous step up the ladder of caste. And in sight of that possibility Shakespeare now has a chance to show Polonius bustling with great ambition. And as soon as he has built that possibility, Shakespeare can achieve the irony of having his busy fool killed by the very Hamlet whose father-in-law he dreamed of being. Every new turning of the plot *makes possible.*

"And it is exactly so in a poem. Each element plays against all the others, and the interplay *keeps suggesting things into the poem.* The exactness and the mastery of a good poet are in the principle of selection by which he lets one thing in and keeps another out. Ideally, he is letting in only those elements that will interplay tellingly toward the total effect. What he is keeping out are those elements that will be merely random, and therefore inert.

"For a good poem has dramatic structure—or call it fictional method, if you prefer. The elements of the poem are, in a real sense, a cast of characters. The metaphors, for example, must perform very much as a scene in a play or in a novel performs itself. One of the most fundamental weaknesses of bad poetry is the lack of such a structural sense of motion—the sense of entrance, development, and motion toward a climax."

"I don't understand what you mean by a metaphoric climax," says the Citizen.

"It's hard to say," says the Poet. "I can only try to catch it in another metaphor. I think of it as a series of releases, like arrows shot into the air on different trajectories. All the way through a good poem those arrows of suggestion are being shot into the air. The implications of an image in line one, the suggestion of an overtone in line two, a shadow of irony in line four, the tone of a countervoice in line seven. One might wonder—were he to stop and think about it—where all those arrows might be going. One can almost have a sense of hearing them whistle through the air. Then, suddenly, at the true final moment of a good poem, all those arrows thud into the bull's-eye at the same instant. All of them come in at slightly different angles, but when all of them hit dead center and at the same instant—*that* is climax."

"And when they don't?"

The Poet shrugs. "You can try revision. If that doesn't work, there is always the wastebasket."

"You seem to be seeing a poem as a machine for marksmanship."

"Think of it rather as a machine for making choices. Having written three words, the poet must *choose* a fourth. It doesn't just happen: it must be chosen. And having written four, he must choose a fifth. And so on for all the elements of the poem—every image, every metric emphasis, every last comma must be selected for admission. The good poet is defined by the quality of the choices he makes—by the exactness of his demands, and by the rigidity of his refusal to make cheap choices."

"That," says the Citizen, "is a large order."

"Happily, it's a huge order. Why go to art for anything but the hugest and most lovingly involving difficulties? Why die in a puddle when there are oceans to drown in? The object of a poem is not to make itself salable, but to feel out the perfected rhythmic structure that will release the experience of the poem in the most relivable and in the most revealing way."

"One more thing," says the Citizen, "and I'll take my confusions home and try them on. You speak of a poem as a machine for making choices. A good machine involves both input and output. If what you have described is the input, what is the output?"

"Knowledge," says the Poet, without hesitation.

"Knowledge?"

"Knowledge. The indispensable *experience of knowledge* that defines a civilized human being. The poem takes a man through the moment of experience to the moment of insight. It arouses and adds to his total sentience."

The Citizen tugs his ear thoughtfully. "Let me think about that," he says.

"Let me urge you to," says the Poet.

POETRY AS KNOWLEDGE
DIALOGUE WITH A REALIST

"At our last session," says the Citizen, "you were claiming that the end product of a poem was knowledge."

"I'll stand by that," says the Poet. "But I also said, 'The indispensable *experience of knowledge* that defines a civilized human being. The poem takes a man through the moment of experience to the moment of insight. It arouses and adds to his total sentience.' Those were my exact words."

"They were," agrees the Citizen.

"Then let me add explicitly what is already implicit in them—that the experience of knowledge in a poem is always a self-delighting thing. As Horace put it, the end of poetry is 'to teach and delight,' or, more exactly rendered, 'teaching while delighting.' "

"Very well," says the Citizen. "Those were your words, and now we have more words. But what do they mean, if anything? Suppose it all turns out to be just one more way of saying that you poets have a good time messing around with words?"

"The best of times," says the Poet. "I like to mess around with words."

"But," says the Citizen, "you just hate to say it flatly."

"I have just said it flatly."

"Like the old alchemists," the Citizen continues, ignoring him, "you toss off a lot of fancy mumbo-jumbo to make a simple-minded process seem mysterious and profound."

"Are you saying that poets are like those alchemists, or that critics are?"

"Well, the critics, I suppose," says the Citizen.

"And," says the Poet, "what if one out of every so many critics actually is that sort of mystifier (though I'll bet you have never read one that really qualifies that way)—need his abuses damn all critics, including the good ones?"

"What I mean," says the Citizen, "is——"

"I have twice granted you," says the Poet, taking his own turn at bulldozing the conversation, "that poets love to 'mess around' with words. I could argue that language is one of the profoundest and most singular of human activities, and that any man messing around with words is playing with one of our most essential tools of knowledge and one of our most essential human experiences, but let's leave that out of it for now, and let me ask you a counterquestion. You are, as you told me in our last session, a chemical engineer. Don't you like to mess around in the laboratory?"

"Everyone putters some," says the Citizen. "That's not the same thing as work."

"What do you call work?"

"Call it anything that gets a job done or adds to knowledge."

"But isn't it possible for a putterer to stumble onto something he could not have found in any other way?"

The Citizen grimaces. "Legend to the contrary," he says, "precious little gets discovered by accident these days. But all right, let's say an accident can happen."

"Bless them," says the Poet. "I spend all my life puttering around and waiting for the right accidents to happen to me."

"Now wait a minute," says the Citizen. "We are about to get derailed. For the sake of order, I'll withdraw what I said about alchemical mumbo-jumbo. But you were claiming that the end product of poetry is knowledge. I know that the end product of research is knowledge. But even granted that a lucky accident once in a lifetime can stumble onto a piece of knowledge, you can't be serious—not even you—about making freak accident into an epistemology."

"A real mumbo-jumbo word, that big fat epistemology of yours," says the Poet.

"Never mind that," says the Citizen. "The point is that knowledge must be acquired by the orderly process of a trained and careful (which is to say, a self-checking) mind. Knowledge has to be exact or it's guesswork."

"I can't agree with that all the way," says the Poet, "but for the sake of the discussion and to avoid any more dirty work in the semantic clinches, I'll accept it as put. In our earlier sessions we discussed the exactness of a good poem in its own way. Whatever putters toward the poem must finally take its place in a form, and form is a rigorously self-checking thing. We now have to ask, first, if poetry has anything to do with mind in good order, and, second, if that kind of order leads to knowledge. Will you accept that agenda?"

"Accepted," says the Citizen.

"All right, then: has poetry anything to do with mind in good order?" says the Poet. "Let me begin by trying to describe the kind of exact knowledge you go after in the laboratory.

"I once heard an engineer speak on what he called 'creative thinking.' He broke the process down into five steps, which, as nearly as I can recall them, were: 1) define the limits of your problem; 2) undertake the qualitative analysis of your problem; 3) perform the quantitative mathematics required by your analysis; 4) check your mathematics; and 5) find the mechanical implementation of your mathematical solution. Is that a fair accounting of what you mean by mind working in good order?"

"Like you, I could argue a word or two, but for the sake of the discussion, I accept it as a fair accounting."

"Would you also call it creative thinking?" asks the Poet.

"I think you're sneering again," says the Citizen. "Why do you hate to let anyone else use the word 'creative'? The process is certainly creative. It creates knowledge. And exact knowledge."

"I deny any thought of sneering," says the Poet. "I won't even ask why you suspect a sneer. I am concerned only with trying to make a distinction I think you could accept.

"The kind of thinking the engineer described is both useful and admirable. It can lead to some substantial good things. There remain, however, other substantial good things to which it cannot lead, and that second kind of substantial good is most exactly the kind of knowledge that grows out of poetry.

"If you will allow me to call the engineer's kind of thinking 'problem-solving'—understanding that to label an admirable thing; and if you will allow me to call the poet's process 'formalizing'—understanding by that no self-adulatory label: then I think some distinctions can be marked out.

"Those five steps of the problem-solving mind can lead to a lot of answers. But no man can come to the cardinal points of his life and meet them in terms of those five steps. Life-problems do not come up with neat enough limits for that. Can you, for example, get married by defining, qualifying, checking, and implementing the girl? Or if your child has an emotional problem, can you lead him or her to understanding in those five steps? Or when you walk out under the stars and discover how small you are in the universe, can you come to any better knowledge of yourself in those five steps?"

"Hold it right there," says the Citizen. "If you are asking me whether or not I have the answers to life, death, and the buzzing universe, I certainly have not: I admit the limits of my knowledge. But if you are going to take my admission of limitation as your license to peddle the unknown, I won't stand for it."

"The thought," says the Poet, "never entered my head. Who am I to stock solved-in-full universes? The question, you will recall, was whether or not poetry had anything to do with mind in good order. My point is that once you get beyond the limits of a specific physical problem and start dealing with knowledge of human emotions, those five steps of the problem-solving process cease to be mind in good order. If the question is, for instance, 'What is a man?' then those five steps are not apt means of knowing what needs to be known."

"Very well," says the Citizen. "Let's assume that I am that stupid, limited problem-solver, and you tell me just what it is that needs to be known."

"Let me assume instead that you are a human being with more motivations mixed into you than any of us is likely to get entirely straight. Will you, in turn, grant that 'What is a man?' is a question worth asking, and that any order of mind that can aptly engage that question is in good order and leads to substantial knowledge?"

"Fine," says the Citizen. "Granted. Now show me what that order of mind is and what it has to do with poetry as knowledge."

"Let's begin at a low level," says the Poet.

"Thank you for not losing me at the start," says the Citizen with a mock bow.

"Not at all," says the Poet. "As you probably know better than I, electronic brains are now being built that are able to learn. One such machine has taught itself to play checkers, and now beats its own inventor. A more complex machine could be made that would teach itself to play unbeatable chess. The principle, as I understand it, is that the machine is given the basic instructions of the game, then told to file away every situation that leads to a losing game, and never to repeat any situation in that file. It follows, therefore, that by the time the machine has made every possible mistake (which it will never repeat), it will make only moves that are not mistakes and it will, therefore, be unbeatable, though it may be played to a draw. Interestingly, if my information is correct, the machine has to be told when it has won, lost, or played to a draw. *It can win but it cannot know it has won.*"

"It shouldn't be too hard to build in that recognition," says the Citizen, "but keep going."

"But what are the limits of the machine?" says the Poet. "I was once seriously asked by an IBM man why I thought an electronic brain could not write a poem. Let me say at once he was not suggesting that a machine could write a poem. He knew it couldn't, but he was interested in my reasons for believing it could not. I suggested a simpler demonstration. Let's leave out the order of mind that writes a poem. I suggested, instead, that if he would build an electronic poker player, and that if he would then back the machine with the total resources of IBM, I would undertake to win the whole shebang from any contraption that would commit itself to five-card stud."

The Citizen shrugged. "You wouldn't even have to be very good. There are just more variables in poker than a machine could be set for."

"That," said the Poet, "is just my point. Poker is not mechanically predictable. The players must guess out and outguess one another. Yet, certainly, the whole process involves much more than simple chance. Over the long pull, the same players always turn out to be the winners. They know something that makes them winners. No matter that they cannot classify what they know, and cannot break it down into five, or twenty-five, or a million exact steps. They know something and their performance attests. Nor is there any set order in which their knowledge is to be acquired. It is the knowledge of experience. The good players have made themselves sensitive to an environment: they *feel* their way to that knowledge. And it is, you will grant, useful knowledge."

"Very useful," says the Citizen ruefully. "But what has all this to do with 'What is a man?' "

"Quite a lot," says the Poet. "If a poker game involves more variables than even an electronic problem-solver can file away, how many variables are there in life itself to defy the oversystematic mind?"

"Hold on," says the Citizen. "You beg the question when you say, 'oversystematic.' If it is *over*systematic, then it is excessive, and I will not be left to defend excess. It is up to you to show that it is, in fact, excessive, and if you can demonstrate that, I grant your point."

"Right you are," says the Poet. "I'll withdraw that phrasing. Let me say instead that whatever is involved in these variables will not yield to the idea of *exactness* as involved, say, in physical measurement."

"Very well," says the Citizen. "At the present stage of our knowledge there are all sorts of things we cannot be entirely exact about, but if you are going to throw out exactness, what are you going to put in its place?"

"I am not throwing out the idea of exactness," says the Poet. "Let us by all means be exact where exactness is possible. There still remains an order of mind that can lead to knowledge of the inexact. It is that order of mind that must engage the question 'What is a man?' And poetry, I argue, has a great deal to do with that order of mind. Poetry is in fact a means to the knowledge one must have before he can ask that question meaningfully. I used poker as a low-scale example. Let me jump high up the scale, and take an example from Greek mythology."

"Oh, come now," says the Citizen. "I'm pushing fifty these days with twinges of mortality between the martinis, and I can testify that chemical engineering doesn't do anything about the chemistry of that thought. Nor do I want to think of my kids as particles of energy caught into atoms made up into molecules of organic goo. But why drag in all those gods and goddesses and their queer shenanigans?"

"Read Greek mythology as a series of queer shenanigans and you end up with an anthology of odd tales, all of them interesting enough in themselves. But what really goes on in those tales is a drama of the psyche. They go, let us say, by parables. And parables are a profound and meaningful way not only of speaking but of acquiring knowledge. Everything in those parables of Greek mythology comes together in endless interrelationships to make a drama of the unconscious. What the myths do is dramatize the inner urgencies, frustrations, longings, triumphs, defeats, and cross-motives of every man. Hence the number of terms in psychiatry that have been drawn from them. The myths dramatize man's knowledge of himself.

"Take, for example, the story of Pygmalion. Is it simply an odd tale about a sculptor who created a statue so beautiful that he fell in love with it? Through love of what he had himself created (expressed in his prayer to Venus) he gave life to his creation and the statue became his wife. Is that simply a tale? Does not every man at some time to some extent fall in love with an image he has himself created? In science you would call such an insight a law: that every man at some time to some extent falls in love with an image he has himself created. I am satisfied to call it simply knowledge, and to find joy both in the knowledge and in the way it has revealed itself.

"That is no sort of knowledge for the problem-solving mind, perhaps. We must read the myth with our minds keyed to a more various and more supple allegorical mood.

"That tale, moreover, is simply a beginning. The generations of Pygmalion and of his statue-wife are also part of the sequence. From them was born a daughter and from her was born Cinyras, a mythological king of Crete. And the daughter of Cinyras was Myrrha, who conceived an unconquerable passion for her father and stole into his bed at night to lie with him.

"Note how the passions answer one another. Pygmalion fell in love with the image he had himself created, and through his godly passion (his prayer to Venus) he brought that image to life. His great-granddaughter fell in love with the image of her creator—her father—and through an earth-passion with no touch of godliness in it, brought about her father's death (for he took his life when he learned what had happened), and she was herself turned into a tree (with its roots as a further drama of the earth-trace).

"Certainly the second tale, taken with the first, has added something to our knowledge—has added a great deal perhaps—but let us simply say that it has demonstrated an enduring connection between two kinds of human passions.

"Nor does it end there, for Myrrha was pregnant, and when she turned into a tree (a myrtle, evergreen), the great bole of the tree that contained her womb split open to give birth to Adonis, the most beautiful of men, who grew to be the beloved of Venus herself.

"Is all this talking about life? About what it is to be a man? Certainly it is not the sort of talk that seeks the equations of the physical sciences. What happens in the mind of a man when he speculates on the allegorical possibilities of Adonis? Why should the most beautiful of men be born of a line so marked by opposite passions? Are not all men, when they stand most understandingly in themselves, born of the passions that give life and of the passions that destroy?

"Adonis, moreover, is marked for doom by the fates. Venus does her best to protect and to warn him. Above all she enjoins him from hunting dangerous beasts (could Myrrha, who was both his mother and sister, be figured forth in that thought?). But Venus must return to heaven, and she has hardly left before Adonis attacks a wild boar and is killed by it. (And what about that boar? Is it a literal beast, or is it the dramatization of a force already in the blood of Adonis, and of every man?)

"I submit that mind in good order is functioning here. And, further, that this order of mind leads to knowledge. These dramatic elements are full of the seeds of self-knowledge. Their growth is so rank and so many-branched that the knowledge they reach into will not be made systematic in the sense of the physical sciences. But it is still knowledge—more knowledge than those five problem-solving steps can reach to."

"As usual," says the Citizen, "I am left with a lot of thinking to do before I quite know what I think. But one question sticks in my mind. You said that parables are a profound and meaningful way not only of speaking but of acquiring knowledge. I will probably end up by granting in my own mind that there is this order of knowledge you are talking about, and that the reader acquires that knowledge from his thinking about them. But suppose I did a piece of research and then wrote it up as a parable? The parable—or the myth, as I should perhaps say—is not the way *I* acquired the knowledge, but only my way of having some fun with the knowledge I had previously acquired. How can you say a poem creates knowledge, when the knowledge is from the poet's previous experience of his own life, the poem being simply the way he expresses what he has already learned?"

"No," says the Poet. "I do understand your question, but that simply is not the way it works. Remember that we began with poetry as the *experience* of knowledge. A poem is never about ideas: it is always and only about the *experience* of ideas, about what happens inside a human being when an idea begins to work in him and motivate him.

"It is true that every time we enter an experience, we bring to it our past experiences. The new encounter does, nevertheless, remain an experience in itself.

"In a poem, it is exactly the poem itself that is the experience. The poem happens to the poet. He enters it without knowing where he will come out. Nor does that fact open the poem to a charge of inexactness—you enter a job of research not knowing where you will come out, but always trying as exactly as possible to pursue the demands of your own developing body of knowledge. It is a mistake in any piece of writing—and a mistake, may I say, on which students in Freshman English flounder endlessly—to think of the writing process as if one had two bins, one of which is labeled 'Thoughts' and the other of which is labeled 'Words,' the problem being to pull a Thought out of one bin and then, from the other one, the Words that match it. Whatever emerges in a piece of writing emerges *as* words, forms, images, and rhythms.

"Because those four elements are natively multiple, as we have discussed, it will not do to be downright about them. What will it serve a man to look into his own psyche and shout, 'You there—get down to brass tacks or shut up!'

"In the poetic experience of knowledge one must be willing to hearken to the allusive. That much granted, I can go on to say that the poet does not know what he is going to know until he finds himself knowing it in answer to the demands of his form, as the words and the metaphoric elements suggest it to him, and as the rhythm both enforces and elicits it from him. It is the process of answering those demands and of being moved forward by those suggestions that is his experience of his form.

"What I cannot defend, unless you are willing to grant it, is the value of form as the kind of experience that goes most deeply into whatever a man is. Dance, ritual, religious ceremony, public ceremony, or poetic encounter—if the form is sound, it is of what is deepest in a man. Nothing is more powerfully of man than the fact that he naturally gives off forms and is naturally enclosed by them. To acquire knowledge of aesthetic form is to acquire knowledge of man. And with that I rest my case."

"No rebuttal," says the Citizen. "At least not yet. I have too much to think about. But wherever I come out in my own ponderings, let me say I have enjoyed this give-and-take."

"So have I," says the Poet. "But while you are in this benign mood, may I ask you to grant me one thing?"

"Name it," says the Citizen.

"That I was not sneering at any time in the course of all this."

The Citizen nods. "Granted," he says.

"Thank you," says the Poet. "That point does matter to me."

CONTROVERSIES

EDNA ST. VINCENT MILLAY

EDNA ST. VINCENT MILLAY,
A FIGURE OF PASSIONATE LIVING

[*November 11, 1950*]

Political historians remember 1917 as the year in which the United States went to war to make the world safe for democracy. Literary historians recall it as a time of great stirring in American poetry. Ezra Pound and his followers were busily imagizing. T. S. Eliot stood between "Prufrock" and "The Waste Land." Baudelaire was becoming an excitement in advance circles. Yeats was at the point of his best writing. Hopkins was about to be published. Joyce and Gertrude Stein had already brought their techniques far enough forward for e. e. cummings, as a Harvard undergraduate, to have written an extremely perceptive assessment of their experiments and aims. In short, The Age of the Manifesto was upon us. Schools and movements were everywhere. The next ten years were to see them flower and fade quarterly, leaving behind them stacks of unread little magazines.

Into all this excitement and search for a new way of writing stepped twenty-five-year-old Edna St. Vincent Millay, who had just been graduated from Vassar and had just published a volume of verse called *Renascence*. Miss Millay brought forth her ballad stanzas, her archaic embellishment, and her sonnets in the grand manner. Perhaps not surprisingly, even her traditionalism was enough to excite a school into being. Edna St. Vincent Millay became a name for a kind of lyric to be imitated wherever the female heart beat fast.

Her popularity, easily won, was to continue through the Twenties and—perhaps a sign of dangerous limitation or perhaps a sign of fundamental power—was to reach beyond the "literary" to something resembling the "public." Her reading appearances were to become tri-

umphs of trailing gowns and far-flung gestures. The legend of her loves
was to illuminate dreams from Keokuk to Salt Lick.

Now Edna Millay is dead, and somehow the Twenties, when some
of you were very young and some of us were children, are suddenly
sent splintering into antiquity. What a long way back it is to yesterday
when Edna St. Vincent Millay was The Village and The Village was
Edna St. Vincent Millay, and you went back and forth all night on
the ferry, and I, still in knickers, read about it in Medford, Massachusetts, and daydreamed the wonders of the life being lived just off
Washington Square.

Or else it was just silly and adolescent with shouting on street cor-
ners, and dreary recitals by bearded poets, and a great deal of very high
level small-talk by flat-chested girls in excruciating dresses. But, silly
or not, it was a time of tremendous vitality, and certainly no one lived
it more passionately and beguilingly—or so at least it seemed to me,
and so it must have seemed to thousands of adolescents like me—than
Edna St. Vincent Millay.

There are always two of every poet: one a person, the other a presence contrived by the poems. Whatever the person is, the presence is
something else, an aspect of the person or a series of aspects. The
reader of Edna Millay is easily confused in this since the person and
the presence seem so bound up together, the legend of her living so
much a part of the poems. One reads the poems and thinks he could
walk down the street and identify their author on sight.

It is impossible, of course, to say whether or not Edna Millay's
poems will "survive"—whatever that means—but in the very imme-
diacy with which one makes a person of the presence may lie the best
testimony to a creative achievement. For it is not good enough simply
to dismiss the issue by saying that the poems are autobiographical. Or
if it is, it is only good enough if one realizes that autobiography is not
transcribed so much as it is invented. No one can write all of himself;
he must select aspects, and every selection invents. Whatever powers
and whatever limitations are to be found in the poems, their achievement is that they invented Edna St. Vincent Millay.

Almost, one is tempted to say nostalgically, they invented a decade.
One knows the thought is absurd and yet one half-thinks it. One may
as well say the raccoon coat invented the plastic age. No, what I am

thinking is that she invented it (or somehow brought it alive) to me and certainly to many of my generation busy at their first fumblings and exaggerations.

I must have been nearing fifteen, a happy prowler in the dark stacks of our public library, when I began to pull down poetry from the shelves. About all the poetry I had behind me was Kipling and I was not sure but what he was too "young"—by which I meant I had read him more than six months ago. Then I found "The Man with a Hoe." That was a wonderful discovery: "Who loosened and let down that brutal jaw?" I would demand of my sisters. *Spoon River* was another: "Petit the poet, tic-tic, peas in a dry pod"—it was enough to make me feel like a critic. Then one day I opened *The Harp-Weaver* and came on "The Goose Girl":

> Spring rides no horses down the hill,
> But comes on foot, a goose-girl still
> And all the loveliest things there be
> Come simply, so it seems to me.
> If ever I said, in grief or pride,
> I tired of honest things, I lied;
> And should be cursed for evermore
> With Love in laces, like a whore,
> And neighbors cold, and friends unsteady,
> And Spring on horseback like a lady!

Now there was a thing you could really recite: grief, pride, curses, whores! This was life! I began to read Millay avidly, to spout her endlessly. "What lips my lips have kissed." Mine hadn't kissed anything but the cheeks of aunts, but wasn't that part of the drama? "Euclid alone has looked on Beauty bare." How rich that was!

> Let all who prate of Beauty hold their peace,
> And lay them prone upon the earth, and cease . . .

What a sudden sense of life they released! Even the too-muchness was right. In retrospect, of course, one knows that it was exactly the too-muchness that was right, but what an excitement it was then to curl up with it in a corner of the stacks and wait for the time when you could recite it to a girl with the moon beside you or, perhaps more accurately, to the moon with a girl beside you. Certainly the moon comes first.

"The Goose Girl" still strikes me as the most typical of Edna Millay's poems, of the kind of presence she sought to invent. Its measure is cut to absolute simplicity; one thinks immediately of Housman, whose hand has surely touched Edna Millay's first poems. And immediately one senses a difference in the simplicity. "The Goose Girl" bears many surface resemblances to Housman's "Cherry Trees." The meter, the kind of language, the easy flow of the symbols, the imagery, all have a great deal in common. Yet Housman's poem remains convincing, and somehow "The Goose Girl" does not.

The difference occurs not in the way of saying but in the attitude of the saying, a point Robert Frost once made especially well in speaking of "the way the poet takes his subject, the way the poet takes himself." One is finally forced to distrust the way Edna Millay takes herself in this poem. One can believe without reservation that Housman wanted to walk out quietly to observe the cherry trees. His feeling for the false bloom of snow upon them is evoked beyond question. But can one feel the same conviction in the evocation of Spring as the Goose Girl and the Lady on Horseback, or is the author being consciously picturesque? And when we are told that

> All the loveliest things there be
> Come simply, so it seems to me,

not only the archaic use of "be" but the knowledge of Miss Millay's archness in so many of her other poems makes us wonder if this is not simply another pose. We doubt, and immediately the poem confirms our doubt by the burst of rhetoric that fills up the next five lines. This is not an experience, we conclude; it is a pose.

And poem after poem confirms the feeling that it is a pose; there is always that element of the overdramatic, a fabrication of the words rather than of the feeling, of a posture rather than of an experience. It is, one suspects, exactly this in the poems that once set twenty years of undergraduates to imitating them. Something in the overstatement of the poems fitted our own imbalance. Perhaps that explains why I fell violently in love as a sophomore at Bates College with our local Edna, or, more precisely, with the best of our local Ednas, for even at so small a school as Bates there were at least two dozen of them. Certainly something powerfully suited to our needs grew at that edge of bathos.

> I screamed, and—lo!—Infinity
> Came down and settled over me.

Or in the coy first hungering for great sophistication:

> After all, my erstwhile dear,
>   My no longer cherished,
> Need we say it was not love,
>   Just because it perished?

It swaggered with us like our first self-conscious cigarettes, an endless, very fine portrait of ourselves being very wise.

It seems impossible now that we could have been so moved by such lines. Or is it simply that we can never again be so moved by anything? Whatever the truth of it, we were moved, we were filled, we were taken.

Then somehow it was all over. The Twenties had ended even for those of us who were too young to do more than overhear the tail end of their legend. Symbolically, Edna Millay's power to thrill and carry the reader seemed to end with them. For what made the poems immediate was the passionate youngness of their author. And suddenly it was years later and the youngness had fled. One read Auden and Spender instead, and as each of the new Millay books appeared— *Wine from These Grapes, Conversation at Midnight, Huntsman, What Quarry?*—one wondered what had happened to the breathlessness and carry that used to be in the poems.

The simple fact seems to be that, having outgrown her youth, Edna Millay had outgrown the one subject she could make exciting. *Conversation at Midnight* was her attempt at intellectual reportage of an age, but it provided no subject for her gift. It seemed as if she had stopped living in order to talk—to talk endlessly and dully—about life. There is still here and there the intense preoccupation with herself, her body, the pose of her body; but where once we read of the body in love we now read:

> Over the sound of flushing water, which
> For some strange reason, science having gone so far,
> Even in the houses of the extremely rich
> Still roars in a room, and everybody knows where you are . . .

> Instead of bright children on McDougall Street,

> Sons-of-bitches at Hialeah
> hacking their initials in the royal palms . . .

Instead of the endless energy of the girl, we are presented the matron posing before her dressmaker who turns her about and is made to cry: "*Que Madame est maigré.*"

Then came the war, and the social consciousness that had first driven her to write some of her worst poetry in "Justice Denied in Massachusetts" (the Sacco-Vanzetti trial) betrayed her into such books as *Make Bright the Arrows*. These are tragic books from which the last vestige of gift has disappeared; nobly to be sure, for reasons that all men of good will must be tempted to condone. But finally poetry must be protected from even the highest motives. Perhaps especially from the highest motives. Moral indignation is no substitute for art. In these poems, unfortunately, only that substitution speaks: line after line of exhortations from the vocabulary of humanism, page after page of moral platitudes, but not a phrase of poetry. We agreed that there were no islands left, we wept for Lidice, but the poems could not find our feelings. The facts themselves were so desperately more moving.

But to enumerate a poet's failures is not to judge him. A writer must be judged by his best. Edna Millay's best came at a time when many needed her excitement. Whether her capture of that audience was a good or a bad thing for the course of poetry one cannot say with any conviction. Certainly her intimate treatment of the frankly sensuous was some part of an age's contribution toward broadening the range of subjects permissible to poetry. That much is surely good. Certainly, too, the kind of poetry she set herself to write has found no followers except among the dim mediocrities of the Poetry Societies. And that cannot be good. But neither merit nor lack of merit defined her position in the poetry of the Twenties. It was not as a craftsman nor as an influence, but as the creator of her own legend, that she was most alive for us. Her success was as a figure of passionate living.

Unfortunately, passion is nonreflective. At its slightest her passion made her the mother of the O-God-the-pain! girls of the O-World-I-cannot-hold-you-close-enough! school. And even at its best it is not likely that her work can be popular so long as poetry continues its present development toward the ambivalent consciousness and the pessimistic intellect. Perhaps her poems must be forgotten. Or perhaps they will become, like *The Rubaiyat* and the *Sonnets from the Portuguese*, poems that generation after generation of the young will be swept away by, gorgeously, overwhelmingly swept away by, and then outgrow.

But today none of that seems to matter. One finds himself less inclined to criticism than to nostalgia. At least it will be so for all of us who were very young and very merry and aren't exactly that any more, but who once long ago opened those little black books with their titles pasted to the binding, and suddenly found the wind blowing through everybody's hair and a wonderful girl running to us through the wind. "*Que Madame est maigré.*" But what a whirling all-night time it was!

LETTERS TO THE EDITOR

[*December 2, 1950*]

⁎

When I saw an article about the late Edna St. Vincent Millay I was greatly excited. After reading it I am so angry and disappointed that I find myself writing to reproach you for printing such a petty and malicious requiem, which dwells insistently on the lesser works of a truly great lyric poetess.

John Ciardi intimates that at the time of Miss Millay's great fame only the adolescents and malcontents of humdrum living were moved by her poems. Had he read the critical estimate of her work at that time he would have realized that she was acclaimed by mature critics not for her attitudes but for the lyric perfection of her verse. It is unfair to dwell exclusively on or to quote only the mediocre.

E. W. PARAMORE
East Norwich, N. Y.

⁎

John Ciardi's article betrays an almost neurotic eagerness to disclaim and deplore his early enthusiasm for a now unfashionable—but immortal—kind of poetry. Why is it any more "coy" for her to use some of the phrases he quotes (notably not her best work) than for

him to present himself as a presumably appealing adolescent in knickers in the Public Library of Medford? What in heaven's name have the "incredible" dresses of the period to do with the matter? The clothes of every age are incredible to the following one. He ignores Millay's best poems, her most poignant lyrics. With his estimate of the later, socially conscious works most persons of taste must agree. The article in general assumes an air of condescension difficult to justify. Because thou art harsh and obscure, shall we have no more silver jets of melody?

KATHARINE DAY LITTLE
Boston, Mass.

⁎

I did not know Edna St. Vincent Millay personally and I was never a great admirer of her verse. But it seems to me that she was a true poet both in her earlier and later works. She at least possessed the lucidity which most of her contemporaries lack.

GEORGE SYLVESTER VIERECK
New York, N. Y.

⁎

Edna St. Vincent Millay grew old. And John Ciardi, too, has grown old, as he unwittingly reveals in his critique. But Edna's poems will forever remain new and fresh so long as we have new and fresh minds to read and to react.

EDMUND S. WHITMAN
New York, N. Y.

*

Somehow or other, Miss Millay's faults as a poet—and she had many—are confused with Mr. Ciardi's trials in growing up. Quite a few others of us grew up as his contemporaries and managed to take Edna in our stride. Being no longer adolescent, our appraisal of her work is more measured.

Instead of identifying her with her worst poems, which any spirited adolescent would and probably should like, we would be inclined at this date to measure her best poems against the accepted best in modern poetry.

LOUISE LITTLE STURGIS
New York, N. Y.

*

Edna St. Vincent Millay was no ivory-tower resident. She was a tremendous booster of American show business. She thought "radio has the opportunity and, if skilfully employed, the power of giving to its listeners through the medium of poetry, as great a happiness and as deep an enrichment of their lives as it has given through the medium of music." She listened to the radio on an old table model. She switched the dials to symphonic music, news round-ups, and sports programs. She followed the fistic battles of Joe Louis. Once when her radio broke down she traveled twenty miles in order to hear the blow-by-blow account of a Louis fight. She was miserable when Charlie McCarthy went off the air. On one occasion she wrote a poem in praise of the dummy's brilliant behavior and sent it to Edgar Bergen via Western Union. The poem read:

Last night I heard upon the air
A little man who wasn't there,
He wasn't there again today,
I hope he'll never go away.

She brought considerable fragrance to the air waves with her magnificent poetry readings from the former NBC studios at 711 Fifth Avenue. In the beginning (circa Cockaday Circuit) the NBC program nabobs thought there would be a limited, somewhat "precious" audience for the Millay readings. They discovered otherwise when the fan mail rolled in. West Point cadets, Scranton coal miners, Tacoma lumberjacks, Arizona cowpunchers, Texas oil drillers —these and many more demanded a repeat performance by the glorious writer.

Years later the world was privileged to hear her memorable dramatic poem *The Murder of Lidice*, her first document written expressly for radio. One of the greatest works ever to be written for the air, it cried out against the horrors of dictatorship. In burning single syllabled words she called upon all freedom-seeking people to fight the barbaric invaders. It was an eloquently moving performance with Paul Muni, Clifton Fadiman, and the late Alexander Woollcott against a background of special music by the NBC Symphony Orchestra. Radio came of age that day.

JO RANSON
New York, N. Y.

LETTERS TO THE EDITOR

[December 9, 1950]

*

It seemed a little odd to read an essay entitled "Edna St. Vincent Millay," by John Ciardi, only to find that it dealt with his youth rather than her poetry. John must have been an awfully cute kid; perhaps your readers are really interested in the story of his adolescence. But why not give it a candid title?

. . . it is not likely that her work can be popular so long as poetry continues its present development toward the ambivalent consciousness and the pessimistic intellect. Perhaps her poems must be forgotten.

So thinks John Ciardi. That's not adolescent thinking; that's real adult thinking. I'm here to tell you that you'll have to do a lot of thinking before you can equal that. And as to the distinguished style of writing—you'll *never* match it. No use to try.

Edna Millay once wrote four lines which come to mind.

Cruel of heart, lay down my song.
Your reading eyes have done me
  wrong.
Not for you was the pen bitten,

And the mind wrung, and the song written.

JOHN TROXELL

Stanford, Calif.

*

I was not surprised at the volume of protest you received on John Ciardi's article. When I read it I was sure that would happen. And it certainly seemed a rather premature rush to express a final opinion; when there is death, there is no more need of haste. One could perhaps pause a while to let the perfume of flowers on a grave have its day of sweetness first, and the flowers themselves a gentle time to wither.

But, aside from that, it seems to me that most of your letter writers miss one point. Perhaps I sense that the more because I shared Ciardi's early passion for Millay—only I was slightly older, just trailing the poet herself in years, so that she anticipated for me what I was about to say. Many of the letter writers agree that her early poems are forgettable. But it seems to me that there is the missed point. Ciardi says those early ones were precious for him—when it was right for his youth to find them precious. So they were also for me. If once there was felt a great surge in a phrase of music and then never more did one find further ecstasy in the same composer—still for that one perfect moment of answer in oneself that composer has been great, and his greatness can never again be denied.

She remains a part of inextricable experience for me. I do not care what the ages' appraisal of her may be, but I think it may come close to Mr. Ciardi's. If the indignant ones will read that article again very carefully, perhaps they will see that Ciardi has demonstrated as precious what the defenders would deny.

JOSEPHINE LYNCH

L E T T E R S   T O   T H E   E D I T O R

[*December 16, 1950*]

*

John Ciardi's article was a fair analysis of Edna St. Vincent Millay's appeal. She *was* Spring incarnate—nothing more. Her tragedy was that this Spring was followed by no fruitful Fall. I shall never forget the eagerness with which I opened my copy of *Conversation at Midnight*—the fragrance of *Renascence* still in my nostrils—nor the disgust with which I consigned that copy to the flames.

But, to paraphrase her own lines, "Need we say it was not poetry, just because it ceased?" Let her continue to live in lines like these:

I would I were alive again,
To kiss the fingers of the rain,
To drink into my eyes the shine
Of every slanting, silver line,
To catch the freshened, fragrant breeze
From drenched and dripping apple trees.

ETHEL TORNÖE OLNEY
San Anselmo, Calif.

LETTERS TO THE EDITOR

[*February 17, 1951*]

EDITOR's NOTE: *The following letter is from Norma Millay, sister of the late poet and her literary executor.*

I have read several replies to an appraisal of the poetry of Edna St. Vincent Millay by John Ciardi; the original article has now been sent me, and I find its originality striking, to say the least. It has already been said that Mr. Ciardi handed us his confessions under a misleading and inviting title, but no notice seems to have been taken of the poet Ciardi showing beneath Miss Millay's stanzas like a grimy slip. I have counted eight original mistakes in the few quotations he allotted her, and his French, which he twice makes her "make" someone say, is so original as not to have been invented.

I appreciate of course that the author worked against time, that he wished to get his article into print while a sense of personal loss was being keenly felt throughout the country for its beloved poet.

I quote the author in his appraisal: "And suddenly it was years later and the youngness had fled." Whose youngness, Mr. Ciardi? Are you sure? Can it be that *you* had become too old to understand "The Fitting," a later poem you attempt to interpret for us, while you state you had stopped reading her? You lament that she no longer wrote "of the body in love" and give us evidences of its passing by some strange examples—very strange: a direction in a play for an off-stage sound; an observation made by one of the characters who had been drinking for hours, obviously selected by you for the words "son of a bitch" (you were always so alert to words like "curse" and "whore" —remember?—so that one wonders what "Euclid alone has looked on

Beauty bare," that called for the embellishment of the youth Ciardi, moon and girl, really meant to you); and your third example, and this I struggle to believe, is "The Fitting." You write of this: "Instead of the endless energy of the girl we are presented the matron posing before her dressmaker—." This, a poem of a body so in love that it is losing weight noticeably thereby and, quite the opposite to "posing," the lady does not dare recognize herself in the mirror for fear of disclosing her mind, wholly occupied with the coming evening and *him,* "While they murmur busily in the distance," they, snipping their cold shears against her.

Had Mr. Ciardi been thoughtful enough to state in a subtitle that "The Goose Girl" strikes him as "the most typical" of Miss Millay's works, readers could have gone on at their own risk. In this poem, by the way, the word is "forevermore" not "for evermore"; there is a comma after "horseback"; a period after "still." Mr. Ciardi's selection of the typical Millay shows the type of reader, I should say, rather than a work representative of a poet whose sonnets, collected some time back, numbered 161 while we were told of several sequences not included.

Edna St. Vincent Millay began writing poems in the Nineties; wrote poetry in the first decade of this century in its Teens, in the Twenties, in the Thirties, in the Forties, and in the Fifties until she died—because she was a poet. And there are undeniable evidences that she is widely read, understood, and deeply loved.

I wish to add that I believe the misquoting of poetry to be due usually to a too personal enthusiasm, but that in writing by a person connected with the English department of any school it becomes ignorance together with an arrogant disregard for authenticity and should be disclosed as such. Mr. Ciardi's inability to understand the work of a poet is his misfortune.

NORMA MILLAY

Austerlitz, N. Y.

THE UNICORN

A CLOSE LOOK AT THE UNICORN

[*January 12, 1957*]

Anne Morrow Lindbergh's great personal distinction, together with the popularity of her six earlier volumes, some of poetry and some of prose, made it clear from the start that her latest volume of verse, *The Unicorn and Other Poems*, would sell widely. Poetry nevertheless is no reliable consort of either personal distinction or of book-store success. Everyone is in trouble when he looks at the stars, and under the stars I am as humanly eager to grant Mrs. Lindbergh the dignity of her troubles as I am to enjoin my own.

One of my present troubles is that as a reviewer not of Mrs. Lindbergh but of her poems I have, in duty, nothing but contempt to offer. I am compelled to believe that Mrs. Lindbergh has written an offensively bad book—inept, jingling, slovenly, illiterate even, and puffed up with the foolish afflatus of a stereotyped high-seriousness, that species of aesthetic and human failure that will accept any shriek as a true high-C. If there is judgment it must go by standards. I cannot apologize for this judgment. I believe that I can and must specify the particular badness of this sort of stuff.

I open to the first poem, a simple two-part piece titled "The Man and the Child." Stanza one develops the theme "It is the man in us who works"; stanza two, the theme "It is the child in us who plays"; and the two themes are resolved in the single final line, "It is the child in us who loves."

A simple pattern of idea but certainly not a bad one as such. One need only imagine what Blake might have done with such a structure to realize that poetry can remake any theme or series of themes if it can manage to deepen and to reinvigorate them. The measure of the poem is not in its assertion but in the performance of its own insight. As a definition of "performance" let me offer "the emotional enlargement of the starting insight by its re-creation within the artifice of the poem."

What of Mrs. Lindbergh's performance? Here are her starting lines:

It is the man in us who works;

Who earns his daily bread and anxious scans
The evening skies to know tomorrow's plans;
It is the man who hurries as he walks;
Finds courage in a crowd; shouts as he talks;
Who shuts his eyes and burrows through his task;
Who doubts his neighbor and who wears a mask;
Who moves in armor and who hides his tears.
It is the man in us who fears.

I certainly must record as a first general impression that the details of the man's behavior seem exquisitely foolish. I wince over the opening clash of cliché in "who earns his daily bread," stumble over the tortured and rhyme-forced inversion of "and anxious scans" (Mrs. Lindbergh might at least have put commas around "anxious"), and proceed from there to a dull nothingness, only to be brought up with a real grating of the nerve by the absurdity of line eight, in which I am told that the man moves in armor and, so encased, goes to the trouble of hiding his already hidden tears. Or perhaps Mrs. Lindbergh thought of the man as wearing armor but with the vizor raised. But what can be the figurative force of "to move in armor" if it does not mean "to go carefully and completely on guard"? Knights in armor raised their vizors only in moments of relaxation or as a gesture of courtesy. Clearly neither possibility can apply here. And clearly, too, Mrs. Lindbergh asks no such questions of her language and metaphors. The more evident principle of the writing seems to be that "tears-fears" is an easy rhyme and that any other consideration may be thrown overboard so long as the jingle is saved.

At this point I have had enough of the first poem. I turn to the second and read the first two lines:

Like birds in winter
You fed me;

I wonder why there is no comma after "winter" and I am left to guess
what I later confirmed, that Mrs. Lindbergh does not understand
English usage of the comma. But, more urgently, who is "like birds in
winter"? Grammatically rendered, the lines can only mean "You, like
birds in winter, fed me," *i.e.*, a kind of coming of the ravens. Four
lines later, however, the context makes it clear that these lines must
be taken to mean "You fed me as one feeds birds in winter."

Once again I have had enough. I turn to the third piece, "The Little
Mermaid," and I read:

Only the little mermaid knows the price
One pays for mortal love, what sacrifice
Exacted by the Sea-Witch, should one choose
A mermaid's careless liberty to lose.

Only the little mermaid—and Mrs. Lindbergh. But by now I am becoming accustomed to mindlessness, as I am to Mrs. Lindbergh's way
of lunging for rhymes, for any rhyme. So I am prepared to pass over,
as familiar ground, the rhyme-forced redundancy of "sacrifice," the
similarly dictated inversion of line four, and the faulty parallel construction of the second clause.

There still remains a small harvest of clichés. From the next twelve
lines of the poem I cull: "smoky cauldron," "restless waves," "dim
pellucid depths," "unheard music," "light as foam," and "moon bright
nights." The poem continues on to the overleaf but I do not. I begin
to skip.

I try page eighteen and find this metaphoric flight in the first four
lines:

Burning tree upon the hill
And burning tree within my heart,
What kinship stands between the two,
What cord I cannot tear apart.

I am not at all sure I know how that second burning tree got into Mrs. Lindbergh's heart, but to save time let me grant rather than dispute both the trees and the assertion that a kinship "stands" between them. I am next asked to believe that this kinship, by apposition, is a "cord" and that the cord, by carry-over of the parallel construction, "stands" between the two trees. I can only assume that Mrs. Lindbergh intends the construction "a cord stands between the two trees" to mean "a cord is tied from tree to tree." But if this is her intention —and no other seems remotely possible—I must certainly remind her that freshman English students are required to take remedial courses when they persist in such illiteracies. Mrs. Lindbergh continues with "What cord I cannot tear apart." Once again the grammar is faulty (as it is in poem after poem of those I sampled). Whether "cord" be taken as some sort of rope or as some sort of umbilicus, "to tear it apart" can only mean "to shred or to rip it," whereas the only possible sense in this context is not "to shred" but "to break." Am I to assume that Mrs. Lindbergh is actually illiterate? The contrary evidence is not overwhelming. But what is more evident—once again—is the fact that she is constantly in trouble with the simplest of rhymes (here "heart —apart") and that, lacking first a sound grammatical sense and second anything like a poet's sense of words and their shades of meaning, she is defenseless against her rhyme-schemes and will commit any absurdity while entangled in her own harness.

Nor is "absurdity" too strong a word. I can certainly sense the human emotion that sends Mrs. Lindbergh to the writing, but I can only report that what emerges in the writing is low-grade poetry and low-grade humanity. As a person Mrs. Lindbergh must certainly have richer resources than these, but whatever those personal resources the fact remains that they simply do not make their way through bad writing. I must believe that the art of poetry is more important than Mrs. Lindbergh or than you or than me,* and that bad observance of that art is an assault on one of the most enduring sanctions of the total human experience. Believing that, I believe it to be absurd, and a violence against language, to write, as Mrs. Lindbergh does, for example, of a submerged stone "clogging" a stream. "Clog" is a distinct, mean-

* See letter from Miss Milda W. Defandorf, p. 83.

ingful, and useful word, and as such it is as delightful to the senses as is the feel of a well-made pair of pliers in the palm. For the first three reasons the word is part of the total possibility of human understanding and communication. For the consequent sense of delight, it is a part of the relish and art of language. For a person of poetic pretensions to misuse language itself in so slovenly a way is certainly akin to Original Sin, and in the absence of the proper angel I must believe that it is the duty of anyone who cares for the garden to slam the gate in the face of the sinful and abusive.

Certainly it is the same sinful insensibility that permits Mrs. Lindbergh to offer for sale the following lines—as pedestrian, tone-deaf, and silly a proposition in intellect as ever befuddled a high school valediction:

> For beauty, for significance, it's space
> We need, and since we have no space today
> In which to frame the act, the word, the face
> Of beauty, it's no longer beautiful.

(Characteristically, note the construction "space [dimensional] in which to frame the word [oral].")

Or again in the following, in which the reader is asked to believe, among other things, that earth lies between its own surface and some neighboring planet:

> The planet in the sky,
> The sea-shell on the ground:
> And though all heaven and earth between them lie.

Or, finally, and as a sort of ultimate absurdity, what must certainly be the neatest trick of the literary season:

> Down at my feet
>   A weed has pressed
> Its scarlet knife
>   Against my breast.

Compare the now classical examination answer that read: "Dante was a great transitional figure: with one foot he stood in the Middle Ages, while with the other he saluted the rising sun of the Renaissance." The student could perhaps be forgiven—he was racing the clock. But what will forgive Mrs. Lindbergh this sort of miserable stuff?

L E T T E R S   T O   T H E   E D I T O R

[*February 2, 1957*]

*

I, for one, resent John Ciardi's "contemptuous" attack upon Mrs. Anne Lindbergh and her book of poetry *The Unicorn and Other Poems.* I do not believe that Mrs. Lindbergh fancies herself a "great" poet (after all, there are few who can claim that distinction), nor do I think she pretends to be a profound thinker. I think of her as a human being with the same problems, likes, dislikes —in fact, all the feelings that any of us might have. These human feelings Mrs. Lindbergh has very ably put into words. Maybe the arrangements of some of these ideas into poetry sound trite to the hardened ultra-sophisticate, but I am sure that to many these poems express what Mrs. Lindbergh intends them to without using a lot of double talk and futile phrases that mean nothing either to the reader or the writer. Why not take this book of poems for what it is, an expression of Mrs. Lindbergh's own thoughts. Don't dissect it for techniques.

ILA M. K. FLANDERS
South Natick, Mass.

*

I thought Ciardi's review of Mrs. Lindbergh's poems the most literate, authoritative, and expert I have ever read in this difficult field of criticism. I have a wild respect for good poets, and he so deftly and accurately made the points that had to be made that, contrary to my long-established custom, I had to write this fan letter.

HERMAN KOGAN
Chicago, Ill.

*

Even assuming that Mrs. Lindbergh's poetry is perfectly bad, there is no need to keep the critical machine grinding away and spitting forth every offending bit. What's the use? Professor Ciardi cannot give the ultimate verdict anyway. Posterity will do that. And it's amazing how some poets who mixed their metaphors and committed solecisms have nicely stood the test of time.

GEORGE P. NYE
Roslindale, Mass.

Unlike John Ciardi, who only "sampled" Mrs. Lindbergh's verses before he ridiculed them, I have read his comments fully and thoughtfully. Ciardi exceeded his privileges as a poetry editor to insult a sincere and sensitive writer. The roles of prosecuting attorney, judge, reviewer, and editor should not be vested in one person. A reviewer who finds that he has "nothing but contempt to offer" may decline the assignment. But he may not assume that his disdain absolves him from the formal duty of reading the book or the customary courtesies of criticism.

GEOFFREY BRUUN

Ithaca, N. Y.

*

It does seem to me that there is a point beyond which no reviewer can pass with impunity. Is there not a place where personal vindictiveness is paramount, and the "truth" about the work second-ary? Both of the above-mentioned articles seem to me to fall in a very doubtful class.

GEORG PLUCK

Grass Lake, Mich.

*

The Idols of the Market Place are always present in the communications of men, and perhaps I put too derisive and personal a meaning upon the word "contempt." Mrs. Lindbergh's may indeed be a very poor book, and then, by analysis, it should doubtless be shown to be so. I cannot believe, however, that Mr. Ciardi really means that as a reviewer of Mrs. Lindbergh's, or any other book, he has "in duty, nothing but *contempt* to offer." He must have intended some other word, since the duty of dispassionate, just criticism would have to be of a nature and quality to preclude contempt.

ROBERTA TEALE SWARTZ

Wellesley, Mass.

LETTERS TO THE EDITOR

[*February 9, 1957*]

*

Apparently Mr. Ciardi did not like *The Unicorn and Other Poems*, by Anne Morrow Lindbergh. I would like to recommend to Mr. Ciardi a paragraph from the lead article in the same issue, "The Greek Freedom," by Edith Hamilton.

Arrogance, insolent self-assertion, was of all qualities most de-tested by the Greeks. *Sophrosune* was the exact opposite. That was the Greek ideal and the result was their freedom.

FORREST A. BROGAN

Hamden, Conn.

*

Didn't the folks at Harvard ever teach Mr. Ciardi that one may chide a lady but no gentleman ever slaps her in the face?

EDWIN L. POOR
Saratoga, Calif.

*

I know nothing of Mr. Ciardi or the repressions that have soured him. I can only say that the grossly insulting language he used in his comments on Mrs. Lindbergh's recent volume is offensive. I cannot imagine them as legitimate criticism.

V. A. ROBERTSON
San Diego, Calif.

*

I, unlike Mr. Ciardi, can either take Anne Lindbergh's poetry or leave it alone. He can do neither. I think the clue to what is chewing on Mr. Ciardi is given at the outset, where he mentions her personal distinction and popularity and the good sales that attended her other volumes of verse. To Mr. Ciardi this is not to be endured. He reminds me of a beaten fighter who in desperation starts fouling his successful adversary.

ALBERT R. MARTIN
St. Joseph, Mich.

*

May one compliment Professor Ciardi on his flair for destructive criticism. Using bluntness with the verve of a butcher he blue-pencils her work as if it were but the schoolboys' theses he is so used to reducing.

CHARLOTTE LOUISE GROOM
Cincinnati, Ohio

*

Why don't you find a new poetry editor?

MARGARET G. CAREY
Minneapolis, Minn.

*

Perhaps your readers would have found Mr. Ciardi's remarks more enlightening had they not suffered through the idiotic verse in SR these past months. How is it possible for him to set himself up as such an authority, when at the same time he is publishing such uninteresting trash?

MRS. M. H. PERRY
Pomona, Calif.

*

I shall watch SR for a poem by Mr. Ciardi, and if he doesn't make his ideas walk like good tin soldiers (with their *vizors down*) he'll come a cropper. And God spare him if he should ever step on a snake! In all fairness, it should leap to his masculine chest and pierce him to the heart.

MARIE J. HOLT
Newport, R. I.

*

If Mr. Ciardi craves clarity of thought and meaningful use of words and punctuation marks, he should not waste his time on Mrs. Lindbergh, who is surely a minor offender, if one at all. Let him address his demands to e. e. cummings, T. S. Eliot, and their tribe.

NEWELL H. DAILEY
Pella, Ia.

*

Readers of SR expect more of Mr. Ciardi's talents than his reminder to the poetess "that freshman English students are required to take remedial courses when they persist in such illitera-cies." I remind Mr. Ciardi that, in Mrs. Lindbergh, he's dealing not with a college freshman, but with a distin-guished woman. She has a right to ex-pect distinguished, non-freshman criti-cism.

ED WATERS

Los Angeles, Calif.

*

While Mr. Ciardi aligns his marks of punctuation and his exact words, I'll purchase a copy of *The Unicorn and Other Poems* and read it, content in the knowledge that a critic's opinion is not necessarily better than mine.

ELIZABETH L. DERR

Mt. Vision, N. Y.

*

I have just finished the review of Mrs. Lindbergh's book:

From Mr. Ciardi's words, I gather
He'd other things be reading, rather.

Please note proper placing of commas.

JO HEMPHILL

Washington, D. C.

*

We were not there to see, yet know,
    your tears . . .
The earnest men are gone and only
    hardy
Scalpels like acute Ciardi
Remain?: You've loved a world that,
    graceless, jeers?
We fools, who broke our skulls on
    Plexiglas
Because your image of a man looked
    high,
Weep in the wings for you and watch
    you fly

Through freedom from the brutish
    pedant-class
Mismated metaphors grow much
    more serious
In the grim gaze of the Categorical
    Imperious;
And only time
Can force a rhyme
Of "clever lad"
And "cad" . . .
None but the grounded heart may
    guess your tears.

WM. K. FIELDING

Ware, Mass.

*

Before I read Mr. Ciardi's review of Anne Morrow Lindbergh's book of poems, I had thought it a fine and lovely thing. I still think so. He calls his re-view, "A Close Look at the Unicorn." He has looked too closely. He cannot see the forest for the trees.

Poetry is not a dead body to be laid upon a table for dissection. It is a liquid, living, moving thing. Mr. Ciardi won-ders why there is no comma after "winter." In digging into a poem with the dissector's keen, unfeeling blade in his search for commas he failed to find the comet.

C. M. A. ROGERS

Mobile, Ala.

*

My first reaction was shock. How could any one individual be so cruel? And my second—Why should a magazine that goes to a reading group of kind people have ignored us in favor of one horrid person?

ALICE ROBINSON

Claremont, Calif.

*

I find myself greatly distressed by the furious, violent, savage attack on one who essays to learn by doing. Grant that the work is amateurish and below the standards of Mr. Ciardi's excellence. But I ask, not being a critic, only a reader, must one be a brutal human being in order to be recognized as a brilliant critic—and be a poet, too?

I. S. GALINDO
Los Angeles, Calif.

*

This review was unwarranted in its tone and temper. Many collections of mediocre poetry appear regularly; they are usually passed over lightly or ignored. Why Mrs. Lindbergh should be singled out for such a "production" is puzzling. It suggests personal animus, or other more obscure motives.

NAME WITHHELD
New York, N. Y.

*

It makes us realize how much we miss Amy Loveman. Such an article could never have slipped by her editorial scrutiny. I am a poet (minor) and have often appeared in your pages. I agree with much that Mr. Ciardi has to say about Mrs. Lindbergh's book—but *not* with the words he chooses to express his judgment of the "standards."

Mr. Ciardi himself is a competent poet, but his petulance and egotism unfit him for the role of critic. John Ciardi is only one individual. What of *The Saturday Review* and its distinguished editorial board?

MARY BALLARD DURYEE
New York, N. Y.

*

Every now and then John Ciardi manages to spoil an issue of my favorite magazine. I am not a poet nor a critic. (I don't believe Mr. Ciardi is either.) I am sorry that I am not because I'd like to think my opinion matters when I say Mrs. Lindbergh's poems have beauty for me.

In all my years of reading SR I have never seen such cruel carping criticism of even the trashiest book. This seems even to attack Mrs. Lindbergh personally.

ELEANOR GRAY EGGEN
St. Paul, Minn.

*

In this devastating review Mr. Ciardi says, "For a person of [Mrs. Lindbergh's] poetic pretension to misuse language itself in so slovenly a way is certainly akin to Original Sin." Twenty lines above Ciardi writes, "I must believe that the art of poetry is more important than Mrs. Lindbergh—*or than ME.*" My! MY! No high-school freshman gets by with that.

MILDA W. DEFANDORF
Milwaukee, Wis.

*

Mr. Ciardi's painfully silly and craftily barbed attack on Mrs. Lindbergh's *Unicorn* reminds me forcibly of the compulsion of a small boy to throw his whole stack of snowballs at the first animate object that comes into range.

DOROTHY BOICOURT
Kansas City, Mo.

*

It is not necessary to use a sledgeham-
mer to demolish a fragile shell.

E. B.

New Haven, Conn.

*

Though I know virtually nothing about
Mrs. Lindbergh, I doubt if she feels the
need of any apology from Mr. Ciardi.
But he certainly owes her one—and
owes one also to SR and its readers.

WM. D. HAMMOND

Grosse Pointe, Mich.

*

Mr. Ciardi sounds like a rejected lover,
and a very young one at that.

ELIZABETH HOWLAND

Lafayette, Ind.

*

I suggest you let some other reviewer
take over women poets, especially if they
are successful.

NAME WITHHELD

St. Paul, Minn.

John Ciardi and the Readers

EDITORIAL BY NORMAN COUSINS

[February 16, 1957]

John Ciardi's review of Anne Morrow Lindbergh's *The Unicorn and
Other Poems* has produced the biggest storm of reader protest in the
thirty-three-year history of *The Saturday Review*. Hundreds of readers
have hastened to tell us of their pointed disapproval of Mr. Ciardi's
review; four have written in his support. Many of the letters have
raised questions about our editorial policy and procedure. How is it,
they have asked, that the review was allowed to appear? Would the
review have been published if the editor was not abroad at the time?
One note inquired whether the editor wisely took off for Africa the
moment the issue containing Mr. Ciardi's review went to press. Where
does the editorial board stand on the kind of review written by Mr.
Ciardi?

In fairness to Mr. Ciardi, before he is gobbled up alive by our readers, some points ought to be made clear. First, he did inform the edi-

tor, before the latter went abroad (there being no connection between the two events), of his intention to write a highly critical review of Mrs. Lindbergh's book. Mr. Ciardi was told that so long as he was Poetry Editor he would continue to enjoy the same authority over his department possessed by other members of the staff. He would have direct access to the columns of the magazine. We would stand behind his right to unobstructed critical opinion; but this did not mean he could count on our automatic support for his views.

It is only with the greatest personal pain that we occasionally publish certain reviews dealing with books or the other arts. We find ourselves in total disagreement, but we bite our critical lip and send the copy to the printers. It is impossible to edit an independent journal of criticism if the contributors feel free only to mirror the pet ideas of the editor. Our job is to build up a roster of critics with integrity, authority, vigor, and a point of view. The magazine belongs to them and the readers to no less an extent than to the editorial board and the stockholders. The quickest way to devitalize a magazine, we feel, is to claim a monopoly in these pages for the tastes of the man who is lucky enough to be editor.

Once in a great while our restraint breaks down and we indulge ourselves to the extent of a dissenting opinion. This happened recently in the case of the movie *War and Peace*. Earlier it happened with respect to Father Huddleston's *Naught for Your Comfort*, which we considered one of the most important books of the year but which our reviewer picked to pieces, to our infinite dismay. For the most part, however, we try to maintain silence and a decent respect for the opinions of the authorities to whom we go in good faith and who write for us in equally good faith.

Now, back to John Ciardi.

There is an important difference, it seems to us, between the present controversy and previous controversies involving the magazine. In most other cases, we have been called upon to back up our contributor in an argument with an author or a publisher or a branch of government or an organization. In this case, the controversy is inside the magazine itself. Mr. Ciardi's differences are with our readers. Therefore, both parties stand on equal ground so far as we are concerned. We have written to Mr. Ciardi to say that we will protect his access to our columns but he must not expect us to side with him as a matter of course or editorial duty. We also told him that we were disturbed by the implication in his defense that few of his critics knew anything about poetry. He also dismisses too lightly, it seems to us, the protests involving the question of good taste in the manner of his attack. We don't see anything inconsistent between good criticism and good taste. Strength doesn't always depend on violence.

Our main argument with Mr. Ciardi, however, involves the basis of his criticism. It seems to us that his critical yardstick for Mrs. Lindbergh's book was better adapted to the measurement of prose than poetry. By applying a rigorous test of meaning to each phrase, by insisting on precision in punctuation, by X-raying the intent of the author throughout, he has given literalness far more sovereignty than it needs or enjoys in verse. The important questions about a poem are not limited to its word-by-word or line-by-line content or structure. Does anything come to life in a person when he reads a poem? Is there a door of awareness that comes unlocked? Are there rhythms and sounds no one of which may have particularized meaning but which say something in the aggregate and produce a response that could not be produced in any other way? It seems clear that Mr. Ciardi's reply to these questions in the case of Mrs. Lindbergh's book would be in the negative. Even so, it would have made for a stronger review if he had used these questions as the context for the full development of his critical opinions. This is not to say that structure and detail are irrelevant. But they are not the whole show either.

Nor can we accept the adjective "illiterate" when applied to Mrs. Lindbergh or her books. There are few living authors who are using the English language more sensitively or with more genuine appeal. There is in her books a respect for human responses to beauty and for the great connections between humankind and nature that gives her work rare distinction and that earns her the gratitude and loyalty of her readers, as the present episode makes clear.

This editorial is not intended to chastise Mr. Ciardi. From the moment he joined *The Saturday Review* staff he added real salt to our stew. We have never caught him in an ambiguous moment. He lives as he thinks and writes, with vast energy, freedom, conviction. He has won the very real affection and respect of the entire staff. We believe that in the months and years ahead his relationship with our readers will be no less rewarding to them and to him.

LETTERS TO THE EDITOR

[*February 16, 1957*]

*

John Ciardi's "A Close Look at the Unicorn" is criticism of the sort that prompted my first subscription to the *Review*, about three years ago. It is criticism based on convincing references to principles, not merely on subjective preferences. Above all, it is braced with specific illustrations. The result is a review both informative and instructive.

EARL CLENDENON
Chicago, Ill.

*

Such terms as "contempt," "illiterate," "foolish afflatus," "slovenly," and "miserable stuff" denote rabies rather than ratiocination.

ROSE CROSS
Nashville, Tenn.

*

Why take a baseball bat to club a butterfly?

M. E. KNEVELS
Orange, N. J.

*

Mr. Ciardi devotes an entire paragraph of his long piece to Mrs. Lindbergh's misuse of the word "clog," and declares it "akin to Original Sin." Mr. Ciardi is neither God nor the Pope; but he sure is a pharisee!

NAME WITHHELD
Cambridge, Mass.

*

Mr. Ciardi must be very inexperienced, very young, and very pleased with himself. Also he has, without doubt, some personal grudge.

LAURA W. CLARK
Buffalo, N. Y.

*

It should not require half a dozen columns of such shrill vituperative writing to damn any book of verse, especially one this slight in dimension and quality.

ADELLA P. SHEA
Chula Vista, Calif.

*

We think you owe to Mrs. Lindbergh's thousands of admiring readers, and to literature itself, an unbiased review of her book. May we suggest one of the critics who felt her volume was one of the year's best poetry books?

MAY FORDE
Evansville, Wis.

*

I believe Mr. Ciardi has, in spite of the conceit that leads you into such absurdities as this review, pepped up the poetry department of SR.

MARION SMITH
Grand Rapids, Mich.

*

It is the wonder of the year to me how anyone with the intelligence I supposed Mrs. Lindbergh to possess could allow such stuff to be offered to the public.

ISABEL BOYD
St. Petersburg, Fla.

*

In an article which contains Mr. Ciardi's favorite word, I, thirty-six times, he only demonstrates that the most obvious example of inflation is his own self-importance.

WALTER HAYES
Claygate, Surrey, England

*

I believe that Mr. Ciardi's "Close Look" gave us a closer look at Ciardi than it did at the Unicorn. So much heat! So little light!

ELAINE W. COGSWELL
Berkeley, Calif.

*

It leaves one with a sense of degradation for having read it, and printing it ill becomes the dignity of The Saturday Review. In the days of William Rose Benét one never had to be ashamed of the poetry page.

DANIEL R. HULL
Woodbury, Conn.

*

Much as I admire John Ciardi's honest, fearless, and often brilliant criticism I cannot help regretting that, in the case of Anne Lindbergh's book, he gives his readers the impression that he is reviewing the personality of the author and not the poems.

KATHERINE GARRISON CHAPIN
Washington, D. C.

The Reviewer's Duty to Damn

LETTER TO AN AVALANCHE

[*February 16, 1957*]

A few weeks ago I reviewed in these pages Anne Morrow Lindbergh's *The Unicorn and Other Poems.*

Then came the avalanche. As it happens I am sitting the year out on a Fellowship to the American Academy in Rome and the avalanche descended on the New York office. The cable connects, however; the airmail has been flowing; and I have been receiving generous samples from the avalanche. SR tells me that hundreds of such letters have been received. The sampling that has been forwarded to me shows a remarkable consistency in language. The following phrases will serve to illustrate the whole range: "shocking . . . cruel . . . horrid person hitting below the belt . . . a mean low person . . . unfairness shouts aloud . . . totally unjust . . . gross discourtesy . . . lack of plain human decency . . . petty harshness . . . it leaves me with a sense of degradation for having read it."

The issues here—the first issues at least—are clear enough, but before addressing them, let me assure the avalanche of its own numerical strength and consistency. Of the hundreds of letters my review evoked, I have seen only two that might be called favorable. If there is reason in numbers, those who have been moved to object are certainly right. I am not yet persuaded, however, that the avalanches of indignation are an intellectual measure I can respect. If the excellence of poetry were determinable by a national election, I have no doubt that Edgar Guest would be elected the greatest poet in the English language—by a landslide. I doubt that he is, and I doubt the pertinence of the present avalanche.

The first issue is clearly enough the ever-present *ad hominem*. I have attempted to show by principle and evidence that Mrs. Lindbergh writes not simply bad poetry, but contemptibly bad poetry. The answer to that proposition, according to the avalanche, is: "You are a mean low horrid person." The avalanche may be right about me. But my character has nothing to do with the proposition I have put forth, and with the principles I have attempted to introduce as measures of Mrs. Lindbergh's poetry. These principles are not my invention. They would have existed in human reckoning had I never been born. Clearly, therefore, they do not depend on me for their validity. It may even be that I am unworthy of the principles I have offered for discussion. It is still the principles themselves that are at issue. If I have misstated these principles, let the statement be corrected; if I have misapplied them, let my procedure be challenged; if I have misused evidence, let my error be shown.

A second charge, already implicit in some of the phrases I have cited, is made explicit in the following passage from one letter:

> Mrs. Lindbergh is (as everyone except Mr. Ciardi knows) a sensitive and intelligent person; she would have understood a more subtly worded criticism; and so would the readers of *The Saturday Review*, who are now more prejudiced against Mr. Ciardi than against Mrs. Lindbergh. . . . It is not necessary to use a sledgehammer to demolish a fragile shell.

I think this would be a valid criticism were it a fact that the premise of my review was to make Mrs. Lindbergh understand, or that she is indeed a fragile shell. I shall have more to say below about the fragile shell, but one of the main reasons for selecting *this* book for damnation in so many words was the very fact that it was obviously destined for considerable sale and general acclaim; that far from being a fragile shell, it was almost certain of solid sales and praise, as poetry goes. For better or worse I thought it necessary to make my disagreement strong enough to counterbalance the general vague approval the book was bound to receive elsewhere.

The fact that I have expressed myself as contemptuous of Mrs. Lindbergh's poetry is, as far as I am concerned, a necessary accuracy. I regret—I have already regretted it in my review—that my final considered judgment leaves me no other choice. I think these are slovenly poems. The title under which I sent in the review was "The Slovenly Unicorn." I do not understand why the title was changed by other *SR* editors. Slovenliness I have always held to be the most contemptible of aesthetic sins. I think I have established the existence of slovenliness in these poems. If I have failed to establish the existence of such slovenliness, my charge must, of course, fall through. If I have established it, and if slovenliness is indeed (as I believe it to be) contemptible, what choice have I but to consider these poems contemptible? I am sorry if that conclusion hurts Mrs. Lindbergh, but I am even sorrier that she writes such stuff. I should, of course, be delighted to have her grasp my objections and profit by them. More urgently, however, I am trying to establish as a policy of this magazine that poetry is a serious, dignified, and disciplined human activity which is not to be debased in the name of a counterfeit sentimentality that will not bother to learn the fundamentals of its own art.

It is that line I mean to defend. That, and the proposition that the discussion must go by principle. I am not aware of any compulsion within myself to assault the character of persons not known to me, and I do not believe that I have done so. I chose to affirm principles. It is certainly significant to me that I was able to find only two letters in the total avalanche that showed even so much as an awareness that a principle was involved.

An avalanche, moreover, is not only a descending mass; it is a release of stored-up forces. "Insulting," says one letter and then cites the "idiotic verse" I have chosen for *SR* since I became Poetry Editor. One letter speaks of "the animus which darkens" my criticism, then goes on to say that I "should have attacked cummings and Eliot if what you crave is clarity of thought and meaningful use of words." One reader was moved to look up my own poems, and concludes that my recent poem to Dylan Thomas in this magazine is no good. Another says practically nothing about the present review but gleefully reports having found an unfavorable review of my own last book of poems in the most recent issue of *The Hudson Review*. (You missed another in the *Yale Review* a few issues back.) One argues that it is all wrong to "dissect" poetry in this way because it is "too living a thing for close criticism." (I thought that particular bit of nonsense had been disqualified even as a topic for sophomore bull sessions.) Another calls my review a "rude piece of writing" and goes on to schoolmarm me in the following way: "I shall watch SR for a poem by Mr. Ciardi and believe me if he doesn't make his ideas walk like good tin soldiers (with their *vizors down*) he'll come a cropper." (Dear Faithful Reader—I have had three poems in SR during the last year. I certainly hope none of them walk like good tin soldiers. Please send cropper.)

I have said that an avalanche is a release of stored-up forces. The alignment of those forces is not peculiar to SR; it is in fact descriptive of the fundamental split in all general discussion of poetry today. One vocal group believes basically that poetry must avoid all "difficulty," that it is offensive to discuss aesthetic principles, that to anatomize an art form is to destroy it, and that the real purpose of art is "to breathe forth BEAUTY." In practical application this attitude tends to become a kind of surviving Genteel Tradition.

The poetry of the surviving Genteel leans heavily to the big abstractions loudly proclaimed, to bluebirds, to "yet I know's" and "do but command's," and to the wonder the wonder the wonder of being fifty in a vague suburban way. For present purposes, let me summarize the opposite attitude with a line and a half from Browning: "Thoughts may be/ Overpoetical for poetry." Poets and readers of this persuasion (I have already described it in some detail in some of my earlier articles and need not repeat all the specifications here) tend to find the output of the Genteel Tradition to be mushy and mindless. And there is the division: one group wants poetry pretty, vague, and easily effusive. (Because easy effusion is subject to telling ridicule, the Genteel are naturally inimical to close criticism. The trouble is they can seldom if ever survive it.) The other group wants poetry to be real, physical, and disciplined. The stored-up forces of the present avalanche are simply the forces of the offended Genteel: when I took over as Poetry Editor of SR a year ago I began systematically to uproot Genteel poetry and to substitute whatever you want to call the other kind. I never imagined everyone would like it, but that remains my policy and it will be my policy for as long as I am its Poetry Editor.

One last charge delivered by the avalanche is that a reviewer commits a social impropriety, a somehow cowardly action, in expressing contempt for poems written by a socially gracious lady, *even if the poems justify such contempt*. It would be much better, runs this argument, to ignore the poems in silence. Clearly, however, to grant this argument is in effect to deny the reviewer the right to offer any but favorable reviews—a situation already dangerously prevalent in all our mass media.

I must insist in rebuttal that a reviewer's duty is to describe the book as accurately as he can. Twice in quite a number of years as a reviewer I have reviewed a book not simply harshly but contemptuously. It occurs to me that twice in something like fifteen or twenty years is not exactly a general compulsion to character assassination. If I come on another book as bad as Mrs. Lindbergh's, by an author whose name passes as that of a serious writer, I shall certainly review it in the same terms of contempt. I have only two reservations to make: the first is that the author's reputation be such that there is reasonable danger that the poems will be taken seriously; the second is that the more unfavorable a review happens to be, the more meticulously it must be documented.

What is the reviewer's contract with the author, the publisher, and his own readers? I think the author and the publisher are one in this: they, as part of their promotional process, offer the book for sale, and as part of their promotional process they send me a copy with the request that I state my considered opinion of the work in print. I do not ask for the book: it is sent to me. Moreover, if I say anything especially favorable about the poetry, there is an excellent chance that my remark will be excerpted and used in promotion for this book or on the dust jacket of the next. My contract with my readers is simple enough: to be honest. Had I liked this book, I should certainly have said so, and all hands would have been happy. I did not like it, and I tried to say exactly how much I did not like it, and for what reasons.

I may be wrong in thinking Mrs. Lindbergh writes dismal stuff. But I have asked no one to take my word for it. Rather, I have tried to document point by point what I submit to be the slovenly incompetence of the writing.

Let me confess, moreover, that I had long been waiting for the proper chance to do an out-and-out unfavorable review. I was in no sense lying in wait for Mrs. Lindbergh. I had simply decided as basic policy that it was necessary for SR from time to time to publish a review in which a bad book was called bad in so many words and for carefully detailed reasons. In the course of the last six months or so, I have passed over many possible subjects on the grounds that they were too insignificant to be worth a real assault. Mrs. Lindbergh's book happened to fill the bill perfectly. To the extent that she cares anything at all about this review my pre-set decision was a misfortune. The real misfortune, however, is that these poems were ever written. I was especially ready to sail into them, first, because they provided an excellent opportunity to define further that sort of pernicious poetry I mean to have none of in SR, and, second, because they provided an opportunity to offer an essential challenge to the whole pussyfooting process of book reviewing in our national mass media. It is even possible that in my zeal to press these two charges I overstated my objections to Mrs. Lindbergh's poetry. I cannot feel that I did, however, and I must still rest my case on the critical methods of the review itself.

The fact is that reviewing in the United States seems to have succumbed to a mindless sort of approval of everything. The very fact that the author is a human being seems to plead that to dislike his writing would be to offend him. I have long been appalled by the national review standards (and lack of standards) and I have long been determined to do something about them as Poetry Editor of SR. I was especially delighted, therefore, to find in the current issue of *The American Scholar* an article by Geoffrey Wagner entitled "The Decline of Book Reviewing." Mr. Wagner argues tellingly a number of points I have often argued less well: (a) that different reviewing standards are often applied on the same page of a given periodical, (b) that it is almost impossible to find an unfavorable review in our mass media, and (c) that the reviewers themselves are forced to cheat their real opinions or to quit. Here is part of what Mr. Wagner says on that last point:

Who has not heard complaints from some friend who read a eulogistic review of what turned out to be a rotten novel? While there can be no question of the reviewer today not being allowed the free play of review, one cannot help observing that the big

review media seem to employ extremely unexacting and opti-
mistic men and women. There is even the suspicion abroad that
a reviewer is dropped like a hot potato should he consistently
"pan" the books he is sent. (The sourpuss! Some poor devil has to
sell these things.)

Mr. Wagner goes on to point out how this process cannot help but
corrupt the reading tastes of the masses. He then cites two instances of
double-standard reviewing that fascinate me in their implications:

> Readers have seen *Marjorie Morningstar* reviewed on the front
> pages of *The New York Times Book Review* in a friendly notice
> by Maxwell Geismar, only to be followed by his sharp "criticism"
> of the same book in the pages of the *Nation*. Readers are also able
> to compare, if they wish, Edgar Johnson's kid-gloves review of
> Gordon Ray's recent book on Thackeray in *The New York Times
> Book Review* with his distinctly less cordial approach to Ray in
> *Publications of the Modern Language Association of America* for
> last March.*

* The March 23, 1957, issue of *SR* carried on the Letters to the Editor page the
following remonstrance from Mr. Geismar: "It is too bad that John Ciardi, who is
so right in principle, should be so wrong in language and feeling—an odd thing for
a poet. To make matters worse, he has now repeated a silly tale about my two
articles on Herman Wouk, and he brings to his fevered defense a rather frivolous
article on book reviewing by Geoffrey Wagner in *The American Scholar*.
"From what bit of inaccurate gossip Mr. Wagner himself picked up this Wouk
affair, I don't know. But if anybody had read my two articles with care, the following points would be clear: 1) The first review of *Marjorie Morningstar* in *The
New York Times* could hardly have been called a 'friendly notice.' It was in fact
a particularly severe review which the *Times* featured without changing a word,
and I received—certainly not so many letters as Mr. Ciardi has—but enough to
record its honesty and integrity; 2) My second article on 'The Age of Wouk' in
the *Nation* was a sequel to this review—not a contradiction of it. That was why
the *Nation* suggested it to me; and it dealt not with Mr. Wouk or his novel in
themselves, but with the *Time–Life* version of this artist as the apostle of a new
American literature. It was a satire.
"Come, come, Mr. Ciardi! It may also 'fascinate' you to know that I am including both articles in a forthcoming collection of critical essays because I happen
to be proud of them, and see no fundamental difference in their values, or in
those principles of criticism which I, too, share with the exacerbated Poetry Editor
of *The Saturday Review*."

I think I need hardly argue that the state of things Mr. Wagner describes is real, and dangerous to the standing of good literature in our society. I would add one further charge against the American book reviewer: he has destroyed his own vocabulary. Our review media use the same terms for discussing the junk produced along the Spillane–Wouk axis as they do for the efforts—good or bad but at least seriously undertaken as living art—produced along the Hemingway–Thomas Mann axis. The publishers and their jacket-blurbing tradition are certainly partners in this guilt. (One of these days I mean to do a survey of book-jacket prose and let the chips and advertising contracts fall where they may.) Between them and the natural laziness of all sentimentality, book reviewing has confused even its own inner standards. Lacking any true sense of good and bad writing, lacking any standard by which they may feel justified in damning bad writing, the reviewers have tended to settle for gentle, meaningless, polite noises. They have become readers without conviction.

I damned *The Unicorn*, first, for the reasons stated in the review itself—because the poetry struck me as miserable stuff and because I am not willing to concede that personal distinction can compensate for slovenly performance. (Had Mrs. Lindbergh's performance been on Broadway instead of in the bookshops, imagine what the drama critics would have done to her.) I did so, more importantly however, because her book was bound to have a wide circulation and to receive many vague accolades. I cite a single example: SR in its issue of December 22 (my review, already written, was awaiting publication) undertook its annual "critics'" poll of the best books of the year. *The Unicorn and Other Poems* was tied for second place with three votes. You may be sure that the votes Mrs. Lindbergh received were all from "newspaper critics" and included none from the panel of experts who had been polled. (That distinction between "newspaper critics" and "experts" is not accidental.)

I submit that when a book I believe to be as certainly meritless as *The Unicorn* comes that close to winning even an informal national poll as the best book of verse of the year, then I conceive myself to have a duty to state my objection to this sort of stuff with no apology to the author or to the traditions of the Genteel. Should I wait till it wins the Pulitzer? I think it is time, rather, to cry Hellfire. Or there is no pulpit.

The principles on which I reviewed *The Unicorn* are the principles on which I hope to see all *SR* poetry reviews based, and I urge those same principles on all the nation's review media. With the exception of the "notice" (which is not a review really, but simply a basic statement that the book exists, with one or two personal comments by the reviewer), I shall hope that reviews in these pages conform to the following principles. I cannot, of course, control what the reviewer writes. I can and will "kill" reviews that ignore these principles, and I can and will call more and more upon the reviewers who observe them.

1. The reader deserves an honest opinion. If he doesn't deserve it give it to him anyhow.

2. No one who offers a book for sale is sacrosanct. By the act of publication and promotion, the citizen–human-being forfeits his privileges as a noncompetitor. Having willingly subjected himself to judgment he must accept either blame or praise as it follows. If in doubt, assume that the book is signed by Anonymous.

3. Evaluation must be by stated principle. The reviewer's opinion is only as good as his methods.

4. A review without reference to the text is worthless.

5. Quotation without analysis of the material quoted is suspect.

6. If you cannot document a charge, pro or con, do not make it.

7. Poetry is more important than any one poet. Serve poetry.

8. Limitations of space often make it difficult and sometimes impossible to apply these principles as carefully as one would wish. No space limitation, however, is reason enough for forgetting that these principles exist.

LETTERS TO THE EDITOR

[*February 23, 1957*]

*

From its very beginnings I have taken SR, delighted in it, and depended on it. Editors, department heads, and reviewers have come and gone. Changes have been many, but usually toward growth. Never have I written you a letter. Never until the January 12 number have I found a reviewer, also a department head, guilty of gross discourtesy. But Mr. Ciardi's affront to Mrs. Lindbergh showed just that. The whole thing "smells to Heaven." Poetry is not involved.

MARGARET C. METCALF
Duxbury, Mass.

*

I exploded, shooting sparks like an angry Catherine wheel. When my initial reaction had somewhat subsided, I knew Thomas Wentworth Higginson had said (in preface to Emily Dickinson's poems) better than I am able exactly what I felt. "When a thought takes one's breath away, a lesson on grammar seems an impertinence."

ALICE BULLOCK
Santa Fe, N. M.

*

I have long been a great admirer of Mr. Ciardi's writing, both creative and critical, but I am compelled to take issue with this article. Mrs. Lindbergh's book is a great disappointment and not up to acceptable standards of poetry. But I do believe that kindness and courtesy should be incorporated in the rules of any profession, not just toward Mrs. Lindbergh because she is a gentle soul and has suffered more than most women and I shrink from seeing her chin quiver, but because, in the long run, kindness *and* honesty make the best policy.

JEAN CLARKE CALDWELL
Beverly Hills, Calif.

*

Please tell me, in mournful words, who is John Ciardi that he should set himself up as the Godhead of Poetry? Does he write poetry? I am such a simple soul and woman that I enjoyed *Unicorn.*

SARAH L. STILL
Boston, Mass.

*

The whole caliber of your magazine has been lowered by the official sanctioning of his tantrum.

SARAH S. RAMBERG
Southampton, Pa.

*

Mr. Ciardi's detailed and well-considered critique is a highly commendable piece of work. There are, unfortunately, very few critics today who are conscientious enough to take their duties seriously. By seemingly attacking the author, Mr. Ciardi is defending poetry. Only an inferior critic is tolerant of mediocrity. The vituperative letters prove that their writers have opinions; Mr. Ciardi's critique proves that he has taste. But, as Schiller said so well: "Mit der Dummheit kämpfen Götter selbst vergebens."

GUY DE VRY
Hollywood, Calif.

*

A literary review with standards can ignore a bad book or it can give it an unfavorable review. If the book is written by a well-known author, and seems likely to gain wide readership, a review is indicated. To read such a book and to write an unfavorable review is an irksome task to say the least, and I, for one, am grateful that Mr. Ciardi has done this with Mrs. Lindbergh's book, and done it so well.

The correspondence concerning Mr. Ciardi's review reveals an alarming lack of understanding of the nature of poetry and the function of criticism on the part of some of your readers. Poetry, and let us have no metaphysical nonsense about

it, is the communication of an idea (or feeling, or poetic vision, or moral truth, or what you will) through the medium of language to an audience.

MAX E. BAKER
New York, N. Y.

*

I cannot build up much sympathy for Mrs. Lindbergh. Any person who has the temerity to assume that another person will pay to read his (or her) creations is inviting the wrath of that person. And, as all the letters flattening Mr. Ciardi took such pains to point out, Mrs. Lindbergh is well paid for the abuse said wrath gave rise to.

JAMES A. JACOBSON
Waukesha, Wis.

*

Approximately two dozen letters are published in SR Feb. 9—all of them deliberately and maliciously aimed against Mr. Ciardi's judgment. I declare myself on his side.

1. A critic is entitled to be as vitriolic as he damned well pleases if his ire is of such a pitch as to merit his outburst.

2. His points are in keeping with all modern principles of good grammar, meaning, and punctuation.

3. Mrs. Lindbergh and her supporters have no right to hide behind their sex in order to avoid the criticism that he would offer under the same circumstances to male poets.

4. His darts are sharp and, therefore, hit home. The reader's blood runs faster when he reads Mr. Ciardi's attack.

WAYNE K. WALTER
Las Vegas, Nev.

LETTERS TO THE EDITOR

[*March 2, 1957*]

EDITOR'S NOTE: *Up to the time* SR *Feb. 16 went to press with John Ciardi's "The Reviewer's Duty to Damn," we had received half a dozen letters in his support against hundreds of criticism. Since that time the readers' mail has swung sharply in his favor. Not for the purpose of attaching any significance to numbers, but purely in the interests of a factual accounting, we now report an overall three-to-two balance in Mr. Ciardi's favor.*

*

You have no right to use the editorial page to criticize John Ciardi. I am canceling my subscription.

ARNOLD WHITMAN

Brooklyn, N. Y.

*

How can you support Mr. Ciardi? Please cancel my subscription.

HAROLD DAWES

Los Angeles, Calif.

*

I sent a subscription order to SR on the strength of Mr. Ciardi's criticism of Mrs. Lindbergh's verse.

NAME WITHHELD

Oyster Bay, N. Y.

The hysterics of Mr. Ciardi's review were bad enough, but in his defense he points up a serious danger to your fair editorial policies. Mr. Ciardi writes, "They (the poems) provided an excellent opportunity to define further that sort of pernicious poetry I mean to have none of in SR." If a person of Mr. Ciardi's questionable maturity is to be allowed to choose the *type* of poetry to be published in SR, then you can cancel my subscription.

JANET HUSTON

Truro, Mass.

EDITOR'S NOTE: *We are regretfully canceling Miss Huston's subscription.*

*

If you will accept contributions, I'd like to reimburse SR for every cent of cash lost in canceled subscriptions—either by those who disapprove of it for having published Mr. Ciardi in the first place, or by those who are outraged that the magazine should have published all the letters from readers criticizing him. This controversy alone is worth more than the cost of a dozen subscriptions.

DONALD R. MATSON

Chicago, Ill.

*

As a member of the Society for the Preservation of John Ciardi, I predict that following the first emotional surge you will get a steady stream of letters defending him. On several occasions I have written Mr. Ciardi lambasting him a bit. His replies have been the courteous, well-considered words of a man who is interested in ideas but not in personalities.

While I think Mr. Ciardi was a bit rough, still he was right. He is a gentleman and as such gets pretty warm when his loved ones are abused, and the muse is one of his loved ones. Furthermore, he is a darned good critic and a fine poet. He completely separates Mrs. Lindbergh as a person and as a poet. While I personally would be a bit more moderate, still I say, "Long live Ciardi!"

CARLIN ADEN
Tacoma, Wash.

*

This widespread criticism of Mr. Ciardi's review suggests a disturbing paradox. The violent personal vilification of Mr. Ciardi is the very kind of attack which the public claims to find in his review. The great majority of your letter writers seem to us to have reacted to that review with all the insensitivity to its purpose which they condemn in Mr. Ciardi. Such popular insensitivity in defense of a volume of so-called "sensitive" poetry bears out the point that Mr. Ciardi was making regarding the appeal and the audience of *The Unicorn.* The well-meaning sloppiness of thought that was the subject of this review is fighting back with all the sloppiness of non-thought at its non-well-meaning command.

MAX NATHAN, JR.
STEPHEN J. JELIN
New Haven, Conn.

If Mr. Ciardi had been shooting at a flea his artillery would certainly have been out of place, but Mrs. Lindbergh has achieved a public stature somewhat greater than that of a flea. It is for this reason first of all that she deserves Mr. Ciardi's criticism. Good poetry cannot be selected by popular vote, even in a democracy. An educational system which introduces children to the great world of poetic literature through the works of Helen Hunt Jackson can scarcely produce a poetry-minded people.

I am convinced that the final paragraphs of Mr. Ciardi's review will survive, amidst the *mots justes* of Shaw and Woollcott and those other acid-tongued reviewers of the past whose passing has been as loudly mourned as their writings were loudly anathematized while they lived.

NEIL FREEDMAN
Pittsburgh, Pa.

*

We are delighted that someone in the modern world has the intelligence to realize and the honesty to uphold the lately abused principles of literary criticism. Mr. Ciardi's painstaking review of Mrs. Lindbergh's "popular" verse is a masterpiece of clarity in pointing out the slothfulness into which idols too frequently fall.

POLLY BENSON
BETH MEARS
Sweet Briar, Va.

*

Because this reader has always felt that building a doghouse for one's dog does not entitle the builder to the classification of architect, thank you for John Ciardi's review, for projecting into the *SR* many rocks and pebbles of the anti-Ciardi "avalanche"; for stating your editorial position so clearly; and for the candid brilliance of Mr. Ciardi's rebuttal (in "The Reviewer's Duty to Damn"). It is high time somebody did something about poetry, for the sake of poetry, even if the "personal distinction" of a Mrs. Lindbergh, a Miss Vanderbilt, a Spellman et al., must suffer in the process. Where that distinction is based on newspapers' and popular magazines' build-up it is a greater reason for expecting SR to give a serious report, if the net product of those who look at the stars (to paraphrase Mr. Ciardi) is passed on to us as serious stuff.

BRUNO TORZIA
Bayonne, N. J.

*

I am writing to you to express my appreciation of John Ciardi, both as critic and editor. His review was an honest, thorough, and craftsmanlike job, one that deserves to go under the name of literary criticism. It is my hope that no restraints will be placed on Mr. Ciardi's critical reviewing and editorial policies.

GEORGE GORDIN, JR.
Washington, D. C.

*

In Mr. Ciardi's boundless scorn for what he calls the Genteel Tradition in poetry, he apparently would wish it banished and replaced with his choice, i.e., an inbred, superspecies of poetry, virile, highly disciplined, ruthless and "real." For Mr. Ciardi's sake, it's too bad that reality cannot be so neatly regimented, separated and labeled. Instead, life stubbornly persists in endless variety.

If poetry is to reflect life truly, then it must give expression to great range—surely to the abstract, the homely, and the Genteel, as well as to the concrete, the intellectual, and the sanguine. The

throttling action arising out of Mr. Ciardi's dogmatic, either/or attitude towards his admittedly beloved Muse would, if successful, ultimately kill the thing he loves.

IRINA STARR
Los Angeles, Calif.

*

Is it possible that John Ciardi is mistaking his prejudices for principles? It has happened. And could his prejudices possibly be based on a schoolboy fear that poetry is not a proper work for a man, transmuted now into a compulsion to prove that women can't write it?

It would be interesting to apply the criteria of his review of Mrs. Lindbergh's book to the work of a more firmly established American woman poet—say Emily Dickinson. On the grounds of mixed metaphor, faulty rhymes, inverted sentence order, individualistic punctuation, and ambiguous grammar she would fail his test at every point. Nor is she afraid to write "beauty" with a capital B. Do we give her a zero along with Mrs. Lindbergh and the illiterate freshmen?

ANNA MARY WELLS
New Brunswick, N. J.

*

Let me say this for Mr. Ciardi: he has a right to list his principles of judgment —he is doing his damnedest to honor them. There must be, however, many words concerning what seems to me to be a hidden issue of great importance— for poetry—that neither Mr. Ciardi, the Editor, nor the readers have touched upon. No one has stood up to say, "Good Lord, 400 letters and only four in his favor!" My question is: Where are the poets? Where are the voices of all the people who have a vital interest in a discussion of this variety? Where are the words of all those who have profited by Mr. Ciardi's ideas, either through direct personal contact, or through his influence on poetry in general (I have special reference here to his notable anthology, *Mid-Century American Poets*)?

RALPH SCHNEEBAUM
Brooklyn, N. Y.

*

What a relief to have a reviewer speak his mind as well as John Ciardi has spoken his both in the review and his defense of it. Don't fire Ciardi! He may purify the reviewing profession. It needs it.

J. EDWARD CAROTHERS
Schenectady, N. Y.

*

Seldom have I read a review that was more complete. It was well conceived and logically carried out, based not on Mr. Ciardi's so-called "vituperance," but on evidence drawn directly from his source. His thoroughness, which must be complimented, is impersonal; it must be in any critic. But just as the critic has a duty so the reader has a responsibility —that of making a sincere endeavor to see through the eyes of the critic, objectively and impersonally without prejudice and self-consciousness.

C. L. GODAR
St. Louis, Mo.

*

It is the age of the sentimental idiot. Mr. Ciardi's sane and angry voice will be relished by a minute minority.

WILLIAM GAULT
Pacific Palisades, Calif.

May I speak out in behalf of John Ciardi? I, as a psychoanalyst, suspect that Anne Morrow Lindbergh represents an illusion to the American public, a sort of object of hero worship; and when one takes the hero apart and reveals the hero for what it is, the reaction is anger. The destruction of an illusion is painful, and the readers, rather than feel their pain, grow angry and vituperative toward Ciardi. It is a reaction that the psychoanalyst encounters daily in his practice. Poor Mr. Ciardi is the goat. May I applaud your sound willingness to let him differ. Voltaire would shake hands with you.

WILLIAM RICKEL
Dayton, Ohio

*

More power to Mr. Ciardi, who has principles and upholds them. My only criticism is that he apologized too much in his review and labored too much in his rebuttal. I am a recent and (heretofore) reluctant reader of SR. My reluctance is no more.

HELENA M. STAINTON
Ithaca, N. Y.

*

I believe public taste is improving and SR is in a rather special position to help things along. For that reason I should hate: 1. To see Mr. Ciardi get sore and quit; 2. To see him get fired; 3. To see him compromise with his conscience and issue a memorial edition of James W. Riley. Keep at it, Mr. Ciardi, but for Pete's sake remember that you don't need a cannon to get a scared cow off the street.

WILL JONATHAN
Tacoma, Wash.

*

Wish to God more mealy-mouthed critics were like Mr. Ciardi!

RICHARD POPE

Detroit, Mich.

*

I should like to congratulate SR on its choice of Poetry Editor. At last we have felt a breath of fresh air through the pages of your magazine. Though we have subscribed to the SR for many years, I must confess that we have become a bit bored with the reviews. They lack vigor, vitality, and lively controversy. Too often, as Mr. Ciardi rightly says, the reviews sound like blurbs for publishers' dust jackets rather than thoughtful, exacting considerations of the art work.

MRS. HANS J. VAN BAAREN

Toledo, Ohio

*

Congratulations to Mr. Ciardi for having the courage to call a spade a spade. As a fellow teacher who is vitally interested in seeing only that which is great art praised and that which is rubbish written only for the edification of mediocre minds exposed, I can only say, bravo. Again, Mr. Ciardi, bravo!

NICHOLAS PETE NICHOLS

San Antonio, Tex.

*

I had always believed that SR's readers constituted the most loyal band of magazine subscribers in the country. I am frankly shocked that they would now try to punish the magazine by subscription cancellations as the result of one of the most important literary controversies in recent years. What has happened to our perspective? Why do we have to fly apart like this in an argument! I don't

see what purpose is served by hurting the one magazine that is honest and courageous enough to keep all the channels of a debate open. How many readers agree with me?

MARTHA ARNHEIM

Philadelphia, Pa.

*

Here is one reader, at least, who—far from being agitated one way or the other by the Ciardi–Lindbergh controversy— is profoundly grateful that it took place. I have respect for everyone involved— Mrs. Lindbergh, Mr. Ciardi, the readers, and the magazine itself. Where else could one find people excited and concerned enough about poetry to make it into the national issue that it has become? My gratitude for an important and stimulating intellectual experience.

RICHARD G. THOMPKINS

Boston, Mass.

*

I have been a subscriber and a steady reader of SR for about ten years. When I read a book review I want to know accurately what the book is about, whether what it tries to do is worth doing, and whether it has done well what it set out to do. A politely vague pat on the back is of no value whatever. It is not that I like "slashing" or malicious reviews, but I do want a well-informed and judicious report, applying proper critical standards. This is what I generally get out of John Ciardi. Let the genteel sentimentalists go hang; it is not they who will save either the world or your magazine.

ROBERT B. DOREMUS

Madison, Wis.

*

Mr. Ciardi wields a most chastening club in his endeavor to demolish the "delicate shells" housing popular poetic myths and to club the flitting "butterflies" of blatant poetic resplendence. It is well we have such a Virgilian guide (and I have the utmost faith in Mr. Ciardi's taste and discretion) in this contemporary Inferno of images and shapes obfuscated by rank commercialism. It is men like Mr. Ciardi who alone can revitalize the flagging creative disciplines in the United States.

VINCENT R. TORTORA
Lancaster, Pa.

*

I never met Mr. Ciardi, but have made a few attempts at getting some poems, which were not the technical modern type, published in *SR*. None was ever published, of which I'm glad now, because they would seem out of place in a highly literary magazine.

Nevertheless, I received nothing but kindly and generous encouragement and humble advice from Mr. Ciardi when he returned these poems. He took the time to write me sincere letters filled with the warmth of a good-natured personality,

and there was no reason why he should single me out to be a receiver of his kindliness. I am sure there are many others like me who could say the same.

NAME WITHHELD
Weehawken, N. J.

*

SR never had it better, especially in the wary observation of "the wonder the wonder the wonder of being fifty in a vague suburban way."

MARY BELL
Cicero, Ill.

*

I'm tired of seeing overrated writers dutifully applauded by sheeplike critics. There's too much equivocating, too many vague phrases such as "I rather think this book has come close to the mark" in today's criticism. Mr. Ciardi shines in the murk. He has had the guts to say clearly and firmly, "This is a bad book." It's a pleasure to read a reviewer who demonstrates courage, integrity and intelligence. I vote for John Ciardi.

MARGARET RICH
Brooklyn, N. Y.

The Morality of Poetry

EPILOGUE TO AN AVALANCHE

[*March 30, 1957*]

The American culture has developed a number of institutions that systematically encourage, and even give social prestige to, the shallowest possible view of poetry. Our Poetry Societies fluctuate between the society columns and the book-review page, but tend always to special-ize in the frothy genteel. Some of our leading "quality" magazines still regularly publish as poetry a kind of counterfeit sentimentality that might once, with some minor changes of vocabulary, have made its way into the pages of *Godey's Lady's Book.* A number of our sovereign states still appoint a poet laureate—always, as far as I can determine, a writer from the vanity-press lists.

My acquaintance with the poetry features of our newspapers is far from total, but I have looked about me, and I have yet to find a single regular columnist or feature writer on any of our large-city newspapers who is competent to discuss more than the spelling of poetry. (I must certainly exclude that rare good man, Harvey Breit, from whom one can always expect both perception and wit.) Occasional reviews by guest specialists in the Sunday *New York Times* and *Tribune* begin to discuss poetry in viable terms. Yet after some years of sampling the editorial-page poems of the daily *Times* and *Tribune* I have not yet been able to find a poem that rises above a heavy-footed mediocrity. In fact, by a kind of Gresham's Law, the bad poetry drives out the good. Real poets refuse to submit their work to those pages.

The trouble with all of these institutions, and with their too-general endorsement by the School System, is that they make it possible for a well-intentioned person who is "interested in poetry" to be offered any number of socially endorsed counterfeits without ever experienc-ing a real poem. If the canvases at the Metropolitan and at the Mu-seum of Modern Art were to be locked up, and made available only in newspaper reproductions, the consequent death of aesthetic standards would be about comparable to what these institutions are doing to the sense of poetry in our culture.

If this sort of thing is what the "general reader" thinks he wants in the name of poetry, let him have it. The right to be wrong is a blessed democratic gift, and may the Constitution guarantee it forever. But if it is no offense to accept counterfeit money, it is still an offense to try to pass it on. Let the admirers and the writers of hobby-verse be-lieve what they please, but they have no right to expect the poets to confirm their foolishness. Unless the poets hold counterfeit sentimen-tality in contempt, they become incapable of uttering their own devotions.

A stunning example of the poet's necessary contempt occurs in Yeats's "Adam's Curse." I am writing from Rome without my books about me and I must quote from memory throughout this article, but I believe I can avoid major misrepresentation:

> A line may take us hours maybe;
> Yet if it does not seem a moment's thought
> Our stitching and unstitching has been naught.
> Better get down upon your marrow bones
> And scrub a kitchen pavement, or break stones
> Like an old pauper in all kinds of weather;
> For to articulate sweet sounds together
> Is to work harder than all these and yet
> Be thought an idler by the noisy set
> Of bankers, schoolmasters, and clergymen
> The martyrs call the world.

Yeats is insisting clearly enough that the best of the world's work is done by the poets, whereas those spokesmen of the literal values, bankers-schoolmasters-clergymen, are no more than a "noisy set." W. H. Auden in his elegy "In Memory of W. B. Yeats" says it differently but says about the same thing. He notes the brokers "roaring like beasts on the floor of the Bourse" (the "noisy set" scorned) and carefully disassociates poetry from them:

> poetry makes nothing happen. It survives
> In the valley of its saying where executives
> Would never want to tamper. It flows south
> From ranches of isolation and the busy griefs,
> Raw towns that we believe and die in. It survives,
> A way of happening. A mouth.

And he adds later in the same poem that time, nevertheless, "Worships language and forgives / Everyone by whom it lives."

Yeats, in his poem, goes on to a related affirmation when he has one of his characters say:

To be born woman is to know,
Though it's not taught to us in school,
That we must labor to be beautiful.

I take this to mean—among other things but emphatically—that the values Yeats defends have to do with the rescue of one's human attention from trivia and mindless conformity in order that that attention may be applied in a life-shaping way.

One could mine English poetry, past and present, for similar examples, but these will serve to make clear enough the existence of a basic difference between (in Yeats's terms, and I mean to keep those terms throughout the present discussion) the world on the one hand and poetry on the other.

If I have succeeded in establishing an acceptable distinction, I have attempted to do so in order to suggest that the real difference is a difference of morality. I have no ambition to define the world's morality for it, nor can I in any all-inclusive sense define the poet's for him. It may still be valuable, however, to discuss some principles of the poet's morality that are crucial to the success of a good poem while remaining generally unrecognized by the world as true primary values. An awareness of "this other morality," moreover, will provide one way of measuring the essential difference between the work of a poet and that of a hobbyist in metrics.

Let me skirt, for the moment, all argument for or against popular morality. I simply make the point here that poetry is independent of that morality, as it is of general good character or social standing. Villon, despite all his failures as measured by the world's morality, emerges as a poet, and Robert Southey—every reader's choice as the best Sunday-school teacher in English Literature—does not. If there ever was an original Tom o' Bedlam, his song is forever in the memory of the English language, but who reads the songs of Henry the Eighth? Baudelaire wrote "immoral" poetry and Swinburne found himself in serious trouble for translating it into Victoria's English, but Baudelaire will remain part of the indispensable knowledge of the human race long after students begin to forget which country Victoria was queen of in which century. Like it or not, poetry has never depended upon the approval of the world's morality, manners, or caste systems. The fact seems to be, in fact, that more poems die of decency than of any other one cause.

Assume, if you please, that Baudelaire was indeed an immoral man. If, then, his work has become one of the values and resources of the race—a fact that seems clearly beyond argument at this point—what gives it value? To be sure, he was a poet and knew how to use words, metaphors, rhythms, and poetic structures to marvelous effect. But for the sake of the argument, let us even assume the monstrous untruth that poetic gift is merely ornamental and not of the essence. By what values did this "immoral" man seek the truth of his own life?

Peter Viereck's poem "Poet" contains some pertinent observations on this point. The poem is a tribute to Baudelaire based on two sentences taken from Baudelaire's "My Heart Stripped Bare": "All created form, even that created by man, is immortal. For the form is independent of the material, and it is not the particles that make up the form."

Clearly, this is a statement of devotion. In speaking of creation "even by man" Baudelaire is certainly putting man next to godliness by virtue of the fact that he, too, can give immortal shape to things, his own life among them. But to make a thing that will endure forever is a terrible responsibility. The very title of Baudelaire's piece—"My Heart Stripped Bare"—identifies one essential element of that responsibility: the maker must be uncompromisingly honest. Social niceties, received views on conduct, respect for established social habit, all the lures of easy sentiment must be brushed aside. Propriety and social glibness may be the measure of all things at a cocktail party or at the Thursday Group Meeting, but the human unconscious that reads the poem in the still midnight of immortal feeling is beyond social gesture. Be damned to all else; the poem must be real to its midnight.

And, exactly here, we may identify the first antisocial morality of the poet. It is, of course, antisocial only in short-range terms. It is *against* its contemporary (and ever-shifting) proprieties in order to be *for* what is longest and truest in man's awareness of himself. The genteel, then as now, will not find Baudelaire bearable, but centuries from now that midnight-man will still be there to read and to learn some of his own life from the reading.

Viereck's treatment of this theme speaks the essence of that morality which compels the poet without quite being recognized as a morality by the world at large. In what precedes the passage I quote here, Viereck develops the theme that the poet, by the disciplines of his form and of his imagination, holds things in order. Viereck compares Baudelaire to a king who had ruthlessly driven all shabby elements from his court and kingdom. The instant the king dies the exiles begin to plot again the old chaos of the slovenly:

> Words that begged favor at his court in vain—
> Lush adverbs, senile rhymes in tattered gowns—
> Send notes to certain exiled nouns
> And mutter openly against his reign,
> While rouged clichés hang out red lights again,
> And refugees report from far-flung towns
> That exclamation marks are running wild,
> And prowling half-truths carried off a child.

The whole of Viereck's catalogue of aesthetic (and intellectual) corruption is worth study, but it is especially to the point that he has selected clichés as the central prostitution. It has always been an astonishment to me that people of the highest moral principle in the world's terms will yet abandon themselves willingly to the immorality of the cliché.

For a cliché is not only a sinful slovenliness; it is an enemy of mind and hope, and it is not only a prostitution but a theft. Nor can the case be put, honorably and accurately, in milder terms. Every morality must be bound by both a blessing and a damnation, and on this point, within the morality of poetry, only damnation will serve. Our mass-media journalism, our collapsing educational system, and the insanities of the Madison Avenue–Hollywood axis have already put us in sufficient danger of becoming a mindless generation. If our poets and would-be poets are to be encouraged in such slovenly thefts within their own imaginations, then a primary cultural force for good intellectual order is seriously weakened. The ultimate sin of the mind is the failure to pay enough attention.

It is exactly at this point that one may locate the essential difference between the kind of morality that binds the poet and that which seems to operate in the general culture. The Christian tradition recognizes seven deadly sins, which I take to be another way of labeling seven moral failures. Of them, the culture at large seems to have an adequate sense of pride, envy, wrath, avarice, gluttony, and lust, but seems to be relatively unaware of Acedia. We translate Acedia as "sloth," but that translation tends to blur the essential meaning. "Sloth" tends to suggest mere physical slovenliness. Acedia is quite something else—it is the failure to pay sufficient attention to one's devotions. It has many faces, but its essence is an intellectual haphazardness that springs from not caring enough. In the Middle Ages, interestingly, it seems to have been the sin most feared by the monks: the fear that they had not paid enough attention to God.

No failure of poetic morality (and of artistic morality in general) can be more fundamental than the failure to pay enough attention to the nature and requirement of one's chosen form. To perform sloppily for high causes and high moral issues is both an affront to the cause and issue, and as thoroughly bad as performing in this way for low causes and issues.

So to the fundamental difference between one morality and the other: the world tends to recognize six deadly failures and to pay little attention to the seventh. The poet, finally, has to care only about the seventh. It is not at all necessary for him to scorn the other six, but granted that he has talent enough, his work will finally live only if he has kept his attention in disciplined and self-consuming order.

Let the writers on "subjects"—and those would-be defenders of poetry who seek in it the loose affirmation of shabbily stated principles of high moral purport but low aesthetic integrity—let them learn once and for all that the only subject of any poem is the kind of attention it brings to bear on the universe or on its least sliver. A poem may or may not have a "surface subject," but if it does not have as its central activation a motion of the attention that creates an ordered form then it is no poem, and what it does is shabbily done.

I have several times before used an example from the poetry of Elizabeth Bishop to illustrate what I mean at this point. The passage I have in mind is from a longish poem called "The Fish." Miss Bishop describes how she caught the fish, held it out of water, and began to look at it. Here is what she says about the fish's eye:

I looked into his eyes
which were far larger than mine
but shallower and yellowed,
the irises backed and packed
with tarnished tinfoil
seen through lenses
of old scratched isinglass.

I read that passage to a convention of schoolteachers once and said that, as far as I knew, it was the best job of looking at a fish's eye in the whole range of English poetry. To which, of course, one teacher replied: "So what? What is so important about looking at a fish's eye?"

The fact is that anything significantly looked at is significant. And that is significant which teaches us something about our own life-capabilities. The function of detail when ordered by a human imagination is to illustrate the universe. One comes away from Elizabeth Bishop's poetry not simply with a miraculously observed and drawn image, but with a new idea of the possibilities of his own senses. The eye of the ignorant sees nothing. Only mind can apprehend the visible, and the eye can only register what the mind is able to perceive. Elizabeth Bishop's description literally lets us see a fish's eye, but beyond that literalness it teaches us what we ourselves will be capable of if we manage our imaginations with sufficient devotion, and if we are sufficiently ruthless toward any cheapening substitute for the real thing.

To achieve that ability to experience and to transmit experience in experienceable terms is the labor and the devotion and the morality of the poet—his "labor to be beautiful." An element of that morality is to scorn loose talk about the "large significances" of the poem. The poet is ready for "large significance" only as he has learned his art. To try to short-cut to the big-message by way of slurred details is to guarantee that the poem is a counterfeit. A poet is responsible for every last detail he allows into his poem. Nothing is too small to matter. There are accidentals, to be sure, but every accidental must be passed on by his principle of selection, and it is of the essence of his moral commitment that he insist on keeping that selection uncompromising. I submit it to be true of all of English poetry that only those poets who have most cherished the close fact of things and the discipline of their art have been able to make enduring statements of human values. Art is the mentality of human passion. Without mind enough, which is to say without gift enough and discipline enough, passion is mush.

The true poet can have only scorn for those who call upon him to deliver pretty stereotypes. If that is what one wishes, he can buy it with four-color illustrations from Hallmark. One thinks, for instance, of those who cried throughout the war years for another poem like "In Flanders Field"—as if the poets among those who were sitting in the blood or the boredom of the actual war could turn popular affirmations off and on at will like the smile of a politician.

The true poet can submit to anything before he can submit to the falsification of sentiment. But whether one concurs in the "surface subject" or not, if he cares at all about poetry he must realize that the surface subject is not the poem. I would grant, as in the case of a poet as talented as is Roy Campbell, that it is possible for the kind of mind offered in the poem to be so repulsive that one can almost regret the fragments of gift it possesses. That, however, must be left for another discussion, the basis of which would be that such a man as Campbell has gift but abuses it. The fact still remains that a poem written in true devotion to itself—rather than in some sort of split devotion to an overriding sentiment—cannot be anything but an affirmation. There is no such thing as a negative creation if the creation is built on a ruthless devotion to order.

There is also society's reward in this, whether or not society is willing to be aware of it. The very fact that there have always been men among us who have chosen to be ruthlessly moral about language may well be the greatest single blessing a man inherits by being born into a civilization. No one guards the language as poets do—guards it, refreshes it, and restores it. (In speaking of language, one of course assumes the subject to include the perception and the discipline and the joy of what language is capable of expressing. One intends, in fact, nothing less than the total process of living with real awareness.) Without the poets to guard the language it would fall apart in the mouth, and with it the very possibility of social communication. When a language falls apart a nation is finished.

Let one example illustrate. I find hardly a schoolboy these days who can distinguish between "intra-" and "inter-" or between "democracy" and "republicanism." Yet almost all can distinguish meaningfully between "glory" and "grandeur." They can do so because Poe drew that distinction so well in "To Helen" that the words grew firm on the public tongue. May something teach that schoolboy—and his mother and father—more of the distinctions time will require of all of us. Poetry could do it, if the world would allow poetry to come to him as the real force and order of living that it is when it observes its own morality. It seems doubtful that the world is so inclined, and that fact must go down as the world's loss.

For poetry is no social ornament to be applied as part of a "finishing school" gloss. It is a way of life and it is a discrete and irreplaceable means of knowledge. It is as much a way of knowing as is science, and the kind of knowledge it vitalizes, stores, and makes available is forever beyond the range of science. It is rather for poetry to instruct science if humanity is to be rescued from its own pushbuttons.

Poetry takes as a primary value an awareness of one's own aliveness. A man becomes a man by learning the history and the miracle and the joy and the difficulty of his own attention and of his moral commitment to it. Poetry is what best makes available to a man exactly those life responses and that entrance into the possibilities and the devotions of his own attention—if he will guard it ruthlessly from everything including his own sentiments and his own surface decency. From the tribal chant to Genesis, and from Genesis to the next truly devoted and truly shaped poem to be created in human history, poetry has added and will add to the richness of man's awareness of what it is to be a human being on a tilted planet.

That awareness is no matter of "message." It is the life-dance of the poem, the shape and motion and force of the truly fulfilled form. A good poet does not take a poem: it takes him. He happens to it, and he does not know what has happened until it has been done. He goes into the poem and he comes out of it at some unpredictable point. But wherever he emerges, he emerges wiser and truer and more alive. And throughout the total process he lives ruthlessly by his trained attention, by his devotion to his principle of selection.

And only such devotion will serve him in his act of being a poet. For those who wish to flirt with the poem in easier and more passing terms the one critical mercy is to be silent. If, however, there comes a time to speak—then, as the sin is deadly, so must the judgment be damnation. That high moral affirmation battered into bad rhyme and slovened out of shape in the name of rhetorical-seriousness is not poetry but aesthetic immorality. It blurs our apprehension of life itself. Ignorance is no excuse for it, and sincere good intention cannot plead for it. It pretends to care, it may believe it does care, but it simply does not care enough.

LETTERS TO THE EDITOR

[*April 20, 1957*]

*

I cannot refrain from paying tribute to John Ciardi's "The Morality of Poetry." The number of thinkers who have moved me as deeply could be counted on one hand. In my humble opinion he has contributed a historic gem of aesthetic principle.

GORDON D. GRAY
Painesville, Ohio

*

I think Mr. Ciardi is a superb poetry editor and how I *love* his views! I just simply think it's a privilege to read his words. I hope he writes more and more.

JANE NUGENT GREEN
St. Paul, Minn.

*

Looking through Fowler's *Modern English Usage* this morning I came across a passage on the subject of the word *prig.* According to Fowler Mr. Ciardi is a prig. I think SR is fortunate to have him. I have not missed an issue in weeks.

HELEN STEVENS
Peterborough, N. H.

*

A poet has no enemy but the clergyman, schoolmaster, and banker *in himself.* Not any other man is able to endanger his work.

NANCY STONE
Haddonfield, N. J.

*

What *are* you trying to do? You are letting Bennett Cerf *out*—and keeping John Ciardi *in.* The former—informative, intelligent, refreshingly human, and often more than a little amusing. But

Ciardi! A fanatic of the first class if I ever encountered one.

MRS. ANNA G. KIMBLE
Mission, Kan.

*

As Mr. Ciardi omits all mention of the singing word, almost everything he has to say is equally applicable to prose and therefore seems to me to be so general that as criticism of poetry it is a shade less accurate than the accuracy he demands of poetry.

MRS. EDMUND ROWLAND
Drexel Hill, Pa.

*

As an old devoted reader, I take the liberty of sending a message to Johnny. Tell him to get out of that classroom he berates so suspiciously much. Tell him to relax, because when all's said and done (by all the academicians in the world, in or out of classroom), poetry is a folk art. Like all folk arts, it is as various as the livers of life who create it and as variously responded to as the livers of life who react to it. Poetry is above and below all systems of criticism, and there is nothing duller than poetry *criticism.*

LAURA BEHELER
Santa Fe, N. M.

*

Mr. Ciardi's scheme to prove his assumptions by throwing acid blinds all— even Mr. Ciardi. I show every devotion to a Great Teacher, but have only contempt for a Grand Inquisitor. There is no surer way to establish protestants than Mr. Ciardi's dogma.

JOE M. TOCKMAN
Colorado Springs, Colo.

*

I was very happy while reading Mr. Ciardi's recent dissertation. Though a high school student, even I have noticed how empty and sentimental some of the recently published "poems" are. To the writer of this poetry it probably expresses some abstract meaning very clearly, but to the reader it does NOT. SR should perform a public service by making copies of the Ciardi article available to these not-so-lucid laureates.

LARRY PRATT
Hays, Kan.

*

Come now! Christ hasn't risen—not really. Why does SR devote so much valuable space to that insignificant but noisy person, Ciardi? On the cover, yet! Poetry does not pretend to be immortal —readers do not look for "great" poetry. Editors just publish the best that comes in, each according to his magazine's readership's theoretical educational and income level, not necessarily personal standards. Back to your corner, John, until you get dry.

MRS. L. C. PETERSON
Roseburg, Ore.

*

This man Ciardi again! I fear for his blood pressure.

RUTH WILLIAMS
Coopersburg, Pa.

*

After recent attacks upon John Ciardi, I want to say how grateful I am to him, especially for his advice on learning how to write.

DOROTHY SCHULZE
Minneapolis, Minn.

EXPOSTULATION AND REPLY

Norman Cousins forwarded the following letters to me while I was still in Rome. In an accompanying note he asked me to reply to them because he believed that SR policy was involved.

I saw little point in engaging J. Donald Adams on the terms he set forth, and I said so. With my reply as printed here, however, I sent a note to Peter Ritner, then SR's Feature Editor, insisting that he phone Adams, asking the man to reread his letter in a cooler moment, and then to decide whether or not he really wanted it to be published. When the letter did appear in SR, I wrote to ask Ritner if he had in fact contacted Adams. My question, however, seems to have been lost in a mass of other details. I do not know for certain, therefore, that Adams was actually offered a chance to withdraw his letter, but I am left to assume that the offer was made and rejected.

LETTERS TO THE EDITOR
J. DONALD ADAMS
[*May 4, 1957*]

*

I have hitherto held back from entering the discussion provoked by your Mr. Ciardi, but his latest blast, bleat, or burp (take your choice) has stirred up my adrenal glands even more than his ill-considered attack on Anne Lindbergh. His effusion on "The Morality of Poetry" provides a flagrant example of the obtuseness typical of the academic mind. Its attitudes are by no means confined to our schools and colleges, though they are most frequently found in those precincts. There are professors who haven't a touch of it, just as there are traffic cops who are ruled by maxims, built into their minds as if with reinforced concrete.

I shall make no more than passing reference to Mr. Ciardi's arrogant and boorish assault on a distinguished woman. Mrs. Lindbergh is not a great poet, nor even a very good one—a fact of which she is well aware, and one which gives her a distinct advantage over Mr. Ciardi. But Mrs. Lindbergh is a prose artist of considerable achievement—another fact which only an incompetent critic could ignore. Her book of poems, which Mr. Ciardi chose as a whipping boy to air his views (if they had been burning him up for months, why didn't he give them vent in a general article?), contains one or two excellent pieces, including the title poem, to which Mr. Ciardi made no reference whatever. If he could learn to construct a single paragraph as well written as many pages in Mrs. Lindbergh's books, I should find it easier to read him.

In his March 30 article Mr. Ciardi has some pertinent and pungent things to say, but their effect is marred by his constitutionally academic approach. He is still living in an insulated world, oblivious or disdainful of the average man's craving for beauty in some form— "beauty" being a word which, I imagine, causes Mr. Ciardi severe abdominal pains. I contend it is infinitely better for the average reader of *The New York Times* or *Herald Tribune* (two papers whose services to the cause of poetry make him sniff as if he were passing the stockyards) to read the poems these papers publish daily on their editorial pages than to read no poetry at all. I should like to remind him of Emerson's statement in a somewhat different connection: "There is an ascension in our loves."

Some of this "newspaper poetry," which is synonymous for Mr. Ciardi with a dirty word, and which so offends his delicate nostrils, has, I am sure, wakened many a dull soul (one of those dreadful Philistines) to horizons more shining than any he had hitherto known. I should also like to remind Mr. Ciardi that on Page 2 of *The New*

York Times Book Review, which I have conducted for the past fourteen years, there has appeared more good poetry, even by some of the
standards which Mr. Ciardi professes to uphold, than has been published in any other newspaper or general magazine in this country. In
fact, Mr. Ciardi, in his more inspired moments, has appeared there
himself.

I am fed to the teeth with the presumptuous, half-baked, wet-be-
hind-the-ears, and holier-than-thou attitudes of so many of our academic critics. They need to get about more and breathe, now and
again, a less rarefied air than that which customarily surrounds them.
They are mentally ingrown, intolerant towards anything which does
not square with their dogmatic obsessions as to what they think poetry
should be and do. They are insensitive to the broad human appeals
which move the hearts and stir the minds of many millions of men
and women. And that is why poetry is only now climbing back out of
the swamps and pestholes where too many versifiers, unskilled and undisciplined in their craft, have tried to keep it. This recovery will not
be aided by those who wrap themselves in a critical toga and turn their
backs on the common needs and aspirations of mankind. Many of our
young poets, I am happy to observe—and their work passes constantly
over my desk—are showing their mounting awareness of these needs
and aspirations, and demonstrating it in their work.

As I have said elsewhere over and over again, the time for consolida-
tion in the arts is at hand—the merging of what has proved good
during the years of experimentation and revolt, with what is worth rescuing and preserving from our centuries-old heritage in poetry, painting, or whatever art you are concerned with. The time is here, and the
clock ticks on; perhaps Mr. Ciardi would do well to buy himself a
hearing aid. Finally, the best thing that has been said about poetry in
our time was said by a man well qualified to say it: I refer to Robert
Frost's "The Figure a Poem Makes," which serves as Preface to his
Collected Poems. It might be further helpful to Mr. Ciardi if he were
to reread it.

J. DONALD ADAMS
The New York Times

New York, N. Y.

Mr. Adams, as he confesses, has suffered an adrenal surge and it seems to have led to inflammation of his adjectives. I submit that his letter is the kind of mistake a man may fall into in white heat and then live to regret. I have nothing to discuss with him in these terms. If he has any reasoned points he wishes to make, I shall do my best to answer them in reason.

JOHN CIARDI

Rome, Italy

LETTERS TO THE EDITOR
THOMAS LASK
[*May 11, 1957*]

*

I always thought that a poet's worst enemy was his own bad work, but John Ciardi finds enemies of poetry under every hedge and bush. I'm not quite sure what relevance his backhanded slap against the *Times* had to his main argument, but it seems that the *Times* is help-ing to lower the moral climate in which poets flourish by publishing poetry of "heavy-footed mediocrity." "Real poets," says Mr. Ciardi, "refuse to submit their work to those pages." The following is a list of some of the poets whose works have appeared on the editorial page of the *Times:* Joseph Auslander, Ben Belitt, William Rose Benét, Padraic Colum, Walter de la Mare, Norma Farber, Richard Eberhart, John Gould Fletcher, Lloyd Frankenberg, Oliver St. John Gogarty, John Holmes, Robert Hillyer, Robinson Jeffers, Rudyard Kipling, E. L. Mayo, Edgar Lee Masters, Edna St. Vincent Millay, Kenneth Patchen, Robert Graves, Theodore Roethke, Marshall Schacht, James Stephens, Wallace Stevens, John Hall Wheelock, Marya Zaturenska.

I also add a list of poets, among many others, whose work has appeared regularly in the *Times:* George Abbe, Robert P. T. Coffin, Carleton Drewry, Hannah Kahn, Louise Townsend Nichol, David Morton, Gustav Davidson, Louis Ginsberg, Elias Lieberman, Leslie Nelson Jennings, Sara Henderson Hay, and Harold Vinal. These poets have also appeared regularly in *The Saturday Review.* Is it possible that when they appeared in *The Saturday Review* these poets were dazzlingly original, but that they reserved their heavy-footed mediocrity for the *Times* alone? I notice, also, that two of the poets I have listed have been published in book form by the publishing firm of which Mr. Ciardi is himself the editorial adviser. And some of the foregoing poets even turned up in *Mid-Century American Poets,* edited by Mr. Ciardi.

The heart of the matter, however, is not the list of poets who have appeared in the *Times,* but a realization of the kind of medium the *Times* is. It is not a university quarterly, a "little" magazine, or an *avant-garde* pamphlet printed in black-and-mustard. It is not even a literary weekly. The *Times* is a newspaper. It is not geared to an exclusively literary audience. The man who reads the poem in the *Times* will read it somewhere between Katonah and Grand Central, the young lady between Coney Island and Times Square. To print a dense, difficult poem that will please those professionally interested in poetry would be folly. The *Times* therefore limits itself to short lyric poems in traditional forms and prints what it believes to be the best of the poems submitted to it.

THOMAS LASK, Poetry Editor
The New York Times

New York, N. Y.

*

Mr. Lask's list of poets published on *The New York Times* editorial page is an impressive one. I suggest it might have been more useful as evidence had he told us how far back he reached for his compilation. Were one to find that many good poets in the daily *Times* in any given year (and let us assume that all of the names Mr. Lask offers are honored ones) that would be as much as one good poem a week, allowing for some repetition of names. If, as I suspect on limited evidence, his is a thirty-year listing, and if some of the most impressive of his names are represented by only a single appearance, then the concentration of excellence would obviously be less impressive than the list itself.

I happily accept a correction from Mr. Lask and I will change "real poets" to "many poets." That reading is certainly closer to what I intended. In fairness, Mr. Lask will acknowledge my opening and important qualifications.

I noted in the paragraph from which he quotes that my acquaintance with newspaper poetry features was far from total and that my impressions of the *Times* daily poem were based on "some years of *sampling*" them. Within that sampling, I said, I had yet to find one that rose above heavy-footed mediocrity. I submit that there is no air of edict in setting down an impression so qualified.

Who knows better than an editor how wrong an editor can be? I have made many mistakes I have had to blush for too late, some of them, in my view, serious. I ask Mr. Lask to believe that I have never thought in terms of "friends" or "enemies," but in opinion, possibly fallible and there to be disagreed with, but principled in intention.

I agree entirely with Mr. Lask's identification of "the heart of the matter," and it is just there that our principles are most clearly opposed. My charge against the *Times* daily poem was that it offered —under the prestige of the *Times* banner—a poetic substitute that many readers would be persuaded was the real thing. Mr. Lask replies that *Times* poetry must, in the nature of things, be geared to the commuter psyche of a young man "between Katonah and Grand Central" and of a "young lady between Coney Island and Times Square." Mr. Lask's terms are different from mine, but I submit that they support my charge by repeating it, though in a more engaging way. I cannot see that "dense, difficult" have anything to do with it, and such terms were no part of the original discussion. Poetry is either an experience, large or small, but truly shaped from the life-bound planet, or it is an exercise between zero and mediocrity. I respectfully submit to Mr. Lask that if the nature of the *Times* as a mass medium requires it to publish as poetry only such notes from world and time as the running commuter can absorb, then there is at least a ponderable basis for the argument that it would be a better service not to try to publish "poetry" at all.

I think our real difference is here, and I think the topic is a valuable one for general discussion. My thanks to Mr. Lask for raising the issue and my best wishes to him.

JOHN CIARDI

Rome, Italy

DUNSANY

A DEBATE ON MODERN POETRY

[October 19, 1957]

Dunsany, as noted in Letters to the Editor *for November 9, 1957, died on October 25, 1957, six days after publication of this debate. All but inevitably his death became the signal for some readers to accuse me of having killed an old man. (As a point of fact, he never saw my reply.)*

Dunsany was an old man but a peppery one. In his last years he campaigned for his views of poetry with an energy few younger men could summon. I had seen a number of articles and excerpts from talks he had given on the subject, and I found his views as repugnant as they were firm. Add to his energy the persuasiveness of what had been a great name, and I had no choice but to think of him as a pernicious influence.

On evidence, I submit, he was also something of a rabble-rouser, if anything as vaguely genteel as his audiences may be called a rabble.

His article, "The Poets Fail in Their Duty," was unsolicited and came to SR from his agent, who addressed it to Norman Cousins. NC passed it on to me with a notation that he thought we might do well to publish it. I sent it back with a notation that read simply, "Not while I am Poetry Editor." There was no offense intended or taken in that: by then NC had caught on to my memo style. He did, however, ask me if I did not want to reconsider.

I told him I could not agree to opening the pages of SR to Dunsany's views in silence, for silence would certainly indicate editorial approval. I agreed, however, to permit publication on condition that I be given a chance to speak back. Our disagreement was, accordingly,

set up as a debate, with the consent of Dunsany's literary agent. The
first of the following two articles is Dunsany's; the second is my reply.

The Poets Fail in Their Duty

LORD DUNSANY

What is "modern verse"? Some have said that the writers of it are the greatest since Shakespeare; others feel that Shakespeare is rather out of date. It would be wrong to hamper the hopes of younger men by laying it down that no progress beyond Shakespeare was possible, but it is certainly wrong to mistake mere change for progress and to confuse growth with decay. What then is "modern verse"?

If it be growth we ought not to miss it; if it be decay we should clear it up as soon as possible. It is clearly beyond our intellects, for I have on occasion read to assemblies selections from two writers of "modern verse," and one selection of twelve lines from the first lines of an index, and one piece of deliberate nonsense written by myself, and told them that they could not tell which was which. Nor could they. For the acceptance of any nonsense as being something far superior to all that the nations have treasured has gone so far that no one dares reject any of it, for fear of being thought too unintellectual to understand what, for ought anybody can tell, might be a very profound message. Now, whether it is time and past time that "modern verse" should be cleared out of the way and we should return to poetry, this fear should certainly be cleared away, so that readers may freely use their judgments and find for themselves what the profound message is, if there be any message, or see for themselves that nothing is there. I will quote no names, for I am attacking nobody, but only trying to do my share to stop an intellectual rot resulting from the acceptance of vague and muddled lines that have deserted meter in order to say something that might have a meaning, if only we were a little cleverer and able to find it out; and to restore the melody of meter to the honored place it has held for over 3,000 years. Lines like the following have been accepted for too long:

> Bitter and green an octagonal sun
> Freezes my kidneys with its insistent rays.

Why are meter and rhyme discarded here? Is it because the message is of such importance that meter is a mere trifle compared with it? And what is the message? On the face of it it is nonsense. But then the answer to that is that it is symbolic. And not to accept that is to show ignorance of the importance of symbolism, an ignorance that many people hesitate to exhibit. And symbolic of what? But even to ask that is to risk showing ignorance too; and it is seldom asked. There is no beauty there: what then about truth? Is the sun green? Is it octagonal? Does it freeze? Such questions, if ever asked, are dismissed with the retort that the questioner is being too literal, and, again, that it is symbolic. But the real reason why the sun has been so described is the quest for originality. Others have called the sun golden and round and hot, and these must be contemptuously surpassed, and so descriptions are sought that no one has ever applied to the sun before. They can always be supported by articles in weekly or monthly papers, written in abstruse language and helping on the muddle that is already there in the poem. It can be pointed out that, after gazing a while at the sun, green discs appear before closed eyes, and that the poet, gazing longer and more truly, sees the essential greenness of the sun more clearly than any other. As for its being octagonal, the relationship of an octagon to a circle can be written about in such a way as to confuse, if it cannot quite convince; and if April is a cruel month, as it has been called in modern verse, surely the sun can be bitter and even can freeze. Why the kidneys? Earlier poets would have written of their souls, but souls are démodé, and there is an intestinal trend in modern verse; not only because intestines are new to poetry, and so smack of originality, but because mention of them shows courage and a sense of liberty in breaking away from inhibitions by which Victorian and earlier poets were tamely content to be bound.

I do not think that modern verse originated in deliberate imposture. I think that men with no sense of rhythm and yet ambitious for the fame of a poet wrote their genuine emotions, but poured them out without the clarity that is necessary for their understanding, and when because of the fear I have mentioned already they found that they were accepted, they poured out anything that their pens would write, much as a lady might play with an ouija board. And both the writing and reading of these things were facilitated by some slightly difficult lines of Browning or Chaucer, which because some readers missed their meaning must have given rise to the deadly heresy that poetry should not be expected actually to mean anything. I think a poet has a 90 per cent duty to make himself clear, and a reader a 10 per cent duty to understand him, but not more than that, for poetry is not a mathematical problem, or a puzzle, or something to be decoded. A poet should write for all people, as anyone with a message should make it clear to all, and the greatest are the simplest, and anyone missing the meaning in any story of Homer could go out on to any farm and enquire the meaning of any laborer there, if he told him the story in English and robbed of its gorgeous hexameters.

Who, for instance, could miss this? Odysseus has come to a harbor, where his fame has preceded him, and the king of the little country sends down a herald to invite the famous soldier to a banquet. And Odysseus goes, and at the banquet a herald, or as we should say an after-dinner speaker, talks of his great achievements, how he overthrew the Trojans and burned their towers and killed Priam's sons: and then the speaker sees that Odysseus is quietly weeping, and with a few more words he brings his speech to an end. That is very unlike modern verse. And in addition to the humanity of which it is made, it is all lit up by its meter, which Tennyson described as the lordliest ever molded by the lips of man. But the writers of "modern verse" have thrown meter contemptuously away, with no more tribute to it than to retain the name of verse. In the same way, when the aristocracy of France was overthrown those who had destroyed it wore the gorgeous clothes of the men they had killed, though they saw to it that they were ill fitting, in order to show that they were only dead men's clothes. And revolution is no bad thing to turn to for any metaphor one may require when speaking of "modern verse," for both come from a yearning to be free from a power that has dominated an age or a country for long.

And what a domination the power of poets has been! Their words have gone right down the ages, gripping the thoughts of men, and filling their speech with phrases and fragments of lines, and placing visions before them which all men see. Wearying of Keats's nightingale and Shelley's skylark, the enormous visions of Milton and the sheer power of Shakespeare, and longing to be free from the grip that the Greeks still hold on the ages, some young men are turning away, but turning away to what? Who can take the place of the poets if we throw their statues down? We have our poets today, as every age has had them, but they, also, are powers that are beyond the scope of those who would be free from the grip of old glories. And so some young men of today have turned away not from the poets only, whose power was too much for them, but from poetry altogether: meter is cast away and with it meaning, and the people of our time have been offered a jumble of words so intricate that there may be a meaning there, like a message faintly written and in an unknown tongue; and, as it is hard to see what it is, it is hard to say that no message is there, and no one seems to have taken the risk of rejecting it.

If there is any message in all this modern stuff, let someone tell us what it is in clear language; but if it lies too deep for that, we may be assured that it will do no good to us. The first duty of any man with a message is to hand it on to others, and for this purpose he must tell it so that they can easily understand it. He fails in his duty otherwise. For no message is for the mere amusement of one man. Hence a poet's first duty is clarity. An age needs a few poets who, standing a little aloof from the rush of daily work, yet in touch with the hearts of men, shall show clearly to others their aims, and what is the work they are doing and to what end. And he is a poor poet if they cannot understand him. Indeed, so vivid are visions when they come that almost perforce the telling of them is vividly clear too; so that, when you come upon words that are not readily clear to you, you may suspect that they are not the words of one who has had any vision, and in fact that there is no message there at all.

Messages are things to make clear, not to be wrapped up. If a banker is handed a cheque that is quite illegible he does not assume it to be a cheque for a million pounds, or pay out any large sum. Yet, when it is a thought that a writer claims to offer, the incomprehensible words are too often accepted as being of great value. Let us learn from businessmen not to make such rash assumptions. As a banker would examine a cheque to see exactly what is written, let us never accept a line as meaning something unless we can find out what. And if we can't find out, let's state boldly that no meaning is there. One might of course make a mistake when doing that, but it is not so likely that we shall be mistaken in saying that vague words have nothing to say as that we shall be wrong if we assert that such words have a message, even though we are unable to say what that message is.

I will quote as an example one of those four poems that I have referred to which I have read in public on several occasions. It is unnecessary to say who wrote it. If it is not to be found in the works of the principal writers of "modern verse," then it has not been accepted as great poetry: if it is to be found there, it has been.

HIGH WICKHAM

    In the sun there is shining
    In the empty spaces there is notshining,
    But at the center of the sun there is darkness.
    Shining on the disc,
    Darkness at the center:
    This is the story of the sun.

    In the empty spaces notshining,
    In the empty spaces pitch darkness,
    Which is another way of putting it.
    Pitch darkness where only the planets gobble:
    This is the story of the empty spaces.

It is certainly original; for, as somebody lately wrote of these composers of "modern verse," nobody has written like this before; and then a certain pretentiousness in lines 6 and 11 hints that there may be something there after all. The important thing is for the reader to judge of this for himself, and above all not to think that he is not clever enough to unravel thought that may lie so deep, if there is any there at all. The whole of one line is a plagiarism, but that is no help either way in solving the question of authorship, for the writers of "modern verse" are addicted to that very thing, the lifting of a whole line now and then from another writer. And let not the reader of this believe that he is not intelligent enough to know what is meant by the words "where only the planets gobble," but let him show his intelligence by saying they don't.

Sometimes a word such as chthonic will appear in a modern verse. But is the purpose of that to make the meaning more clear, or is it to show that the writer is more clever than you? I do not say that the word chthonic has no meaning. It probably has. But I have not looked it up to see, because it is not worthwhile. I have no use for it myself, because when I have anything to say I try to make it clear to as many as possible, and this word would not help me to do that, for there are too many people, like myself, who do not know what it means. And then there is another source of the reputation of these writers of "modern verse," which is whatever guess anyone may make while searching for sense among their lines. That would go something like this. Reading such a line as,

How fierce the daisy's protest against June,

one might say that daisies do not protest and are not fierce. But a supporter of modern verse would tell one that in being so literal-minded one misses the point. The poet does not mean the actual flower, he would explain, but rather gives expression to his resentment against the passing of spring, of its ruthless eviction of summer, and so, for those who follow the poem intelligently, the passing of all beautiful things and the usurpation of their places by age and death. And however far this explanation may go, all credit is given for it to the writer of the ridiculous nonsense, a line of which I have here invented.

And sometimes they will throw in a few lines in some foreign language, which look very odd in something pretending to be a poem. What is the purpose of that? Surely not clarity. And if clarity be not the first aim of any man with a message, can he think that his message is of any value? There have been poets who have been accused of having only melody in their line without much to say; and usually, I think, they have been accused wrongly, for if a man is stirred to beauty in any form there is probably something at the back of the impulse that is worthy of the beauty that is to clothe it. But we have no beauty here. Meter is mostly discarded by the writers of "modern verse" in order to give the message that no one can understand. For, if anyone does understand it, the lines fail in their purpose, which would appear to be to show how much profounder and cleverer the writer is than his readers. Write something that it will take a lecturer or a don to explain, and the writer has scored a point. Write something the meaning of which several dons will dispute over, and he has scored two points at this symbolic game. And what exactly does symbolic mean? That is part of the game, a game that is not entirely new; for something very like it must have been played before, to have inspired Gilbert to write these lines:

> If this young man expresses himself
> In terms too deep for me
> Why what a very singularly deep young man
> This deep young man must be.

I have seen plays that are everywhere accepted as being plays in verse, and yet there is scarcely a line of verse in them; nothing more at all to make anyone think there is than a capital letter at the beginning of each line. And certainly the material of them is not the material of poetry, for they are lines that go like this. I parody nobody, but merely give a parallel:

> I hope Harry won't be late for tea.
> No, I don't think he'll be late.
> What train is he coming by?
> The 4:15.
> Is the 4:15 generally late?
> No, not the 4:15.

There is nothing in life that may not be suitable material for the drama, from poetry to the talk of drunken men at a cocktail bar. But neither of these should be falsely described.

There is an American writer who, feeling that there should be some mystery in a poem, gets it by running one word into another and jumbling the spelling. He goes like this:

n
ot eth
eold almos
tladyf eebly
hurl ing
cr u
mb
son ebyo
neatt wothre
efourfi ve&six
engli shsp
arr ow
s

At least he does not make the pretense of beginning each line with a capital; but he does head it, "Poem." To tear with a ruthless unsymbolic hand the mystery from this poem, it goes, unsymbolically, like this: "Note the old almost lady feebly hurling crumbs one by one at two three four five and six English sparrows."

And with its mystery gone one sees, what one might have suspected, that this is not poetry. It is not all modern verse that can be quite so easily decoded. But my object in writing this is to advise all readers to use their wits in decoding the message from all "modern verse" and to see whether it is anything profounder than this one, rather than to surrender those wits to the composers of this so-called verse and to admit that they are cleverer than we are merely because they write something that we cannot understand, or that nou snep ouvon spasc omp rend re, as some of them would say it in scrambled French.

And to what an age they came, and to what men! They came to those who had won the greatest war that the world as yet had known, and they sang to the men who were to rush in and save Liberty when she seemed quite lost, and would have been but for them. Surely a true inspiration came to the most famous, and the most personally popular, of the writers of modern verse when he wrote in 1925:

> We are the hollow men
> We are the stuffed men
> Leaning together
> Headpiece filled with straw. Alas!
> Our dried voices, when
> We whisper together
> Are quiet and meaningless.

And surely Posterity will feel for these writers thus:

> Remember us—if at all—not as lost
> Violent souls, but only
> As the hollow men
> The stuffed men.

The Poet's Duty to Poetry

Nothing is easier on a certain journalistic and platform level than to make an art form appear ridiculous to those who know little or nothing about it. The larger the audience, the lower the brow, and the readier the prejudice against whatever is presented as arty, highbrow, and newfangled.

Maggie and Jiggs have been working this routine for years. Maggie's obvious pretensions to "cultcha" and Jiggs's manly-redblooded-American preference for Dinty, poker, and corned beef and cabbage have combined to prove over and over to the illiterate that opera is a highbrow fraud, and that all operagoers are queer and probably un-Amer-

ican. Still on the comic-strip level, one of the standard gags of syndi-
cated humor turns on the picture that wins first prize at the modern
art show. Variant one: the picture was really hung upside down. Variant two: the judges made a mistake and awarded first prize not to a
painting but to the palette. Variant three: red-blooded boy friend
proves arty boy friend is a fraud—he squirts paint at random and is
awarded first prize by enthusiastic judges. And so on—all of it
howlingly funny provided that one is sufficiently ignorant and sufficiently proud of that fact.

Some distance up the scale the devices become less crude but the
basic suspicion of everything newfangled remains. Whitman was fired
from his government job for writing indecencies. A London reviewer
of the first performance there of *La Traviata* pontificated that the
work would never find a place in the repertoire and that the principal
aria, "Caro Nome," * was nothing but a series of "languid yawns."
Cézanne was damned, van Gogh was told he could not paint, and for
more than fifty years the Prix de Paris went to painters on the level
of this Rockwell-whatever-his-name-is person who does kute-kuvvers
for *The Saturday Evening Post*. It is an old hat Dunsany is talking
through, but his seniority, his early accomplishments, the aura of his
association with great names of another age, and his hammer-and-
tongs mastery of every device of illogic tend to give his charges a
spurious air of authority.

Consider as an exercise in logic Dunsany's opening propositions.
"What is 'modern verse'?" he asks. Then with the air of a man sampling sound and representative opinion he says, "Some have called
the writers of it the greatest since Shakespeare." I don't know who
"some" is and I suspect that if Dunsany made bold to identify this
shadow-man it would turn out that Mr. Some had been invented for
the purpose of the present argument, that he was a nonentity, or that
his original remark was distorted.

"Some" is then assisted in describing the true state of affairs by
"others." "Others," we are told, think Shakespeare "rather out of
date." Now it may be that Dunsany has a specific point in mind, but
if one is discussing in order to clarify ideas, rather than arguing to win

---

* See letter from Eloise Snyder, p. 140.

a point by confusing ideas, these methods of argumentation are generally held to be intellectually dishonest if used intentionally, or signs of ignorance if used unknowingly. For Dunsany is not presenting and evaluating an idea. He is, rather, presenting the class in logic with a fine example of that fallacy labeled *ignoratio elenchi*; and, within that category, of the more specific offense commonly known as the "strawman argument." The fallacy is quite simple. The hidden premise is that "Some" and "Others" in the course of their obviously stupid assertions are truly representative of "all this modern stuff." So, instead of describing fairly that which he seeks not to investigate but to demolish, Dunsany attacks a straw man.

Following this fine round job of flailing the dummy, Dunsany delivers what seems to be offered as a telling proof that "modern verse" is not distinguishable from gibberish. He tells us that audiences he has himself addressed were unable to distinguish between "modern verse" (of his selection) and certain prepared frauds he read in the same presentation. "It," he says (and what a very gorgeous "It" this "It" is: the true and final "It" long whispered as the password by which "Some" are able to identify "Others"; the golden "It" beyond meaning, occasion, or semantic referent)—"It," says Dunsany, "is clearly beyond our intellects, for I have on occasion read to assemblies selections from two writers of 'modern verse,' and one selection of twelve lines from the first lines of an index, and one piece of deliberate nonsense written by myself, and told them they could not tell which was which. Nor could they." No indeed not.

I leave to any interested bystanders the working out of the chain of syllogisms beginning, "Any two selections which an audience I describe as intelligent cannot distinguish from nonsense clearly prove that all modern verse is beyond your intellect and mine. . . ."

Let me instead of pursuing this lovely specimen of murdered reason make Dunsany a counteroffer. He is a man of the theatre who knows very well that anyone who knows his way around a platform can do anything with an audience, especially if he confines himself to confirming minor prejudices. I am myself an old spiel-man. I will undertake for any good fat fee to address any unpacked audience of nonspecialists and to persuade it either for or against modern poetry on demand. All I ask is that the audience sit still for fifty minutes. I would reserve one difference, however. When I set out to work an experimental swindle I will know that I am swindling, and I will not swindle myself into believing my own spiel.

Dunsany goes on with two other devices of standard illogic. The first is the unspecified-charge-in-all-directions. The second is the "excerpt-lifter" with which he supports this general charge. He attacks no one, but he holds it to be absurd that someone (not, of course, T. S. Eliot) called April a "cruel month." The misquotation is Dunsany's. I like to describe this sort of argument to the untrained young who pass through my classrooms as "buckshot marksmanship"—set off a big charge in a general direction and if so much as a single pellet hits the edge of a single truth or half-truth, stand up and claim a bull's-eye. For obviously there are some queer people and some queer theories proclaiming themselves to be "modern." It seems to me equally obvious on the basis of Dunsany's recent defenses of "clarity" that the eccentricity is not wholly on one side.

Dunsany is a sure hand with a loaded phrase. Here is what I take to be his put-up-or-shut-up order to the defenders of modern poetry: "If there is any message in all this modern stuff, let someone tell us what it is in clear language; but if it lies too deep for that, we may be assured that it will do no good to us." For a vest-pocket anthology of word traps one would have to look a long way for the equal of this one. We are told that we must find something called "message" in something called (obviously a dirty name) "all this modern stuff." We are told moreover that it has to be stated in (noble phrase) "clear language" or—or what?—that the statement will be intellectually worthless. No, Dunsany caught himself before committing himself to that unsupportable conclusion. He will not claim that the answer will be false but that "it will do no good to us." Instead of "all this modern stuff" read the sentence substituting for example "all this Freudian stuff." In that case, it would be palpably dangerous to conclude "or admit that it is false," but a tricky debater might yet dodge out from under with "or it will do no good to us." To whom, sir? What do you mean by "message"? To whom must "clear" language be "clear"?

Dunsany is very emphatic in stating the necessity for clarity, but I do not find him truly concerned to recognize clarity when he meets it. Let me return to the "cruel month" and to T. S. Eliot. Dunsany not only misquotes this phrase from the opening lines of "The Waste Land"; he clearly implies that Eliot has written some sort of gibberish. He does so in two ways. First, he mentions these words as incidentally apt to his discussion of a ridiculous passage in which a bitter green octagonal sun is freezing somebody's kidney, and, second, he implies that only a fool would think of calling April "cruel." His exact words are "and if April is a cruel month, as it has been called in modern verse, surely the sun can be bitter and even can freeze."

I am not concerned here to defend or attack "The Waste Land." My one concern is with the charge as made. Dunsany has expressed his interest in clarity in a general way and he has specifically cited this particular usage as both unclear and ridiculous. I shall attempt to show him in "clear language" that there is nothing ridiculous nor unclear about it. Here is the total passage. I quote it to remind Dunsany that poetry exists in its own context and that it is always fairer to keep it there.

> April is the cruelest month, breeding
> Lilacs out of the dead land, mixing
> Memory and desire, stirring
> Dull roots with spring rain.

If paraphrase will serve, I shall paraphrase this passage for Dunsany. First, however, he must remember that "The Waste Land" is a dramatic poem and that the poet speaks through various characters. William Butler Yeats, a former acquaintance of Dunsany's, called such characters "masks." Dunsany has himself once dealt in *dramatis personae*, and will, I am sure, be with me thus far.

The character who speaks these opening lines, then, is saying: "April is (to me) the cruelest month (because) it breeds the life-promising lilacs out of the dead land and thereby mixes memory and desire, stirring the dull quiescent roots (of my lost soul) with (the attractive but ever-false promise of) spring rain."

I do not argue that the foregoing is a "message" that either Dunsany or I am likely to find attractive as a life-view. But we are not discussing a man's right to dramatize the death wish. The question is of clarity, and toward clarity I do make the following points about the passage: 1. It is unmistakably clear to anyone who will read rather than misquote it. 2. The message is not really radically different at this point from the message of many poems by Hardy and Housman, poets that no one will be tempted to think of as excessively "modern." 3. Eliot has not, as Dunsany implies, called April "cruel" and left it there. He has said rather that April is "cruel" in *the sense that* it re-awakens (only to defeat again later) the desires an old man has managed to keep dormant through the winter of his soul. 4. Dunsany really has no trouble understanding this message. He simply does not like what it is saying. He is demanding, that is, that Eliot express Dunsanian values or be adjudged nonsensical and unclear. I must confess that Dunsany's methods of argument do not especially persuade me to admire his values, and I doubt that they would so move Eliot.

I myself cannot, certainly, agree with all of the Eliotian scheme of things. Parson Eliot has always struck me as a bit of a stuffed shirt. Poet Eliot, however, is an artist. Whatever his morality, theology, or general theory, his dendrites are connected to the human race, his artistic "intuitions" (wrong word but right sense) are sound and rich. Dunsany has bewailed the passing of meter and melody. He would have to search a long way to find a better ear than Eliot's. The handling of the three participles in the lines I have quoted, the placement of the participles after the commas in each case instead of at the beginning of the next line, and the consequent way in which that placement ends each line with a caesura followed by a trochee—that is metric handling of a high order. The end of a line always tends to function as a pause, the triple repetition of the final trochees with the feminine final syllable raising the voice against the end-of-the-line check keeps the rhythm suspended, tentative, in motion in a way exactly suited to the "message." Dunsany would know more about metrics were he to study Eliot more carefully.

I shall pass over the strange and misfired attack on an unnamed e. e. cummings. Any reader of cummings can tell at a glance that cummings does not break his language in the way suggested by Dunsany's imitation. I cannot see that a poor forgery qualifies any man as an expert on coinage.

There remains the central question of clarity. Personally I have no interest in making myself clear to Dunsany's prejudices. Dunsany's imagination was formed in another time and attuned to respond to other attitudes and devices. Rejection is a very important principle in "all this modern stuff," but this is not the place to discuss it properly, nor would Dunsany do anything but scoff at the discussion. He prefers the more lordly pose—modern poetry is not poetry, modern painting is not (as Maggie and Jiggs well know) painting at all, jazz is not fit music for a civilized person, modern dance has no "message"—and on and on and on.

It will not do. No art form can be approached with the kind of indignation Dunsany brings to his distortions. There are, as I have already noted, lunatic fringes attached to modern poetry (whatever that is), as there are to every period and parish of art, but the existence of such fringes is no indictment of the center. Toward clarity, however, I will make the following specific proposal for *SR:*

Untermeyer's *Modern American Poetry, and Modern British Poetry* is the broadest anthology of "all this modern stuff." If Dunsany will accept that fat collection as a point of departure, and if he will specify his charges of unintelligibility against any group of poems therein offered by any one poet, citing in his charge what is specifically unintelligible to him, *SR* will attempt to explain to him in print how to read those passages and that poet. This offer will have to be subject to reasonable space limitations and the readers of *SR* will have to be the judges of whether or not the explanation is in clear language. No box tops necessary. Not even a comic strip. This offer, however, is not transferable.

LETTERS TO THE EDITOR

[*November 9, 1957*]

*

John Ciardi is right. It is refreshing to see logic, rather than intuition, regarded as the proper method for dissecting critical views.

CALVERT SHENK
Osage City, Kan.

*

Ciardi's rebuttal contains a measure of truth, but it discredits itself because the tone is unforgivable. If Ciardi's methods are likewise those of *The Saturday Review*—and, obviously, they must pass official muster—one wonders, what is the underlying motive? Why was Lord Dunsany hauled into battle in the first place? Was it only to be set up as a target for waspish heckling?

HERBERT E. MOULTON
Lisle, Ill.

EDITOR'S NOTE: *Lord Dunsany died on October 25 at the age of seventy-nine. He was a good friend of, and to, The Saturday Review for three decades. The editors have the highest respect for him and his work. His article was accepted— not as a peg for Mr. Ciardi's rebuttal— but as a strong presentation of the case for poetry in the classical tradition. The article was submitted by Lord Dunsany's agent, and accepted with the under-* standing *that it would run as part of a debate.*

*

I thought SR knew Caro Nome belongs in an opera named *Rigoletto*, not *Traviata*. I doubt if Ciardi's so smart.

ELOISE SNYDER
Fort Worth, Tex.

EDITOR'S NOTE: *Mr. Ciardi doubts it, too.*

*

All I can say is this. I like what Ciardi says and writes and even though I'll never be able to write it as it should be written, I will say that he writes it and says it the way it should be said and written.

SARGE STERLING
Philadelphia, Pa.

*

Ciardi errs in not admitting that quite a bit of modern verse seems to have no meaning to fairly intelligent and literate people, and is of unintelligibility all compact. I have occasionally come across an issue of *Poetry* magazine in which I could not extract meaning from even a single poem, and I have been reading "modern" poetry for something like forty years or more.

ARTHUR KRAMER
Evansville, Wis.

*

Please do not devote page after page of your otherwise delightful magazine to your self-styled "ultimate-poetry-authority's" opinions on obscurantist verse. The human patience has its limits, after all.

MRS. JOHN R. MENDIUS
Farmington, N. M.

*

When I finished reading Ciardi I literally sat and applauded. In these times it is all too seldom that someone will stand up for intelligence. The common and deplorable trend today consists of trying to lower everyone to the lowest common denominator rather than to give intelligence and education its due as something to strive for and to be lauded when increased.

PRESTON W. KELLY
Iowa City, Ia.

*

d
ea rjohny
oum ay be
rightb uth
e
say sit
better.

GREGORY WALTER
Bywood, Pa.

*

Ciardi's piece is one of the best arguments for critical honesty and tough-mindedness I have seen in print.

SHELDON GREBSTEIN
Lexington, Ky.

I have just finished reading and rereading the Dunsany–Ciardi articles and unhesitatingly award the laurel to Dunsany. His viewpoint is buttressed by the traditions of 3,000 years.

LABAN LACY RICE
Orlando, Fla.

*

I like John Ciardi, his youthful ardor, his bludgeoning vigor, his cocksureness undamped by uncertainties that come with age. I hope he remains forever young and undaunted, for his is a calling that can afford him such luxury without doing him harm.

FRED N. KERWIN
Grand Rapids, Mich.

*

Lord Dunsany has reached the heart of the matter when he says, "a poet should write for all people."

MARY CHERNOFF CORO
Los Angeles, Calif.

*

Please accept a *million cheers* for Lord Dunsany!

PAULINE M. NEWMAN
New York, N. Y.

*

I was quite shocked at the liberties Ciardi took in discrediting the intellectual abilities of Lord Dunsany. I assume that SR would not, in the first place, choose to publish a man who is incapable of handling a subject, as Ciardi seems to feel this opponent is.

GARY SHANKO
San Francisco, Calif.

LETTERS TO THE EDITOR

[*November 16, 1957*]

*

When "A Debate on Modern Poetry" is finally settled, the principles of poetry decided upon may usher in (perhaps in a generation or two) "The Golden Age of Poetry" here in America.

ROY L. MYERS
Eagle Pass, Tex.

*

Lord Dunsany's "argument," as John Ciardi so well points out, ceases to be even interesting. Eliot and cummings aren't the "bad boys" any more.

HELENE WASHER
Chicago, Ill.

*

Bafflegab poetry is endemic to our age of novelty-seeking and gobbledygook. Written by pedagogues with tin ears, it is out of touch with life and purposely strives by its double talk to confuse and bewilder. Dunsany's poetry will be remembered and honored when Ciardi and his ilk are pigeonholed with the Dadaists and Vorticists.

EDWARD REYER
Boston, Mass.

*

My brow lowered considerably when I read John Ciardi's "The larger the audience, the lower the brow." I hope the modern poets, in leaving us simians so far behind, will not in the process of evolving lose contact with each other. Where would they be then?

MRS. RUTH MARTINSON
Anoka, Minn.

*

A thousand cheers for the riotous writings of Ciardi and Dunsany on poetry. We must have these two great humorists debate some other subject soon. I have filed the issue in my bank box to read on the occasion of the next world depression.

GEORGE CLARK
Bakersfield, Calif.

*

Ciardi's article shed fresh light on the use of the *non sequitur*. Ciardi, whom I would rate the Edgar Guest of logical analysis, has engaged to defend poetry from creeping Victorianism and from comic-book culture. May I say he is tilting at windmills with a wet noodle?

The problem is not that modern poetry is hated by the ignorant and by the Philistines, who have *never* liked anything but slop, but its hold has been lost on that audience which poets once commanded—educated people who are perhaps without talent themselves but still in sympathy with the arts.

LAWRENCE LADIN

New York, N. Y.

ROBERT FROST

ROBERT FROST

THE WAY TO THE POEM

[*April 12, 1958*]

STOPPING BY WOODS ON A SNOWY EVENING

Robert Frost

Whose woods these are I think I know.
His house is in the village though;
He will not see me stopping here
To watch his woods fill up with snow.

My little horse must think it queer
To stop without a farmhouse near
Between the wood and frozen lake
The darkest evening of the year.

He gives his harness bells a shake
To ask if there is some mistake.
The only other sound's the sweep
Of easy wind and downy flake.

The woods are lovely, dark and deep.
But I have promises to keep,
And miles to go before I sleep,
And miles to go before I sleep.

The School System has much to say these days of the virtue of reading widely, and not enough about the virtues of reading less but in depth. There are any number of reading lists for poetry, but there is not enough talk about individual poems. Poetry, finally, is one poem at a time. To read any one poem carefully is the ideal preparation for reading another. Only a poem can illustrate how poetry works.

Above, therefore, is a poem—one of the master lyrics of the English language, and almost certainly the best-known poem by an American poet. What happens in it?—which is to say, not *what* does it mean, but *how* does it mean? How does it go about being a human re-enactment of a human experience? The author—perhaps the thousandth reader would need to be told—is Robert Frost.

Even the TV audience can see that this poem begins as a seemingly simple narration of a seemingly simple incident but ends by suggesting meanings far beyond anything specifically referred to in the narrative. And even readers with only the most casual interest in poetry might be made to note the additional fact that, though the poem suggests those larger meanings, it is very careful never to abandon its pretense to being simple narration. There is duplicity at work. The poet pretends to be talking about one thing, and all the while he is talking about many others.

Many readers are forever unable to accept the poet's essential duplicity. It is almost safe to say that a poem is never about what it seems to be about. As much could be said of the proverb. The bird in the hand, the rolling stone, the stitch in time never (except by an artful double deception) intend any sort of statement about birds, stones, or sewing. The incident of this poem, one must conclude, is at root a metaphor.

Duplicity aside, this poem's movement from the specific to the general illustrates one of the basic formulas of all poetry. Such a grand poem as Arnold's "Dover Beach" and such lesser, though unfortunately better-known, poems as Longfellow's "Village Blacksmith" and Holmes's "Chambered Nautilus" are built on the same progression. In these three poems, however, the generalization is markedly set apart from the specific narration, and even seems additional to the telling rather than intrinsic to it. It is this sense of division one has in mind in speaking of "a tacked-on moral."

There is nothing wrong-in-itself with a tacked-on moral. Frost, in fact, makes excellent use of the device at times. In this poem, however, Frost is careful to let the whatever-the-moral-is grow out of the poem itself. When the action ends the poem ends. There is no epilogue and no explanation. Everything pretends to be about the narrated incident. And that pretense sets the basic tone of the poem's performance of itself.

The dramatic force of that performance is best observable, I believe, as a progression in three scenes.

In scene one, which coincides with stanza one, a man—a New England man—is driving his sleigh somewhere at night. It is snowing, and as the man passes a dark patch of woods he stops to watch the snow descend into the darkness. We know, moreover, that the man is familiar with these parts (he knows who owns the woods and where the owner lives), and we know that no one has seen him stop. As scene one forms itself in the theatre of the mind's-eye, therefore, it serves to establish some as yet unspecified relation between the man and the woods.

It is necessary, however, to stop here for a long parenthesis: Even so simple an opening statement raises any number of questions. It is impossible to address all the questions that rise from the poem stanza by stanza, but two that arise from stanza one illustrate the sort of thing one might well ask of the poem detail by detail.

Why, for example, does the man not say what errand he is on? What is the force of leaving the errand generalized? He might just as well have told us that he was going to the general store, or returning from it with a jug of molasses he had promised to bring Aunt Harriet and two suits of long underwear he had promised to bring the hired man. Frost, moreover, can handle homely detail to great effect. He preferred to leave his motive generalized. Why?

And why, on the other hand, does he say so much about knowing the absent owner of the woods and where he lives? Is it simply that one set of details happened in whereas another did not? To speak of things "happening in" is to assault the integrity of a poem. Poetry cannot be discussed meaningfully unless one can assume that everything in the poem—every last comma and variant spelling—is in it by the poet's specific act of choice. Only bad poets allow into their poems what is haphazard or cheaply chosen.

The errand, I will venture a bit brashly for lack of space, is left generalized in order the more aptly to suggest *any* errand in life and, therefore, life itself. The owner is there because he is one of the forces of the poem. Let it do to say that the force he represents is the village of mankind (that village at the edge of winter) from which the poet finds himself separated (has separated himself?) in his moment by the woods (and to which, he recalls finally, he has promises to keep). The owner is he-who-lives-in-his-village-house, thereby locked away from the poet's awareness of the-time-the-snow-tells as it engulfs and obliterates the world the village man allows himself to believe he "owns." Thus, the owner is a representative of an order of reality from which the poet has divided himself for the moment, though to a certain extent he ends by reuniting with it. Scene one, therefore, establishes not only a relation between the man and the woods, but the fact that the man's relation begins with his separation (though momentarily) from mankind.

End parenthesis one, begin parenthesis two.

Still considering the first scene as a kind of dramatic performance of forces, one must note that the poet has meticulously matched the simplicity of his language to the pretended simplicity of the narrative. Clearly, the man stopped because the beauty of the scene moved him, but he neither tells us that the scene is beautiful nor that he is moved. A bad writer, always ready to overdo, might have written: "The vastness gripped me, filling my spirit with the slow steady sinking of the snow's crystalline perfection into the glimmerless profundities of the hushed primeval wood." Frost's avoidance of such a spate illustrates two principles of good writing. The first, he has stated himself in "The Mowing": "Anything *more* than the truth would have seemed too weak" (italics mine). Understatement is one of the basic sources of power in English poetry. The second principle is to let the action speak for itself. A good novelist does not tell us that a given character is good or bad (at least not since the passing of the Dickens tradition): he shows us the character in action, and then, watching him, we know. Poetry, too, has fictional obligations: even when the characters are ideas and metaphors rather than people, they must be *characterized in action.* A poem does not *talk about* ideas; it *enacts* them. The force of the poem's performance, in fact, is precisely to act out (and thereby to make us act out emphatically, that is, to *feel out,* that is, *to identify with*) the speaker and why he stopped. The man is the principle actor in this little "drama of why," and in scene one he is the only character, though, as noted, he is somehow related to the absent owner.

End second parenthesis.

In scene two (stanzas two and three) a *foil* is introduced. In fiction and drama, a foil is a character who "plays against" a more important character. By presenting a different point of view or an opposed set of motives, the foil moves the more important character to react in ways that might not have found expression without such opposition. The more important character is thus more fully revealed—to the reader and to himself. The foil here is the horse.

The horse forces the question. Why did the man stop? Until it occurs to him that his "little horse must think it queer" he had not asked himself for reasons. He had simply stopped. But the man finds himself faced with the question he imagines the horse to be asking: what *is* there to stop for out there in the cold, away from bin and stall (house and village and mankind?) and all that any self-respecting beast could value on such a night? In sensing that other view, the man is forced to examine his own more deeply.

In stanza two the question arises only as a feeling within the man. In stanza three, however (still scene two), the horse acts. He gives his harness bells a shake. "What's wrong?" he seems to say. "What are we waiting for?"

By now, obviously, the horse—without losing its identity as horse—has also become a symbol. A symbol is something that stands for something else. Whatever that something else may be, it certainly begins as that order of life that does not understand why a man stops in the wintry middle of nowhere to watch the snow come down. (Can one fail to sense by now that the dark and the snowfall symbolize a death wish, however momentary, *i.e.,* that hunger for final rest and surrender that a man may feel, but not a beast?)

So by the end of scene two the performance has given dramatic force to three elements that work upon the man. There is his relation to the world of the owner. There is his relation to the brute world of the horse. And there is also that third presence of the unownable world, the movement of the all-engulfing snow across all the orders of life, the man's, the owner's, and the horse's—with the difference that the man knows of that second dark-within-the-dark of which the horse cannot, and the owner will not, know.

The man ends scene two with all these forces working upon him simultaneously. He feels himself moved to a decision. And he feels a last call from the darkness: "the sweep / Of easy wind and downy flake." It would be so easy and so downy to go into the woods and let himself be covered over.

But scene three (stanza four) produces a fourth force. This fourth force can be given many names. It is certainly better, in fact, to give it many names than to attempt to limit it to one. It is social obligation, or personal commitment, or duty, or just the realization that a man cannot indulge a mood forever. All of these and more. But, finally, he has a simple decision to make. He may go into the woods and let the darkness and the snow swallow him from the world of beast and man. Or he must move on. And unless he is going to stop here forever, it is time to remember that he has a long way to go and that he had best be getting there. (So there is something to be said for the horse, too.)

Then and only then, his question driven more and more deeply into himself by these cross-forces, does the man venture a comment on what attracted him: "The woods are lovely, dark and deep." His mood lingers over the thought of that lovely dark-and-deep (as do the very syllables in which he phrases the thought), but the final decision is to put off the mood and move on. He has his man's way to go and his man's obligations to tend to before he can yield. He has miles to go before his sleep. He repeats that thought and the performance ends.

But why the repetition? The first time Frost says "And miles to go before I sleep," there can be little doubt that the primary meaning is: "I have a long way to go before I get to bed tonight." The second time he says it, however, "miles to go" and "sleep" are suddenly transformed into symbols. What are those "something-elses" the symbols stand for? Hundreds of people have tried to ask Mr.

Frost that question and he has always turned it away. He has turned it away *because he cannot answer it.* He could answer some part of it. But some part is not enough.

For a symbol is like a rock dropped into a pool: it sends out ripples in all directions, and the ripples are in motion. Who can say where the last ripple disappears? One may have a sense that he knows the approximate center point of the ripples, the point at which the stone struck the water. Yet even then he has trouble marking it surely. How does one make a mark on water? Oh very well—the center point of that second "miles to go" is probably approximately in the neighbor-hood of being close to meaning, perhaps, "the road of life"; and the second "before I sleep" is maybe that close to meaning "before I take my final rest," the rest in darkness that seemed so temptingly dark-and-deep for the moment of the mood. But the ripples continue to move and the light to change on the water, and the longer one watches the more changes he sees. Such shifting-and-being-at-the-same-instant is of the very sparkle and life of poetry. One experiences it as one experiences life, for every time he looks at an experience he sees something new, and he sees it change as he watches it. And that sense of continuity in fluidity is one of the primary kinds of knowl-edge, one of man's basic ways of knowing, and one that only the arts can teach, poetry foremost among them.

Frost himself certainly did not ask what that repeated last line meant. It came to him and he received it. He "felt right" about it. And what he "felt right" about was in no sense a "meaning" that, say, an essay could apprehend, but an act of experience that could be fully presented only by the dramatic enactment of forces which is the performance of the poem.

Now look at the poem in another way. Did Frost know what he was going to do when he began? Considering the poem simply as an act of skill, as a piece of juggling, one cannot fail to respond to the magnificent turn at the end where, with one flip, seven of the simplest words in the language suddenly dazzle full of never-ending waves of thought and feeling. Or, more precisely, of felt-thought. Certainly an equivalent stunt by a juggler—could there be an equivalent—would bring the house down. Was it to cap his performance with that grand stunt that Frost wrote the poem?

Far from it. The obvious fact is that *Frost could not have known he was going to write those lines until he wrote them.* Then a second fact must be registered: *he wrote them because, for the fun of it, he had got himself into trouble.*

Frost, like every good poet, began by playing a game with himself. The most usual way of writing a four-line stanza with four feet to the line is to rhyme the third line with the first, and the fourth line with the second. Even that much rhyme is so difficult in English that many poets and almost all of the anonymous ballad makers do not bother to rhyme the first and third lines at all, settling for two rhymes in four lines as good enough. For English is a rhyme-poor language. In Italian and in French, for example, so many words end with the same sounds that rhyming is relatively easy—so easy that many modern French and Italian poets do not bother to rhyme at all. English, being a more agglomerate language, has far more final sounds, hence fewer of them rhyme. When an Italian poet writes a line ending with "vita" (life) he has literally hundreds of rhyme choices available. When an English poet writes "life" at the end of a line he can summon "strife, wife, knife, fife, rife," and then he is in trouble. Now "life-strife" and "life-rife" and "life-wife" seem to offer a combination of possible ideas that can be related by more than just the rhyme. Inevitably, therefore, the poets have had to work and rework these combinations until the sparkle has gone out of them. The reader is normally tired of such rhyme-led associations. When he encounters "life-strife" he is certainly entitled to suspect that the poet did not really want to say "strife"—that had there been in English such a word as, say, "hife," meaning "infinite peace and harmony," the poet would as gladly have used that word instead of "strife." Thus, the reader feels that the writing is haphazard, that the rhyme is making the poet say things he does not really feel, and which, therefore, the reader does not feel except as boredom. One likes to see the rhymes fall into place, but he must end with the belief that it is the poet who is deciding what is said and not the rhyme scheme that is forcing the saying.

So rhyme is a kind of game, and an especially difficult one in English. As in every game, the fun of the rhyme is to set one's difficulties high and then to meet them skilfully. As Frost himself once defined it, freedom consists of "moving easy in harness."

In "Stopping by Woods on a Snowy Evening" Frost took a long chance. He decided to rhyme not two lines in each stanza, but three. Not even Frost could have sustained that much rhyme in a long poem (as Dante, for example, with the advantage of writing in Italian, sustained triple rhyme for thousands of lines in *The Divine Comedy*). Frost would have known instantly, therefore, when he took the original chance, that he was going to write a short poem. He would have had that much foretaste of it.

So the first stanza emerged rhymed a-a-b-a. And with the sure sense that this was to be a short poem, Frost decided to take an additional chance and to redouble: in English three rhymes in four lines is more than enough; there is no need to rhyme the fourth line. For the fun of it, however, Frost set himself to pick up that loose rhyme and to weave it into the pattern, thereby accepting the all but impossible burden of quadruple rhyme.

The miracle is that it worked. Despite the enormous freight of rhyme, the poem not only came out as a neat pattern, but managed to do so with no sense of strain. Every word and every rhyme falls into place as naturally and as inevitably as if there were no rhyme restricting the poet's choices.

That ease-in-difficulty is certainly inseparable from the success of the poem's performance. One watches the skill-man juggle three balls, then four, then five, and every addition makes the trick more wonderful. But unless he makes the hard trick seem as easy as an easy trick, then all is lost.

The real point, however, is not only that Frost took on a hard rhyme-trick and made it seem easy. It is rather as if the juggler, carried away, had tossed up one more ball than he could really handle, and then amazed himself by actually handling it. So with the real triumph of this poem. Frost could not have known what a stunning effect his repetition of the last line was going to produce. He could not even know he was going to repeat the line. He simply found himself up against a difficulty he almost certainly had not foreseen and he had to improvise to meet it. For in picking up the rhyme from the third line of stanza one and carrying it over into stanza two, he had created an endless chain-link form within which each stanza left a hook sticking out for the next stanza to hang on. So by stanza four, feeling the poem rounding to its end, Frost had to do something about that extra rhyme.

He might have tucked it back into a third line rhyming with the *know-though-snow* of stanza one. He could thus have rounded the poem out to the mathematical symmetry of using each rhyme four times. But though such a device might be defensible in theory, a rhyme repeated after eleven lines is so far from its original rhyme sound that its feeling as rhyme must certainly be lost. And what good is theory if the reader is not moved by the writing?

It must have been in some such quandary that the final repetition suggested itself—a suggestion born of the very difficulties the poet had let himself in for. So there is that point beyond mere ease in handling a hard thing, the point at which the very difficulty offers the poet the opportunity to do better than he knew he could. What, aside from having that happen to oneself, could be more self-delighting than to participate in its happening by one's reader-identification with the poem?

And by now a further point will have suggested itself: that the human insight of the poem and the technicalities of its poetic artifice are inseparable. Each feeds the other. That interplay is the poem's meaning, a matter not of WHAT DOES IT MEAN, for no one can ever say entirely what a good poem means, but of HOW DOES IT MEAN, a process one can come much closer to discussing.

There is a necessary epilogue. Mr. Frost has often discussed this poem on the platform, or more usually in the course of a long evening after a talk. Time and again I have heard him say that he just wrote it off, that it just came to him, and that he set it down as it came.

Once at Bread Loaf, however, I heard him add one very essential piece to the discussion of how it "just came." One night, he said, he had sat down after supper to work at a long piece of blank verse. The piece never worked out, but Mr. Frost found himself so absorbed in it that, when next he looked up, dawn was at his window. He rose, crossed to the window, stood looking out for a few minutes, and *then* it was that "Stopping by Woods" suddenly "just came," so that all he had to do was cross the room and write it down.

Robert Frost is the sort of artist who hides his traces. I know of no Frost work sheets anywhere. If someone has raided his wastebasket in secret, it is possible that such work sheets exist somewhere, but Frost would not willingly allow anything but the finished product to leave him. Almost certainly, therefore, no one will ever know what was in that piece of unsuccessful blank verse he had been working at with such concentration, but I for one would stake my life that could that work sheet be uncovered, it would be found to contain the germinal stuff of "Stopping by Woods"; that what was a-simmer in him all night without finding its proper form, suddenly, when he let his still-occupied mind look away, came at him from a different direction, offered itself in a different form, and that finding that form exactly right the impulse proceeded to marry itself to the new shape in one of the most miraculous performances of English lyricism.

And that, too—whether or not one can accept so hypothetical a discussion—is part of HOW the poem means. It means that marriage to the perfect form, the poem's shapen declaration of itself, its moment's monument fixed beyond all possibility of change. And thus, finally, in every truly good poem, "How does it mean?" must always be answered "Triumphantly." Whatever the poem "is about," *how* it means is always how Genesis means: the word become a form, and the form become a thing, and—when the becoming is true—the thing become a part of the knowledge and experience of the race forever.

LETTERS TO THE EDITOR
[*May 3, 1958*]

*

In my article on Robert Frost I said I did not know of any Frost work sheets in existence and that no one knows what long blank-verse poem it was that Frost had been working on just before writing "Stopping by Woods."

Since publication of the article my good friend John Holmes, poet, critic, and scholar of Frost, has written to tell me that some Frost work sheets do exist and that it was his understanding from Mr. Frost that the long poem in question is "New Hampshire." I am happy to add this information to the record. If the long poem is indeed "New Hampshire," my guess that it must have contained the germinal stuff of "Stopping by Woods" becomes questionable.

JOHN CIARDI

New York, N. Y.

*

Is there any truth to the rumor that "Jack Kerouac" is a pseudonym for John Ciardi?

CRAIG LEMAN

Corvallis, Ore.

*

Like legions of others, I was delighted with Mr. John Ciardi's beautiful essay, but I was surprised that Mr. Ciardi does not mention the lullaby nature of Frost's poem. He mentions that the poet had been awake all night at work on another composition. At the moment the poem occurred to him he undoubtedly felt the need for sleep and began to create within himself a mood conducive to that end. The whole poem is very soothing and relaxing, which may, in part, account for its universal popularity.

MRS. CORA CARROLL SCANLON

Milwaukee, Wis.

*

Only the "sundry scattered few who consider these things important," as Amy Lowell once said, will know what Frost was talking about.

CHARLES E. CUNNINGHAM

Philadelphia, Pa.

*

LETTERS TO THE EDITOR

[May 10, 1958]

*

The article "Robert Frost: The Way to the Poem," by John Ciardi, is one of the most excellent pieces of explication I have had an opportunity to read. It is simple, thorough, and clear and at the same time provocative of response to the deepest and most far-reaching values in poetry. The essay, just as it is, would be a boon to many students and teachers who together are seeking to find each other as they attend to a poem.

JOSEPH H. JENKINS

Petersburg, Va.

*

Robert Frost's miracle, "Stopping by Woods on a Snowy Evening," comprises four stanzas, sixteen lines, 108 words. John Ciardi's analysis of it runs to ten full columns. This flushes an old question: Does such probing, poking, and picking really lead "The Way to the Poem"?

WILLIAM L. HASSETT
Des Moines, Ia.

*

I have just discovered, by way of John Ciardi's analysis of Robert Frost's poem "Stopping by Woods on a Snowy Evening," that this charmingly simple, eloquent, lyrical little poem, long one of my favorites, is supposedly fraught with duplicity of meaning and symbolism, including a disguised death wish, and that it is not at all about what it seems to be about.

This is really a new high in critical absurdity. If the presentation of this leading, cover-featured article were not so obviously straight-faced, I would have considered this a nice parody of much present-day "criticism." Who is Mr. Ciardi trying to kid? Or is he himself merely kidded? I am sure Mr. Frost must be highly amused or shaking his head in amazement at the awesome proportions his innocent poetic images have assumed ("By now, obviously, the horse has also become a symbol").

MRS. BEVERLY TRAVERS
New Orleans, La.

*

It seems to us that when a poet uses the skill Frost employs in creating a mood, sharing an experience, one should accept it as given, without further analysis. One does not enhance a rainbow by subjecting it to a spectrometric analysis.

JOHN G. GOSSELINK
Hartford City, Ind.

I was a little shocked when I read Ciardi's interpretation of the dark and snowfall in Frost's "Stopping by Woods on a Snowy Evening" as a death wish. I suppose every person must interpret poems like this in terms of his own experience. To me, it seems to say that there is a certain deep satisfaction in stopping to lose oneself in the contemplation of beauty. The experience itself is significant in that it brings the individual into a sense of relationship to basic reality. But one cannot escape too long into these subjective experiences. There is work to do; obligations must be met; one cannot spend his whole life escaping from these practical realities.

J. JOSEPHINE LEAMER
Gardiner, Mont.

*

I am used to most magazines pointing out the obvious, but when SR tells me that a symbol stands for something else (John Ciardi's article on Robert Frost), I am really hurt. Chances are, if I thought a symbol was something other than something else, I wouldn't be reading SR or any other magazine.

MARJORIE DURYEE
Everett, Wash.

*

Why Mr. Ciardi had to pick such, as he himself states, "a simple narrative" to expound upon I'll never know. If one thought of poetry as Mr. C does, the joy of just reading beautiful poetry would be gone completely. One would begin to spend all his time searching for symbols and such.

H. CLAY BARNARD
Sausalito, Calif.

*

I have just finished reading John Ciardi's penetrating analysis of Robert Frost's familiar lyric. This is distinguished service in the cause of criticism. More articles like this and we *will* develop a poetry-reading America.

SISTER MARY DENISE, RSM
Dallas, Pa.

*

Through the years I've read "Stopping by Woods on a Snowy Evening" many times and felt that with each reading I had extracted its meaning to the point where I felt certain that there was no more it could tell me. John Ciardi has exposed new and deeper meanings to me and, as an excellent teacher, has dissected and made clear its very essence.

LLOYD RODNICK
Detroit, Mich.

*

Ciardi has some very interesting ideas. But wouldn't it be better to develop them in a separate essay? It seems to me that the literary woods is too full of heavy limbs falling upon little delicate branches.

GARY THORNBURG
Losantville, Ind.

*

Ciardi's calm, cleanly developed, and illuminating article on Frost's poem surely is a savory example of what his readers have clamored for all these months. In this essay one finds all of Mr. Ciardi's inspiring adherence to principles and none of those bubonic symptoms which many of his readers have denounced. Personally, I am pleased to find also fewer coinings of discordant and sometimes hideous compounds, an indulgence that often spoils the point of what Mr. Ciardi has to say.

EARL CLENDENON
Chicago, Ill.

*

The business of equating this poem with all the current philosophical symbols that are in Ciardi's mind is, of course, Ciardi's privilege. But why should he speak as Frost's analyst?

HARVEY PARKER
Vista, Calif.

*

Ciardi very pedantically makes complete reparation for last year's storm-provoking criticism of Anne Morrow Lindbergh's delicate and deep poetry. Many college and high school teachers will be able to use such an exhaustive analysis in the classroom.

JOSEPH A. McNULTY
Philadelphia, Pa.

*

LETTERS TO THE EDITOR
PHILIP WYLIE

After reading Ciardi's uncomprehending, clinical, anti-poetical "appreciation" of my friend Robert Frost's great lyric, I was so moved, in sundry unprintable ways, that I thought to write Robert: the essay reminded me throughout of a humorless pathologist slicing away with his microtome at a biopsy.

However, what I wanted to say "just came to me" and I simply "wrote it down"—on a Remington Noiseless which I use for all composition, including poetry. It took twenty minutes, from gag to madrigal—some twenty more to add an effort to refute Mr. Ciardi's contention that English is a knobby tongue to rhyme—and I forward the result to you, in the hope that you might print it as one (largely commercial) writer's testament that, to some of us, things do come, we do just write them down, and we know enough English to find little trouble in double-rhyming a ballad, even in what Mr. Ciardi regards as the difficult scheme of Frost's poem. I also felt J. C. should learn that "know," "here," "lake," and "sleep" hardly baffle an idle versifier—and Robert's variation of the ballad form is not beyond the reach even of typewriter poets like me.

Mr. Ciardi, neo-master of critique, finds it easy to demolish the avowedly amateur verses of Anne Lindbergh with his little mechanic's hammer; but he did not realize that when he undertook to acclaim a true poet his implement might bounce from the granite with predictable damage to the self-anointed Thor. Ciardi must be all Ph.D., and of the new academic subspecies.

PHILIP WYLIE

Miami, Fla.

STOPPING TO WRITE A FRIEND ON A THICK NIGHT

In this week's *Saturday Review*
The first bit, Robert, deals with you.
At least, its author, John Ciardi
Tears a poem of yours in two

And shreds the halves. His toy lombard, he
Loads with treacle praise, and lardy,
Salutes your metaphor and tmesis
And fires again to call you hardy.

Art, to him, is just its pieces,
The obvious, his noblest thesis—
Who even calls down holocaust
On his own tongue—the mangling Jesus!

Your blanket snow's thus double-crossed
By one who should be blanket-tossed
And he has miles to go to Frost
And years to learn it's Frost he lost.

Letter to Letter-Writers

[*May 17, 1958*]

I have never known a magazine with SR's knack for calling forth
LETTERS TO THE EDITOR. No one writing for SR need suffer from a
sense that his ideas have disappeared into the void: he will hear from
the readers. I have been hearing of late, and the charge this time,
made by some readers, is that I have despoiled a great poem in my

analysis of Robert Frost's "Stopping by Woods on a Snowy Evening."

The Frost article was self-declaredly an effort at close analysis. I believe the poem to be much deeper than its surfaces, and I set out to ask what sort of human behavior it is that presents a surface of such simplicity while stirring such depths of multiple responses. It may be that I analyzed badly, but the more general charge seems to be that all analysis is inimical to poetry, and that general charge is certainly worth a closer look.

A number of readers seem to have been offended by the fact that the analysis was longer than the poem, which, as one reader put it, "comprises four stanzas, sixteen lines, 108 words" (rather technical analysis, that sort of word-counting), whereas my article ran to "ten full columns."

A first clear assumption in this reader's mind is the assertion that an analysis must not be longer than what it analyzes. I can see no way of defending that assumption. If there is to be any analysis at all, it is in the nature of things that the analysis be longer than the poem or the passage it analyzes. One hundred and eight words will hardly do simply to describe the stanzaic form and rhyme scheme of the poem, without any consideration of the nature of the rhyme problem. Analysis and the poem are simply enough tortoise and hare. The difference from the fable is that the poetic hare does not lie down and sleep. The unfabled tortoise, however, may still hope to crawl after and, in some sense, to mark the way the hare went.

The second assumption is that analysis obscures ("does not lead the way to") a poem, and amounts in fact to mere "probing, poking, and picking." The charge as made is not specifically against any article but against all analysis. The question may, therefore, be simply located: should poetry be talked about at all?

A number of readers clearly take the position that it must not be. "One should accept it (the experience of the poem) as given, without further analysis," asserts one reader. "One does not enhance a rainbow by subjecting it to spectrometric analysis." An unwavering position and an interesting figure of speech. I am drawn to that rainbow and fascinated by this use of the word "enhance." By "spectrometric analysis" I take the gentleman to mean "investigating the physical nature of" but said, of course, with an overtone of disdain at the idea of seeing "beauty" meaningfully through any "instrument." That disdain aside, however, one may certainly ask why detailed knowledge of the physical phenomena that produce a rainbow should "unenhance" the rainbow's emotional value. Is speculation into the nature of things to be taken as a destruction of nature?

Two years ago, looking down on Rome from the Gianiculum, I saw two complete rainbows in the sky at once, not just pieces of rainbows but complete arcs with both ends of each arc visible at once in a great bridge above the city. And in what way did it hurt me as part of my instant delight to register some sense of the angle at which the sun had to hit the atmosphere in order to produce such a prodigy? I must insist on remaining among those who are willing to learn about rainbows.

Such disdain seems to be shared by many of our readers. Mr. Philip Wylie, a man described to me as an author, filed the strongest, or at least the longest, of the recent objections. My "implement," as he sees it, bounces "from the granite (of the poem) with predictable damage to the self-anointed Thor. Ciardi must be all Ph.D., and of the new academic subspecies."

Not exactly factual, since I do not own a Ph.D., but fair enough: giving lumps is a time-honored literary game and anyone with a type-writer may play. Mr. Wylie's indignation is largely against my way of dealing with Mr. Frost's poem, and that is a charge I must waive— he may be right, he may be wrong; no score. One part of his charge, however, is a more general anger at the idea that anyone should go into a detailed analysis of the rhyme scheme of a poem that "just came" to the poet. Once again the basic charge is that poetry is damaged by analysis. One should "just let it come."

Many others have joined Mr. Wylie in his defense of the untouchable-spontaneous. "Get your big clumsy feet off that miracle," says one reader I find myself especially drawn to. "What good do you think you do," writes another, "when you tear apart a thing as lovely as Mr. Frost's poem?" Another: "A dissecting kit belongs in the laboratory, not the library." And still another: "If one thought of poetry as Mr. C does, the joy of just reading beautiful poetry would be gone completely. One would begin to spend all his time dealing with symbols and such."

I must, parenthetically, reject some of the terms of that last letter. "Begin to spend *all* his time," is the writer's idea: that "all" is no part of mine. I shall pass the sneer contained in the phrase "symbols and such." But I cannot accept the responsibility for defending myself when misquoted. One reader, for example, accuses me of stating that a poem "is not at all about what it seems to be about." I can only reply that those are his terms, not mine, and that I have no thought of defending them.

It is that "all" in the first quotation, however, that locates the central misunderstanding. "Once one begins to analyze," the assumption runs, "he begins to spend all of his time 'merely analyzing' and the analysis not only takes the place of the poem but leads to the poem's destruction."

Were there no misconception involved, this reader's anger would certainly be justified. What is misconceived is the idea that the analysis is intended to take the place of the poem. Far from it. One takes a poem apart only in order to put it back together again with greater understanding. The poem itself is the thing. A good poem is a hanging gull on a day of perfect winds. We sit below and watch it own the air it rides: a miracle from nature. There it hangs on infallible wings. But suppose one is interested in the theory of flight (as the gull itself, to be sure, need not be) and suppose one notices that the gull's wings can perform miracles in the air because they have a particular curvature and a particular sort of leading and trailing edge. And suppose he further notices that the gull's tail feathers have a great deal to do with that seemingly effortless mastery. Does that man cease to see the gull? Does he see nothing but diagrams of airflow and lift to the total damnation of all gulls? Or does he see the gull not only as the miracle of a perfect thing, but as the perfect thing in the enmarveling system of what encloses it?

The point involves the whole nature of perception. Do we "see" with our eyes? I must believe that it is the mind that sees, and that the eyes are only the windows we see through. We see with the patterns of what we know. Let any layman look into a tide pool and list what he sees there. Then let him call an imaginative biologist and ask the biologist what he sees. The layman will have seen things, but the biologist will see systems, and the things in place in those systems.

He will also see many things at once. Basic to all poetic communication is what I call *fluency*. Fluency is the ability to receive more than one meaning, impression, stimulus—call it what you please—at the same time. Analysis must always fumble and be long-winded because it must consider those multiple impressions doggedly and one by one. If such itemized dealing accurately locates true elements of the poem, the itemization will have served its purpose, and that purpose must certainly be defended as one that has summoned some of the best minds of all ages. What analysis does, though laboriously, is to establish patterns one may see with.

But there then remains the reader's work. It is up to him, guided by the analysis, to read the poem with the fluency it requires, and which analysis does not hope to achieve. Certainly, whatever is said here, poetry will be talked about and must be talked about. The one point of such talk, however, is to lead the reader more richly to the threshold of the poem. Over that threshold he must take himself. And I, for one, must suspect that if he refuses to carry anything as cumbersome as detail across that threshold, he will never furnish the house of his own mind.

LETTERS TO THE EDITOR

[*May 31, 1958*]

*

I was happy to read the bludgeoning handed to SR's exponent of the New Criticism, John Ciardi. When I read his blown-up "explication" of Frost's delightfully simple poem "Stopping by Woods on a Snowy Evening," I was tempted to write a letter of protest against such arrant nonsense. However, knowing that somebody else could do a better job, I restrained myself. And Philip Wylie did the trick much more effectively than I could.

HALE STURGES

Lakeland, Fla.

As an editor for more than thirty years of an important daily newspaper, I have some knowledge of good and bad writing. By trial and error, we have learned to throw the bad stuff away. May I respectfully suggest that freedom of speech, opinion, or press does not include any duty on your part to circulate Ciardi? Unless, of course, you prefer to be ridiculous.

PAUL B. WILLIAMS
Utica, N. Y.

*

I'm just a simple country feller, but I always thought I understood Frost's poem. Now I don't know if I understand my horse.

ALLEN M. MORTIMER
Martha's Vineyard, Mass.

*

Ciardi is still "the man with the butterfly bat." Frost's poem was so badly mashed, rather than dissected, that some may have difficulty in ever putting it back together, which is a pity.

ROGER B. THOMPSON
Knoxville, Tenn.

*

Mr. Frost's own comment during a talk at the University of California (Berkeley) Greek Theatre might well apply. He said that he was certainly impressed by literary critics who could explain his third, fourth, and fifth meanings when he could only figure out his first and second.

BOB RODINI
El Cerrito, Calif.

*

If Wylie feels so strongly about it, I think he might better have spent his forty minutes organizing an essay on criticism, which, if submitted to *SR*, would probably be published to the edification of all. This would certainly seem more positive an attack than the acidulous little outburst of name-calling to which he treated us. If anything, he proved Ciardi's contention that it takes quite a poet to rhyme in English. His own attempt would even make Ogden Nash weep.

FRANK J. RINALDI
Totowa Borough, N. J.

*

Poetry lovers, let us assume that the poetry editor of *SR*, Mr. Ciardi, was entirely wrong in the spirit and tone in which he once attacked the poetry of Mrs. Lindbergh. But consider this. The man who never did wrong, never did anything. And never will.

DON CLARY
Buffalo, N. Y.

*

Philip Wylie certainly proved Mr. Ciardi's point with that sixteen-line what-you-may-call-it of his. It reads more like the product of a mechanical brain than that of a Remington Noiseless.

JESSE FORBECK
St. Louis, Mo.

*

It seems that Ciardi can do nothing to please some of your readers. The rash of letters vilifying his sensitive and discerning appreciation of Frost's poem must have come from the same readers whose susceptibilities were wounded when he pointed out the limitations of Mrs. Lindbergh's poetry.

FRANK SMOYER
Allentown, Pa.

Analysis of a poem doesn't destroy its beauties; it puts the reader closer to them. The deeper a critic probes, the better he is doing his job and the more valuable he is to us. Ciardi has shown that Frost's poem has depth as well as simplicity and charm. Surely our knowledge of that depth isn't going to lessen our joy in rereading the poem.

JOHN S. SHEA

Camp Irwin, Calif.

The fact that Ciardi gave his reaction to the poem in no way, so far as I can see, prevents others from having a different version of the same poem. Different experiences can make us take a similar situation and feel differently about it. The important thing is that we stop to think about what is being written.

HARRIETTE RING

Batavia, N. Y.

AN INTERVIEW WITH ROBERT FROST*

[*March* 21, 1959]

If ever a man seemed headed for the century mark and beyond, with no diminution of his powers, Robert Frost, on the eve of his eighty-fifth birthday, seemed that man. I flew down from Newark to Miami to find him abundantly well in his winter home and at work in a small strew of manuscripts with Mrs. Theodore Morrison, the devoted companion who, for many years now, has taken the burden of details off his shoulders.

They were deep in the final arrangements of Mr. Frost's forthcoming book but put the manuscript aside to make me welcome. We talked a while. Then Mr. Frost took me on a farmer's tour of his two-acre tropical grove of avocados, mangoes, kumquats, loquats, limes, oranges, grapefruit, pines, palms, and dozens more. He was obviously happy walking in his garden. He had made it himself. He had made something grow and the fact of each tree was meaningful to him.

Back in the house we talked a while, then went out to dinner, then sat and talked till midnight. The next morning we talked again. It was great talk. It always is when Mr. Frost warms to it, for he is certainly one of the master conversationalists of this age. As with any author, a forthcoming book is likely to be first in any conversation, and we began with that.

Mr. Frost: I call it *The Great Misgiving.* My theme is that the only *event* in all history is science plunging deeper into matter. We have

* This piece appeared in SR titled "Robert Frost, Master Conversationalist at Work." I do not know where that editorial change occurred, nor do I feel strongly about it, but I do prefer the simpler original title, which I here restore.

plunged into the smallness of particles and we are plunging into the hugeness of space—but not without fears that the spirit shall be lost.

I am not against science. I always dislike it when people assume that because I am a poet I must be against science. But in taking us deeper and deeper into matter, science has left all of us with this great misgiving, this fear that we won't be able to substantiate the spirit. I've said in "Kitty Hawk":

> That the supreme merit
> Lay in risking spirit
> In substantiation.

Risk is the point. Someone asked me if I thought God *could* take a chance. I said it looked to me as if he had—right from the start.

But only the Western world has really risked it. The people of the East had the great misgiving, but it arrested them. They drew back from the material because they weren't ready to take the dare of it. We in the West have learned to carry the misgiving—in just about the way you learn to carry liquor.

I've been gathering together the poems for the book. The main one is "Kitty Hawk," which is a longish poem in two parts. Part One is a sort of personal story, an adventure of my boyhood. I was down there once when I was about nineteen. Alone, just wandering. Then I was invited back there sixty years later.

That return after so long a time suggested the poem to me. I use my own story of the place to take off into the story of the airplane. I make a figure of speech of it: How I might have taken off from my experience of Kitty Hawk and written an immortal poem, but how, instead, the Wright brothers took off from there to commit an immortality. I knew one of the Wright brothers slightly: I had that little connection with them.

Part Two goes into the thought of the on-penetration into matter and our great misgiving.

Flight is just one more penetration, no more than that. And so one more cause of the misgiving we must all risk; Part Two is the philosophical part.

Then I'm putting in some little poems. I'm including "Cabin in the Clearing." And the one about the Dog, Sirius, the one titled "One More Brevity." And one about Columbus. Those have been published in the magazines. Then there are some little unpublished things. And there's another longish one I did to read to the American Academy of Arts and Letters, titled "How Hard It Is to Keep from Being King When It's in You and in the Situation." That's the kind of long title I sometimes like. I lifted the story of that one out of the Arabian Nights. It's one of the seldom-noted tales that has no sex in it.

It makes up into a pretty full book. It comes to about 100 pages, I'd guess, though I haven't counted them. I have a book out about once in seven years. Some of them have been pretty slim, but this one ought to be a bit longer; I've gone longer than seven years this time and I should have more to show for it.

Question: If The Great Misgiving is the theme of the book, what would you say about the treatment? I mean not "thing-said" now, but more nearly "the poem-ness of the poem."

Mr. Frost: The way the poem goes has been the curious thing of my life. I think the whole thing begins probably in some singsong of our race. Like Mother Goose—in a way we all begin there. The song is so much more important than the thought you have.

There's thought in it; make no mistake about that. But it's as if you were walking along the street and you saw someone you knew coming toward you—someone with whom you always exchange a little banter. There, right away, something comes into your head to say to him. What's the dawn of that? The *act of having the thought* is what gives quality to the poem. The poem *is* the act of having the thought.

In a poem, you don't know what the thought is, but you do know when you've missed it.

Now there's a question—how can you tell when you've missed what you didn't know you were aiming at? I don't know how you know, but the singsong is in it.

For the poem is a thought-felt thing, and the felt part of it seems to exist in waves. The waves are what measure and let you know when you've missed or not. They are the rhythm of it—more than the rhythm: they are *the meter of our race.*

In English the meter is either strict iambic or loose iambic. If it is strict there is only one light syllable between stresses. If it is loose, the meter may have two light syllables between stresses. Then, of course, if it is strictly loose with two light syllables between every two stresses, that is anapestic.

But you can't have three light syllables between stresses. That's not in the meter of English.

There's that to the act of having the thought. There is also the *doubleness* of it. That doubleness, like the singsong of the meter, has something to do with how we are made as human beings. It is some essential part of how we think and are. There is something in all of us of the matchmaker. Man likes to bring two things together into one. He likes to make things into rhymed couplets. Not only poetic rhymed couplets, but the coupling of all sorts of things that reason rhymes together. Rhymed couplets are the symbols of this tendency in man. He lives by making associations and he is doing well by himself and in himself when he thinks of something in connection with something else that no one ever put with it before. That's what we call a metaphor.

I couldn't do without that sense of two-ness. It's a feeling I've had from infancy, a kind of "ulteriority complex."

Some people let that gift lapse within them. A TV man came to see me once about doing a show. He wanted to talk about the necessity for individuality. I found myself thinking of what Job said: "Thou art more to me than my necessary food." But I twisted that around a little for the TV man. I said: "My individuality is more to me than my necessary group."

The TV man couldn't understand what I was saying. He had no sense of doubleness. He wanted to talk about individuality, but really he just wanted to belong to his necessary group.

All of us keep worrying about that. "He doesn't *belong*," we say. That means something to us. But sometimes you have to throw "belonging" to the winds. Those are the times when no one can help you. No priest. No psychiatrist. Nobody.

Question: Can the poem help?

Mr. Frost: A poem is a momentary stay against confusion. Each poem clarifies something. But then you've got to do it again. You can't get clarified to stay so: let you not think that. In a way, it's like nothing more than blowing smoke rings. Making little poems encourages a man to see that there is shapeliness in the world. A poem is an arrest of disorder.

Question: Is that what there is in it for the poet?

Mr. Frost: I've had two main pleasures. I've had pleasure in the form that a poem makes. And I've had pleasure in trying to understand what comes up—The Bomb, Billy Graham, Khrushchev—in everything as it comes up. If you mean to be a man, you have to assess the Sphinx. You have to be riddled by it. You have to find something to say to everything.

And when you say it, you've got to bother them. You've got to say something that will hold them till you can get away.

Question: I'm not sure I understand what it is you have to get away from.

Mr. Frost: The word I want to use for that is "publicality." The poem goes like a marriage. It starts with a thing as private as love, and then moves to the public ceremony of a wedding. It goes from felicity to publicity. I sometimes sicken at the way people celebrate the *publicity* of my poems with no thought for their *felicity*. You have to get away from that publicity, from that "publicality," and get back to the felicity.

The great misgiving here is that you will get beyond the sound of the still small voice in your heart; that the publicity may drown it out. The fear of losing that voice need not be a terror within you, but it should be a misgiving. The risk is that you may perish ignominiously when you lose the voice. That is the risk we all take. The poem is a venture into substantiation. But it *is* a venture—a risk. There must always be a chance that you will lose.

Question: You've said some penetrating things about the venture the poem is. What about the venture the poet is? Not that it is possible to make a distinction in kind, really, but as a matter of emphasis, what have you felt as your "biographical" urgencies as distinct from your "aesthetic" urgencies, if I may put it that way?

Mr. Frost: I've never been much for saving the world. I've never wanted to tell anyone what to believe, but just to start a thought going to see where it comes back. I wouldn't want to be urgent about other people's beliefs; let them come to them of themselves.

The only thing I have ever been publicly urgent about is our high schools. I took a notion there and I want something done about it. I have a feeling our high schools are not up to what they used to be. They lack tone. They've been *speeded* up, but I want to *tone* them up.

Teachers no longer seem to have standing in the community. I get to a lot of places and I get to meet civic leaders at all sorts of gatherings, but no one ever thinks to invite the high school teachers. I want to change that. I want them to be important enough to be asked.

A while ago I was on a TV show in Pittsburgh and I said I wanted endowed and named chairs in the high schools to give the good teachers some stature and position in the town as the Such-and-Such Professor of Something. As a starter, I asked for two in the Pittsburgh high schools, say, a Willa Cather Chair and a Hervey Allen Chair— they both came from Pittsburgh.

A few days later I heard that the foundations had given $15,000,000 for chairs at the University of Pittsburgh—just to show me that they didn't care about the high schools, maybe. That same money could have set up a lot of chairs in different high schools. Say it takes $20,000 to endow a chair—$15,000,000 could have set up seventy-five of them to start with.

I want the foundations to do it and two or three people have shown interest. There are problems to it, to be sure, but nothing that can't be overcome. And I want it done. That's the one public thing I've decided to be urgent about.

Question: If that has been your one public urgency, what do you think of as your personal urgencies?

Mr. Frost: My urgent wish has been to write two or three poems— just a few—that will be hard to get rid of. For the rest, I've always done it poem by poem, as it came to me to do.

What I care about is the hardness of the poems. I don't like them soft. I want them to be little pebbles, but placed where they won't dislodge easily. And I'd like them to be little pebbles of precious stone—precious, or semiprecious.

The difference between just any pebble and a precious stone is that the pebble shines only when it's wet. I want mine to go on shining wet or dry.

Question: A long time back you wrote:

They will not find me changed from him they knew.
Only more sure of all I thought was true.

Would you hold to that in retrospect?

Mr. Frost: The new thing with me has always included the old. Those lines are really about loyalty, aren't they? I know more about loyalty now than I did when I wrote them. But the situation of loyalty is always the same.

I keep seeing articles by people who talk about "Loyalty in Times Like These." But loyalty doesn't change with the times. If you decide to be disloyal *for good and sufficient reason*—perhaps because new loyalties demand it of you—you do so at your own risk. Past, present, or future, disloyalty is always the same as far as the necessary group is concerned. Disloyalty is that for which your gang will take you out and shoot you if they catch you at it. Go ahead and risk it when you must, but let's have no talk of disloyalty made easy—as if you ought to be able to go against your gang and then expect them to kiss you for it.

Question: What about your public life in "the necessary group"? How much public schedule are you carrying as Consultant in Poetry at the Library of Congress?

Mr. Frost: I don't stay in Washington all year. I go there for four separate "intervals" as they call them. Each interval is about a week long. I've done three of them and have my fourth to go.

They are the busiest weeks I've ever put in. I go to my office every day to be consulted and all sorts of people come in. And then there are parties to go to. And then there are public lectures to give. I've given one to chosen children from the nearby high schools—two or three from each school along with one of their teachers. Then I gave one to invited guests of the Library of Congress. And I have a number of them to give when I go back. I have one scheduled for people who specially asked for tickets. Then I'm to speak to a group of graduate students from the Maryland colleges. Then a public lecture in the Folger Library. And then one to the entire staff of the Library of Congress.

I'm doing a big year. Aside from those four intervals at the Library of Congress, I'm to visit about twenty colleges, some for just one day, others for one, two, or three weeks. I have three weeks to do yet at Amherst. And a visit to Mount Holyoke. Then in August, of course, I'll be back at the Bread Loaf Writers' Conference.

I like traveling around to the colleges, though I don't want to do too much of it. I don't want it to be in such a hurry that I find myself saying the same thing all over again at each place.

Question: Do you like teaching?

Mr. Frost: I like trying to shape an idea for the class or for the audience, but I won't read manuscript if I can help it, and I usually can. I evade it. I say, "Let me read it when it's in print; I'll enjoy it more."

I've practiced my evasion. I've held up a set of papers to a class and asked, "Does anyone value any one of these?" Not one of them would say yes, so I threw the whole set into the wastebasket. "I am no perfunctory reader of perfunctory writing," I've told them.

Or I've said, "The first paper you pass in to me is the one you'll get your final grade for." I want them to hold it until they are sure it is the best they can possibly make of it.

And I have never touched a paper with a red pencil. "I'm not here to worry your writing into shape for you," I tell them. "Look to it yourself."

Question: That's what a writer is, isn't it?—a man who has to be able above all else to help himself?

Mr. Frost: There is always that question of help and self-help. I believe in accepting some help, but I value myself chiefly as a self-helper.

There was once a group of ladies in Brooklyn that seemed to want to do something for me. They thought maybe it was too hard to be a poet and that they could help. They had me down to read to them and they asked me, "How do you find time to be a poet?"

I looked them over—there were about five hundred of them—and I asked them if they could keep a confidence. All five hundred said they could, so I told them where I got the time for it.

"Like a sneak," I said, "I *stole* some of it. Like a man, I *seized* some of it.—And I had a little in my tin cup to begin with."

They decided not to do anything for me after all. And better so. If you want to be an artist and need some diversion, it's well to find some puttering to do. Or go get a job on the road. Or in the mills.

I went into the mills. I've done all sorts of things, and willingly, because I couldn't be writing poems all the time—not as a novelist can work at his writing day in and day out—and because I had to make a living. I couldn't bank on the poetry making money.

I only banked on that for one week once. I sold the first poem I ever sent out. I got fifteen dollars for it and I thought, "That's easy." I planned that I'd do one of those every week. I could have lived on that. But it was a long time till the next check.

But that's just the nature of things and I never set myself to quarrel with it. I knew everything must come to market in some way or another. Like a street urchin, I just took things as they came, and thought of anything I got as pure velvet.

There have been those who objected. Somebody said to me once when I was young—a mean person he was—"Do you think the world owes you a living?"

"Oh my goodness no. I don't like to hear you say that," I told him. "But I do think I'm smart enough to make the world *give* me a living for what I can do best."

And it has pretty much turned out that way. I was a pretty foxy boy. I knew the world could set itself to look down on a poet, but I could always be more tolerant of them than they were of me. They tap their heads about poetry. But I just turn my back on it. I don't accept that kind of treatment.

Sometimes I'd find myself in a grim mood during all these years I stood waiting. I'd say to myself, "They think to dismiss me, but I'll thrust myself down their throats. They'll have to take this in the end."

And they've taken the poems. At least a lot of people have. People say nice things about me now when they talk of America having given me a position. They say they often notice how many men there are in my audience. That it isn't all women and children. And they even talk at times about people "stealing" from me.

Nothing could please me more. I once told Judge Learned Hand that the Supreme Court had lost the distinction between being a referee and a handicapper. Hand said he was going to steal that remark and not even acknowledge it.

I'll take that kind of stealing as a reward. That's real appreciation. A librarian told me once that he had a big problem with people stealing books. In his place I'd have been glad they wanted the books badly enough to steal them. What counts, as I see it, is first to have something worth stealing, and then to be stolen from in the right way.

ROBERT FROST

AMERICAN BARD

[*March 24, 1962* *]

On March 26 Robert Frost will be eighty-eight years old. His birth-day will be doubly marked this year. It will be publication day for his first new book in fifteen years, *In the Clearing*. And it will be the occasion for a banquet to be given in Washington, the invitations for which have been jointly issued by Secretary of the Interior and Mrs. Udall and by Mr. Frost's publishers, Holt, Rinehart and Winston. Unless he is prevented by affairs of state, President Kennedy is expected to lead the list of distinguished guests.

For many years now, Mr. Frost's birthdays have been almost national observances. But though each new birthday has brought fresh honors, it is probably the eighty-fifth that will remain most memorable to literary historians.

For that occasion, at a banquet given at the Waldorf by Mr. Frost's publishers, Lionel Trilling read a paper in homage to Mr. Frost and thereby set off a hot if meaningless controversy, while at the same time illustrating an attitude of our more sophisticated critics that, though it passed without comment, remains far more ponderable than the bone that was worried in print during the following weeks.

Trilling saluted Mr. Frost as "a poet of terror." All angry voices to the contrary, I could find nothing wrong with Trilling's choice of words. That he meant nothing but praise is obvious. In fact he com-

---

* In order to conform to the sort of dating necessary in the first of these three pieces on Mr. Frost—necessary in order to keep track of the exchanges with *SR's* readers—I have dated all three of the articles in this section. Since there will be no real need hereafter to keep track of controversies, dating will not be necessary, and I drop all such notations accordingly.

pared Mr. Frost to Sophocles in this sense. What man could fail to feel honored at being so paired? On this point I find Trilling's assessment both just and central to the Frostian genius.

Let the School System make a whited saint of Mr. Frost if it must; and as, alas, it will. The man himself remains an *hombre*. If he is half radiance he is also half brimstone, and praise be. His best poems will endure precisely because they are terrible—and holy. All primal fire is terrible and holy. Mr. Frost could climb to heaven and hear the angels call him brother—*frater*, they would probably say—but he could as well climb Vesuvius and equally hear every rumble under his feet call out to him. The darkness in his poems is as profound as the light in them is long. They are terrible because they are from life at a depth into which we cannot look unshaken. What else is the power of such poems as—to name only a few—"To Earthward," "Reluctance," "Home Burial," "Death of the Hired Man," and "Fire and Ice"?

It was some such homage, I am sure, that Trilling meant to pay, and to worry the word "terror" as if it contained a slur is nonsense. What reader will not prefer the terror of Frost to the sweetness of many of his contemporaries?

What appalled me that night at the Waldorf was Trilling's confession that it had only been within the preceding few years that he had grown aware of the depth and power of Mr. Frost's poetry. And then, as if to toss the whole tribute into the abyss, Trilling added something to the effect that he had been unable to grasp the poems until he came to them through a reading of D. H. Lawrence!

What I think I heard Trilling describe was a failure sufficiently common to the New or Academic Critics to serve as a reproach to all of them. There stood Professor Trilling, one of our leading men of letters, a master of literary subtlety and complexity, paying homage to America's foremost poet by confessing years of professional neglect, and then capping the insult by suggesting that the key to Mr. Frost's poetry lay in D. H. Lawrence, a writer I am bound to believe Mr. Frost would incline to think of as half madman and half charlatan (a guess, let me add, that certainly does not bind Mr. Frost, and that is not at all my personal assessment of Lawrence).

What is there to conclude except that our best critics have suffered too long from a fear of simplicity, and that, misled by the surface simplicity of Mr. Frost's poems, they have dismissed them as being simple—all the way down? It is a rueful irony that brought together America's first truly national poet and a representative of America's first truly formed school of literary criticism, only to show that it took the critic something like thirty years to recognize the real thing when it happened.

By now the New Criticism has pretty much adjusted to Mr. Frost, at least to the earlier Frost. As I mean to discuss in a minute, I find two main stages of the earlier Frost: the poet of passion and the poet of wit and whimsy. The adjustment of the New Critics, as nearly as I have been able to sense it, has been to praise the poet of passion and to dismiss the poet of wit. I wonder what the New Critical verdict will be on this new Frost. For it is a new Frost one finds in these poems; a Frost not unprecedented in his own past, but a new Frost all the same. What Mr. Frost called "editorials" in *Steeple Bush* (published in 1947) were already long on the way toward his new way of writing—or perhaps one should say, rather, toward his new way of taking himself. And the fact that most of these new poems have long been familiar to close followers of Mr. Frost, through his readings and Christmas cards, does take the full burst of surprise from them. Yet put together as they are now in a new book, the poems make bold the announcement that this Frost is impressively different from the more familiar one of the public image.

Trying to parse anything as complex as Robert Frost into categories is a bit like trying to put spirit into a box, but granting the inadequacies of all such boxes, let one be called, as noted, passion, and the other, wit and whimsy. It was basically as a poet of impassioned light-and-dark that Mr. Frost made his appearance on the scene and many of his first reviewers were moved to speak of a background sense of terror that haunts his New England landscape. This Frost burns with the appetites of life. The essence of tragic characters is that they ask of life more than ordinary men are moved to ask. They are terrifying and exalting because they are seared by passion:

I craved strong sweets but those
Seemed strong when I was young;
The petal of the rose
It was that stung.

Now no joy but lacks salt
That is not dashed with pain
And weariness and fault;
I crave the stain

Of tears, the aftermark
Of almost too much love,
The sweet of bitter bark
And burning clove.

When stiff and sore and scarred
I take away my hand
From leaning on it hard
In grass and sand,

The hurt is not enough:
I long for weight and strength
To feel the earth as rough
To all my length.

Call it terror in the Sophoclean sense, or call it the impassioned life force, this is lyricism at a kindling point of the soul. This poet is not only the lover but the demon lover.

His passion, moreover, was always toward the privacy of the self, toward the rescue of the self from the world's demands. So in "Love and a Question," one of his earliest published poems, he dramatizes the world's intrusion upon the privacy of love, choosing for his symbol of the world's demand a needy wanderer who seeks shelter in the bridal house. At this point of his development, the poet frames the question without answering it. The poem ends:

The bridegroom thought it little to give
    A dole of bread, a purse,
A heartfelt prayer for the poor of God,
    Or for the rich a curse;
But whether or not a man was asked
    To mar the love of two
By harboring woe in the bridal house,
    The bridegroom wished he knew.

The same impassioned sense of two-against-the-world cries out in "Not to Keep." And the converse of that theme may be found in "Two Look at Two," a poem in which the lovers, in joy, recognize the exaltation of what is their most private ground.

That theme is everywhere in the early Frost. In "Two Tramps in Mud Time" the question is given a new and terrifying setting, this time to be firmly answered. The speaker of the poem, a farmer, fiercely in love with the muscle and sweat of his labor of chopping wood, feels the world's demand in the presence of two lumberjack tramps who want to take his work from him for pay, because they need the pay:

The time when most I loved my task
These two must make me love it more
By coming with what they came to ask.

And this time the demand is rejected:

Nothing on either side was said.
They knew they had but to stay their stay
And all their logic would fill my head:
As that I had no right to play
With what was another man's work for gain.
My right might be love but theirs was need.
And where the two exist in twain
Theirs was the better right—agreed.

But yield who will to their separation,
My object in living is to unite
My avocation and my vocation
As my two eyes make one in sight.
Only where love and need are one,
And the work is play for mortal stakes,
Is the deed ever really done
For Heaven and the future's sakes.

By whatever force of the rational mind this poet frames his reasons,
the life force in him cries out, "Keep off my acre!"

Perhaps with a touch of whimsy but, if so, with the anger unabated,
that cry rings out again in "The Egg and the Machine." There the
poet meets the intrusion of a locomotive upon his private haunts by
digging up a clutch of turtle eggs. Armed with them as his grenades,
he issues his challenge:

"You'd better not disturb me anymore,"
He told the distance, "I am armed for war.
The next machine that has the power to pass
Will get this plasm in its goggle glass."

That dark, impassioned, and reclusive Frost has not entirely disappeared from these new poems. Whether "The Draft Horse," for
example, is entirely a new poem or one newly brought out of older
workbooks, it moves as darkly and yet as resiliently as any of Frost's
early ventures into shadow. Here it is entire, a poem of terror enough
for any darkness:

With a lantern that wouldn't burn
In too frail a buggy we drove
Behind too heavy a horse
Through a pitch-dark limitless grove.

And a man came out of the trees
And took our horse by the head
And reaching back to his ribs
Deliberately stabbed him dead.

The ponderous beast went down
With a crack of a broken shaft.
And the night drew through the trees
In one long invidious draft.

The most unquestioning pair
That ever accepted fate
And the least disposed to ascribe
Any more than we had to to hate,

We assumed that the man himself
Or someone he had to obey
Wanted us to get down
And walk the rest of the way.

With "The Draft Horse" may be grouped "Ends," "A Peril of Hope," and "Questioning Faces" as poems more nearly in Mr. Frost's first voice, the voice of impassioned love, of dark and of radiance, and above all of a fierce commitment to the private acre of the individual —the essential ground that must be protected from the world's intrusion.

If I am right in taking whimsy to be the second voice in Mr. Frost's developing range, I do not mean to imply that there were not touches of whimsy in the poems from the beginning. There is a happily whimsical touch in "The Pasture," the first poem in the first book (A *Boy's Will*). And more than a touch in as early and as deeply felt a poem as "Mending Wall." There the speaker, thinking to draw out his neighbor, says:

Spring is the mischief in me, and I wonder
If I could put a notion in his head.

and later:

I could say "Elves" to him
But it's not elves exactly, and I'd rather
He said it for himself.

The difference between Frost as the poet of passion and Frost as the poet of wit is one of degree, and the mixture of the two tones in many of the poems may require a considerable adjustment of one's standard "poetic" expectations. As Mr. Frost himself notes in a typical touch of whimsy:

> It takes all sorts of in and outdoor schooling
> To get adjusted to my kind of fooling.

Nevertheless the difference is real. The poet of passion is a singing man and deeply committed. The poet of whimsy is a speaking man and coolly detached, concerned, yes, but evasive, his eye forever on the relation of the individual and society, but warily. "A Drumlin Woodchuck," for example, once more explores the theme of the individual's self-rescue from society, but with a world's difference in the tone. For this poem the poet takes on the *persona* of a wily and complacent woodchuck:

> My own strategic retreat
> Is where two rocks almost meet,
> And still more secure and snug,
> A two-door burrow I dug.
>
> With those in mind at my back
> I can sit forth exposed to attack
> As one who shrewdly pretends
> That he and the world are friends.

Thus protected by the forethought to be devious, all goes well with the woodchuck, and thus:

> If I can with confidence say
> That still for another day,
> Or even another year,
> I will be there for you, my dear,

It will be because, though small
As measured against the All,
I have been so instinctively thorough
About my crevice and burrow.

If the power of poetry lies in its ability to penetrate our feelings to great depth, thereby arousing and revealing our deepest sense of ourselves, it must follow that whimsy, being the shallowest mode of poetry, is the most difficult to make memorable. It may well be the most dangerous mode a poet can undertake. I must confess I am not deeply moved by all of Mr. Frost's whimsical poems. I can smile at his woodchuck, but my smile is partly involved in a shrug. I can admire but I am not moved. For whimsy is not so much a poetic penetration as it is a role, and the role, if charming, is generally slight.

There is always the danger, too, that whimsy may falter into a kind of merely artful performance. Mr. Frost is no stranger to the public platform. He is, in fact, a king of the old pros: he knows how to tickle an audience and he knows how to knock it for a loop. He has developed one of the most assured stage presences of our times. I have sat to hear him through at least seventy-five or eighty, perhaps even more, public performances, and I have never failed to find delight in his manner. The danger to my mind was that the whimsical poems might degenerate into platform jokes, that the *persona* of the poet would forever be "on-stage." Mr. Frost himself, being nobody's fool and no self-deceiver, will have thought about that danger of confusing his magnificent platform whimsy with his essential poetic voice.

Perhaps the most central evidence of these new poems is in the way they demonstrate that he has known how to keep his balance. The voice of that sometimes magnificent whimsy, the voice of seriousness lightly (and largely) taken, as in, say, "Departmental," has been raised to a new resonance here. Neither of the two earlier voices is entirely missing from the present poems. There are sufficient traces still of the impassioned singer. There is a substantial presence of the whimsical and detached sayer. But the new voice is bardic—a speaking voice, philosophical rather than intensely lyrical, but deeply committed. Mr. Frost emerges now as the poet of his people, the poet who speaks America to time.

Mr. Frost has long been proud of what he calls "the position America has given me." Nor did he assume that position by self-appointment. On March 24, 1950, in honor of what was thought to be his approaching seventy-fifth birthday (there had been some confusion about the year of birth, which was long given as 1875), the United States Senate passed a resolution citing his poems for having "helped to guide American thought with humor, and wisdom, setting forth to our minds a reliable representation of ourselves and of all men." Mr. Frost has accepted that role, that position. His lines in the present volume, "On Being Chosen Poet of Vermont," indicate his readiness to accept what might almost be called public office:

> Breathes there a bard who isn't moved
> When he finds his verse is understood
> And not entirely disapproved
> By his country and his neighborhood?

The lines themselves, lightly taken and lightly said, constitute one more "editorial," a half-playful comment. There can be no doubt, however, that Mr. Frost has accepted his bardic burden with whole seriousness. His bardic range, like the range of his whimsical editorials, is America and, in fact, the Western world. But the bardic voice is clearer, firmer, and deeply committed. There are no back doors now through which the wily woodchuck can disappear at will. The bard must stand to his conviction.

That the burden of the bardic role is a dangerous one, much of the history of American poetry will attest. Whitman wrote most of his worst poems in seeking to be the bard of America. Where would he be in present memory had he not had "Myself" to sing about? Sandburg has tried out for the role and blown it to pieces in blasts of windy rhetoric. MacLeish, in my view, let a sublime lyric talent lie in abeyance for more than twenty years while trying to achieve a public speaking voice for America, and missing it. The list of other candidates who have blown or are blowing away in the bardic venture could fill a "Who Was Who" of past acclaim and present neglect.

Perhaps the bardic voice is the one for which contemporary readers are least attuned. How is an audience that was swept to frenzies
by the glandular roil and intensity of, say, a Dylan Thomas, to cotton
readily to this open, rational, philosophical, wry, yet deeply committed kind of saying? It will take time for Frost's achievement to
register, yet, unless I misread, these poems are an achievement to
stand tall beside any passage of the earlier Frost.

Mr. Frost opens his book boldly with a motto compounded from
lines of his "Kitty Hawk" and separately set as a frontispiece:

But God's own descent
Into flesh was meant
As a demonstration
That the supreme merit
Lay in risking spirit
In substantiation.
Spirit enters flesh
And for all it's worth
Charges into earth
In birth after birth
Ever fresh and fresh.
We may take the view
That its derring-do
Thought of in the large
Is one mighty charge
On our human part
Of the soul's ethereal
Into the material.

"Kitty Hawk" is a poem of almost 500 lines begun in homage to
the Wright brothers as the inventors of an age, as the two who finally
gave wings to man and who, it may be said, pointed man's way to
the spaces beyond the earth. The Wright brothers gave man a new
age, and with it, both a new possibility and a new grief. But Mr.
Frost's position is that the risk must be taken. The essence of Western man has always been that he dared risk his venture into the
material. And what other course, the poet asks, is there for man? We

must risk ourselves, we must risk the material. The East refused to risk that substantiation of the spirit, it refused the descent into the material, and it thereby stagnated into griefs of its own.

> Westerners inherit
> A design for living
> Deeper into matter . . .

Dangerously perhaps, but

> If it was not wise,
> Tell me why the East
> Seemingly has ceased
> From its long stagnation
> In mere meditation.
> What is all the fuss
> To catch up with us?

That is hardly the sort of poetry lovesick boys will read to their panting girls, but it is certainly poetry of an order of mind—wise, intense, and elevated.

The poem ends with a salute to science that certainly goes about as far as seems possible toward reversing the position taken in "The Egg and the Machine."

> God of the machine,
> Peregrine machine,
> Some still think is Satan,
> Unto you the thanks
> For this token flight,
> Thanks to you and thanks
> To the brothers Wright
> Once considered cranks
> Like Darius Green
> In their home town, Dayton.

Once the history-of-ideas boys get their hands on that passage, I suspect it will become one of the most widely quoted in all Academe as evidence of how far American poetry has come since Poe's hatred of all science, and from Frost's own early distrust of the machine. Let me hope the history-of-ideas boys will not overlook the reason for Mr. Frost's praise. The Wrights become figures for his homage because they added a new range to the human condition.

It is for the same reason that Mr. Frost praises Columbus in that remarkable poem, "America Is Hard to See."

> Columbus may have worked the wind
> A new and better way to Ind
> And also proved the world a ball,
> But how about the wherewithal?
> Not just for scientific news
> Had the Queen backed him to a cruise.

This is the tone of the whimsical Frost as especially characterized by the witty, down-played use of the word "cruise" to describe Columbus's voyage. Mr. Frost maintains that tone throughout the poem, describing ironically how Da Gama came back with the gold the Queen had invested in, while Columbus found himself in dungeon chains. Yet from that whimsical and ironic surface rise some island peaks of plain statement that come as close to defining America as any man's poetry has done:

> Had but Columbus known enough
> He might have boldly made the bluff
> That better than Da Gama's gold
> He had been given to behold
> The race's future trial place,
> A fresh start for the human race.

> He might have fooled Valladolid.
> I was deceived by what he did.
> If I had had my chance when young
> I should have had Columbus sung
> As a god who had given us
> A more than Moses' exodus.

There then follow the simply stated lines:

> But all he did was spread the room
> Of our enacting out the doom
> Of being in each other's way,
> And so put off the weary day
> When we would have to put our mind
> On how to crowd but still be kind.

It is perhaps such lines as these that best testify to the quality of Frost's vision of America. Long before, he had written "Mowing," in which he said, "Anything more than the truth would have seemed too weak." Even as a bard Mr. Frost will not inflate his devotion beyond reality. There is a darkness of doubt as well as a radiance of hope in his vision of America, and he will speak both truths to his people.

Perhaps Americans have never truly found their America. Certainly that America that was a golden legend to the Elizabethans has never been found. In "The Gift Outright," the poem Mr. Frost and President Kennedy jointly chose for the last inauguration, America is still that dream to be lived into. "The land was ours before we were the land's." The hope is that Americans will someday become truly identified with their "land of living," and certainly the poem itself is the noblest utterance yet to be spoken of the American continent. But in it, Mr. Frost carefully refrained from saying that the identification of Americans and America has actually taken place:

> Such as we were we gave ourselves outright
> (The deed of gift was many deeds of war)
> To the land vaguely realizing westward,
> But still unstoried, artless, unenhanced,
> Such as she was, such as she would become.

"Would become," Mr. Frost says, not "has become." In fact, that difference was President Kennedy's joke. Would Mr. Frost read it now as "has become"? Mr. Frost read it as he wrote it.

In the present volume he continues the same theme in a remarkable poem so central to his intent that he has taken his title from it. "A Cabin in the Clearing" is a dialogue somewhat in the manner of the earlier "The Lovely Shall Be Choosers." Here the speakers are Mist and Smoke, the Mist arising from the land, the Smoke from the man's chimney. Mist begins by saying:

I don't believe the sleepers in this house
Know where they are.

Smoke replies:

They've been here long enough
To push the woods back from around the house
And part them in the middle with a path.

It is a mysterious and compelling poem that follows. The two vapors that accompany the human spirit see the clearing the man and woman have made, but is the clearing there only to maintain a path that joins them to their equally bewildered neighbors? "Nearer in plight their neighbors are than distance." Their plight is that they are not sure either of who they are or of where they are. They have not reached assuredly to either themselves or their land. "They are too sudden to be credible," says Smoke and joins with Mist to eavesdrop on their uneasy sleep, "A mist and smoke eavesdropping on a haze," an uncertainty perhaps already as dim as the Indians whose land it once was in total identification. The poem closes with what I take to be a joint statement by Mist and Smoke (or is it, perhaps, a comment by the poet?):

Than smoke and mist who better could appraise
The kindred spirit of an inner haze?

Are we no more than a smoke and a mist upon the land? No more substantial than that? Is that Mr. Frost's intent? That the land is forever beyond us, and that we shall all in time drift off it while the land remains for some future people to be lost in as the Indian was lost in it? Let no man be in a hurry to fix too tight a meaning to it, but the poem itself, its mood and motion, will not be forgotten.

There are only a few pieces in the present collection that sing in quite so mysterious a music. Some there are but, as noted, Mr. Frost's new voice is toward saying rather than singing. Certainly the longish poem entitled "How Hard It Is to Keep from Being King When It's in You and in the Situation"—a poem more whimsical than bardic—adds a particular gem of wit to the treasury of discursive poetry. Nor are Mr. Frost's more bardic lines "For John F. Kennedy His Inauguration" to be taken lightly as examples of occasional verse.

If the Frost of these poems is less intense than the first impassioned Frost of the lyrics, there is in these a power of mind (the "thought-felt thing") that speaks with a breadth and an elevation that could not have been achieved through passion alone. The bard has largely replaced the lyric poet. In so doing, he has given America a voice it has long needed and will certainly learn to be grateful for.

The question that remains to ask must be addressed to the Swedish Academy. Why has Mr. Frost not received a Nobel Prize? It seems all but inconceivable, and certainly insulting, that an academy willing in the past to honor Sinclair Lewis and Pearl Buck should so spend its honors upon foothills while overlooking our central mountain. I cannot doubt that Mr. Frost would be gratified by a Nobel Prize. Why should he not? He more than deserves it. Why should a man not want what is his by right?

I suspect that the Awards Board of the Swedish Academy, like so many of our New Critics, has been culpably slow in learning to read Mr. Frost's poems. Perhaps the members of that board do not recognize seriousness lightly taken and whimsy seriously taken. If that has been their block, the more bardic of these poems should give them as much straightforward public utterance on man's fate as ever their socially conscious souls may hunger for.

But I suspect rather that their failure has been in their inability to recognize the genius of Mr. Frost's language. Eliot and Yeats, both Nobel Prize winners, wrote in the kind of English a European may come close to learning in his own universities. But Frost's English is of the soil. Only a man with New England in his mouth could write so. Nor is the diction the primary characteristic of Frost's way of speaking; he uses only an occasional New Englandism. Far more than the word choices, it is the rhythm that sings and speaks in New England cadences, the way the rhythm throws the voice down hard on some words and slides it over others. It is the rhythm that makes Mr. Frost the least translatable of poets. But it is also the rhythm that makes him the particular genius of the American tongue.

Perhaps no man raised to another tongue will ever truly hear the subtlety and perfection of Mr. Frost's full voice. But by now, certainly, the Swedish Academy must have heard that truth stated often enough to take note of it, if only by hearsay. The simple truth is that American literature has brought forth none to walk before him. Mr. Frost's recognition by the Nobel Prize committee has been too long delayed. There seems to be no conceivable reason for delaying longer.

ON READING
AND WRITING

WHAT DOES IT TAKE
TO READ A POEM?

"What Does It Take to Read a Poem?" was my first lead article for
SR (then SRL). It was published December 10, 1949, with the title
changed editorially to "What Does It Take to Enjoy a Poem?" I
reread it these thirteen-and-more-years later with some uneasiness
about the downrightness of the tone, but when I manage to squint
past its obvious faults, I find myself feeling almost prophetic as I
reread it. When I wrote it I had no thought that I should one day
be editorializing at SR and finding myself in sometimes embattled
exchanges with SR's readers. As I read it now, however, it occurs to
me that though the piece is in many ways self-limiting, it could yet
serve as an answer-before-the-fact to many of the letters I have since
received.

What does it take to enjoy a poem?
    Let us begin with a really difficult piece of symbolism:

    Hickory, dickory, dock,
    The mouse ran up the clock.
    The clock struck one,
    The mouse ran down,
    Hickory, dickory, dock.

Not really complicated, you say? Consider these questions. What does
it mean? Why a clock? Why a mouse? Isn't it fairly unusual for mice
to run up clocks? What is the point of inventing this esoteric inci-

dent? And since the mouse ran up it and down again, the chances are it's a grandfather clock. What does that signify? And isn't it a fairly obsolete notion? Why did the clock strike one? (To rhyme with "down"? But is "down" a rhyme for "one," or is this another slovenly piece of modernism? Why didn't the poem make the clock strike three and the mouse turn to flee? It didn't, of course, but why?) What is the origin and significance of all these unexplained symbols? Or is this simply nonsense verse? (I find that hard to believe.) And even as nonsense, what is there in this particular combination of sounds and actions (symbolic actions?) that makes this jingle survive a long word-of-mouth transmission in the English voice-box? Why mightn't the poem as easily have read:

> Thickery, thackery, tea,
> An owl flew into the tree.
> The tree's down,
> The owl's flown,
> Thickery, thackery, tea.

I submit: (a) that my parody is a bad poem, that the original is a good one, and that a serious and learned series of lectures might be devoted to the reasons why each is so; (b) that none of the questions I have raised are meaningless and that in fact many critics have made a career of asking this sort of question of less perfect poems; and (c) that neither you nor I know what the poem "means." I further submit that such considerations have frightened many readers away from good poems.

But—and this is the point—the child in whose babble the poem is immediate and alive has no critical theories and no troubles. He is too busy enjoying the pleasures of poetry. The moral is obvious: do not ask the poem to be more rational than you are. The way to read a poem is with pleasure: with the child's pleasure in tasting the syllables on his tongue, with the marvel of the child's eye that can really see the mouse run up the clock, be panic-stricken, and run down again, with the child's hand-clapping, rhythmic joy. In short, 'to read a poem, come prepared for delight.

But if a child can do it why can't you?

That question deserves attention, but before considering it, I should like to say one thing of which I am fairly certain: everyone writes poetry sometime in his life. Bad poetry is what we all have in common. Such poetry generally occurs in three categories: as invective, as obscenity, and as love-yelps.

The obscenity I assume everyone to be capable of documenting. Here is an example of invective:

> Billy Billy, dirty coat
> Stinks like a nanny goat.

And here is a fair example of the love-y lp:

> Have you ever been in love?
> I ask you: have you ever been in love?
> Have you?
>
> I have . . . . I know!

"Billy Billy," you will recognize as a kind of "Georgie-Porgie puddin' and pie," but if you think it peculiar to your childhood or to grandfather's I urge you to look in the encyclopedia under Fescennine for an inkling of the antiquity of man's pleasure in jingling taunts at other men. "Billy Billy," as nearly as I know, was composed in our fourth-grade schoolyard by a former young poet now in the coal business and was used to taunt our local sloven, who has since washed up, cleaned up, grown up, and joined the police force. Almost inevitably it earned its young author a punch in the nose: a fair example of the way criticism operates in our society to kill the poetic impulse. The love-yelp, a reasonably deplorable specimen of its class, was submitted for the Tufts College literary magazine when I was an undergraduate assistant editor. Anyone who will take the trouble to be reasonably honest can almost certainly summon from himself examples of at least one of these forms he has attempted at one time or another, and enjoyed attempting.

If, then, the impulse to bad poetry is so widespread (though I insist that "Billy Billy" is not at all bad), why is it so few people enjoy reading what passes as good poetry? Why is it, for example, that in a nation of 146,000,000 presumably literate people, the average sale for a book of poems is about five hundred copies? Is it that the pleasures and outlets one finds in composing are purely private—that only one's own creation, good or bad, is interesting? Considering the variety of egos that have banded together to pass as the human race, that seems one reasonably good guess, but there is obviously more to it.

First, it seems fairly obvious that the process of growing up in a nuts-and-bolts world inhibits the poetic impulse in most people. Somewhere along the line, they learn to say, "Let's face it; we must be practical." So the literalist on his rostrum demands the rational: "What *does* hickory-dickory-dock *mean*? It has to mean *something*." It does indeed, but not anything you can paraphrase, not anything you can prove. To see what it does mean, you need only go read Mother Goose to a child: you will then be observing a natural audience busy with the process of receiving poetry as it was intended to be received.

Point one, then, is delight: if you mean to enjoy the poem as a poem, stop cross-examining it, stop trying to force it to "make sense." The poem *is* sense. Or if you must cross-examine, remember at least that the third degree is not the poem. Most poems do reveal themselves most richly after close examination, but the examination is, at best, only a preparation for reading the poem. It is never the reading itself.

More precisely put, an understanding of the rational surfaces of the poem (the prose part of the poem) may, in some cases, point a direction toward the poem. The poem is never experienced, however, until it is felt in the same complex of mind and nerve from which it arose—the subconscious. That experience sometimes happens immediately, and is sometimes helped along by our conscious (rational) perceptions. But to substitute rational analysis for the larger contact of the subconscious is to reject the poem. The kind of communication that happens in a poem is infinitely closer to that of music than to that of prose.

Second, poetry must never be read as an exercise in "reading-speed," that deplorable mental-mangle for increasing the rate of destruction of textbook English. The fastest reader is not the best reader any more than the best conductor of Beethoven is the man who gets the orchestra through the *Eroica* in the shortest elapsed time. Why not take a stop watch to the symphony, if speed is your measure? Obviously because music declares its own pace. But so does good poetry. By rhyme, by the word-values of the poem, by the sequence of syllables, and by all these taken together, good poetry contains its own notation. "We broke the brittle bright stubble like chaff" can no more be read at the same rate as "Bury the great duke with an Empire's lamentation" than *allegro vivace* can intelligently be played *adagio*.

Point two, then: leave your efficiency out of it and look for the notation within the poem. Every poem is in part an effort to reconstruct the poet's speaking voice. Listen for it. Listen to the poet on records and at public readings (but know the poems well before you do). You may discover more than you could have foreseen. In any case, when reading a book of poems you must be prepared to linger. That thin volume will take at least as much reading as a detective story.

Third (and of course related to our second consideration): read it aloud. Few poems will come whole at one hearing. Few piano pieces will. But once you have *learned* either, their pleasure is always ready to repeat itself. Even difficult poems are meant to go into the voice-box. Put them there.

Fourth: there are still readers who must be specifically cautioned that twentieth-century poetry is not nineteenth-century poetry. That fact may seem rather obvious, but the point is not frivolously made. Your teachers and mine were products of nineteenth-century culture, and almost certainly the first poems you were given to read were nineteenth-century poems. And praise nineteenth-century literature as you will (and as all must), there yet remains the fact that it tended to take itself much too seriously. The mind of man seemed to suffer the illusion that it lived in a cathedral, and when man spoke he was not only too likely to pontificate, but he was pre-inclined to select from experience only the vast, the lofty, the divine-in-nature. The result was what Cleanth Brooks has called "the poetry of high-seriousness." Opposed to that tradition is the poetry of "wit," poetry in which the mind most definitely does not live in a cathedral but in the total world, open to the encounter of all sorts of diverse elements and prepared to take them as they come, fusing fleas and sunsets, love and Charley horses, beauty and trivia into what is conceived to be a more inclusive range of human experience. Judge the poet of "wit" by the standards of "high-seriousness" and he will likely appear crass and obnoxious; judge the poet of high-seriousness by the standards of wit and he will likely appear a rather pompous and myopic ass.

The point, then, is quite simple: judge the poet by his intent: if you tend to the illusion that you are on your way to church when you pick up a poem, stop off at the supermarket and watch man against his background of groceries for a while. The church is still next door, and I am quite sure that one of the things "modern" (whatever that is) poetry is trying to say is that the cities of our life contain both church spires and Wheaties, and that both of them, for better or worse, impinge upon man's consciousness, and are therefore the material of poetry.

A fifth consideration I can best present by asking a question: how do you, reader, distinguish between your responses to a very bad portrait of dear old Aunt Jane, and a very good one of Old Skinflint, the gentleman who holds your mortgage? The question is one that splits the reading audience straight down the middle. The tenacity with which the ladies of the poetry societies will hold on to Aunt Jane with a bluebird in her hair, and the persistency with which they reject all-that-is-not-bluebirds, reaches so far into the problem of a satisfactory approach to poetry (both reading and writing) that it has been necessary to evolve two terms: "poetry" for that which exists as an art form, "poesy" for that which exists as the sentimental bluebird in Aunt Jane's hair. Confusion is inevitable when these terms are not properly applied. The writers and readers of poesy always refer to their matter as poetry or true poetry, and defend it with as much violence as possible from "the ugly." Here is a piece of poesy—a sonnet of course:

THRENODY

Truth is a golden sunset far away
Above the misty hills. Its burning eye

Lights all the fading world. A bird flies by
Alive and singing on the dying day.
O mystic world, what shall the proud heart say
When beauty flies on beauty beautifully
While blue-gold hills look down to watch it die
Into the falling miracle of clay?

Say: "I have seen the wing of sunset lift
Into the golden vision of the hills
And truth come flooding proud through the cloud rift,
And known that souls survive their mortal ills."
Say: "Having seen such beauty in the air
I have seen truth and will no more despair."

"Threnody" is a fair example of what I have learned to call "prop-room poesy." It fills the stage as a poem might, but it fills it with pieces discarded from other poems and left to gather dust in the prop-room of tradition. It makes a stage of the stage, and brings the stage's own dust on as the play, rather than bringing on the life outside the theatre.

The result may look like a poem, but is really no more than a collection of poetic junk. For example: "golden sunsets far away" (question: have you ever seen a non-golden one nearby?), "misty hills," "burning eye," "fading world," "a bird flies by alive and singing" (question: have you ever seen a non-live one fly by?), "dying day," "the proud heart." . . .

I have tried many times to explain to the enthusiasts of this school that any reasonably competent craftsman could concoct such a poem in a matter of minutes, and with his tongue in his cheek. I said exactly that from a public platform once and claimed I could turn out such an illusion-of-the-sonnet in three minutes flat. I was challenged and given a first line to start with, but I failed: I discovered it is impossible, simply mechanically, to write off fourteen lines in three minutes. It took four minutes and eighteen seconds. The "sonnet" I have quoted above was the poem produced in answer to that challenge, and by way of further experimentation I sent it off to a magazine for "traditional" poetry and had it accepted for publication. In a moment of cowardice I withdrew the poem for fear someone I respected might see my name attached to it. I was wrong, of course; no one whose poetic opinion I could respect would have been reading that magazine.

The fact remains beyond all persuasion, however, that the devotees of poesy are violent in their charges against Modern Poetry (their capitals) as ugly, coarse, immoral, and debased (their adjectives). My good friend Geraldine Udell, business manager of *Poetry, A Magazine of Verse*, the oldest magazine of good poetry in America, once showed me thirty-four letters received in one day's mail accusing the magazine of debasing the pure tradition of English poetry, and enclosing pages of poesy from two magazines of "traditional poetry" as specimens of what should be printed.

It is, you see, Aunt Jane and Old Skinflint with a vengeance. Poesy (which is always anti-poetry) wants it pretty. It wants comfortably worn-out props to which comfortable and vague reactions are already conditioned. Everyone understands the bluebird in Aunt Jane's hair; the response to it is by now so stereotyped that it will do for a birthday card. Poetry, on the contrary, insists on battering at life, and on making the poem capture the thing seen and felt in its own unique complex. It does not repeat, it creates. Therefore, some willingness to dismiss preconception from the reader's mind is necessary if one is to partake of that vital process. One is also required to get himself and his own loose-afflatus out of the way of the poem.

The fifth point then is simple: poesy is not poetry.

A sixth and related consideration follows almost immediately: it concerns the preconception that demands moral affirmation of oneself from a poem, just as poesy demands a loose emotional affirmation of oneself. Consistently adhered to, this application of one's own morality as a test of the poem can lead to ridiculous ends. It would require, for example, the rejection of Milton by all who do not agree with his theology. It might reject beforehand all poems containing the word harlot, since harlots are immoral, and by that test we should have to reject such great lines as Blake's:

> The harlot's cry from street to street
> Shall weave Old England's winding sheet.

Or, shifted to political concern, it might require a new Communist manifesto against any poem in which the lover is rich in his love, since it is bourgeois, decadent, and just plain indecent to be rich.

Similarly, I have observed many present-day reviewers to reject a poem because it seems cheerful ("withdrawal from reality"), because it does not ("defeatist and negativist"), because it is immediately understandable ("facile and slight"), and because it requires reread-ing ("obscurantist"). These are cartoons, of course, but they are car-toons of a real trend. The simple fact is that none of us can hope to be wholly free of preconceptions of one sort or another. I must confess, for example, that I still find Milton's theology a bit silly, and that my feeling prevents me from experiencing *Paradise Lost* as richly as I might. Even Milton's language creates blocks for me that he could not have intended and for which I am solely responsible. For whatever reason, I cannot read of Satan mounted on his "bad emi-nence" without an impulse to smile. I don't know why I want to smile at such a phrase, but I am sure the reason is within me and that it has nothing to do with the poem. I am being blocked in this case by a pre-set subjective response. I must, therefore, recognize the ob-struction and try to allow for it. Unless I can do so, I am not permit-ting the poet his right to his own kind of vision and existence.

Point six, then: the poem does not exist to conform moral, polit-ical, or religious prejudgments. The poem as a poem is in fact amoral. The poem, I say, not the poet. The poet may be the most moral of men, but when he writes poetry he is performing a ritual dance. He may even sermonize, but if the poem is to succeed as a poem, it must be a dancing sermon. What the poem says is always hickory-dickory-dock, that ineffable, wonderful, everlasting dance of syllables that moves the mouse and winds the clock over and over again, and sends the child to sleep among the swinging nebulae. Or perhaps it is hickory-dickory-God, but still what the poem says is what the child dreams: "Look, Universe, I'm dancing." There is no immorality more wretched than the habit of mind which *will* insist on moraliz-ing that dance.

The last necessity for good reading that I shall discuss here is tradi-tion. If you will grant me the existence of an unintellectualized basis for poetry upon which the responses of all readers may meet, we can probably agree that a fair example of such a response may be found in, say, Juliet on her balcony swooning into moonlight at the sound of Romeo's song rising from the shrubbery. Hers is certainly a non-intellectualized response. It is certainly a living response. And a world-wide one: Black Jade in her moony garden in Peiping will respond in an almost identical way to Pao-yii's serenade from beyond the garden wall.

But wait: let us switch singers. Now Pao-yii is in Verona under Juliet's balcony, and Romeo is in Peiping outside Black Jade's garden. Both strike up a song. Why is it that both girls now hear not a swooning love-cry but something closer to the sound of sustained gargling? The answer is—Tradition.

For the fact is we are being educated when we know it least. We learn simply by the exposure of living, and what we learn most natively is the tradition in which we live. But the response acquired effortlessly within one tradition will not serve us in another, any more than speaking pure Tuscan will help us in Peiping.

In order to read poetry, then, one must read poetry. One may of course have read only bad poetry, and in that case he will read badly. The criterion Matthew Arnold set forth as "the touchstone method" may well be applied here. This critical theory states simply that all poetry is judged by great poetry. Poetry may be called great only when it has been acclaimed by so many generations of different poetical taste that its merit and universality are beyond dispute. The way to come to a poem, then, is with the memory of great singing in one's inner ear.

Greatness, however, can be a dangerous measure, for it immediately implies rendering a verdict. I for one cannot lose the belief that it is more important to experience the poem than to judge it. Certainly there is real pleasure to be had from poetry no one will ever think of as great or near-great. Certainly, too, every mental action implies a kind of judgment. Nevertheless, it seems to me more desirable in every way for the reader to conceive of himself as a participant in the action of the poem rather than as a trial judge pondering its claim to immortality.

Time, of course, will hand down that verdict, and in a way from which there is no appeal. It may then happen that the verdict will be against modern poets, and against the principles on which they write. But until that verdict has been achieved, it would be well to bear in mind that the reader is as liable to error as the poet, and that when the poem fails to communicate, the failure may as reasonably be charged against the one as against the other.

EVERYONE WRITES
(BAD) POETRY

The office mailbag bulges daily with envelopes full of bad poems that bear paper-clipped to them laborious little notes that breathe, however shyly, the most grandiose hopes. "Dear Editor," the little notes say in substance, "please tell me that I am a great poet." And between the lines they whisper: "And I will believe it!"

Bad poetry is what we all have in common—bad poetry and a secret persuasion. What man has ever awakened to his ego's passion on the planet without at some time committing a poem, and without cherishing the dream that deep in his soul a poetic talent lay asleep, awaiting only the kiss of discovering circumstance?

Ask John Doe whether or not he can play the violin and he would not dream of answering, "I don't know. I've never tried." But ask him whether or not he can write a poem and it will be a rare and saintly-humble John Doe indeed to whom it occurs that the poem requires at least as much technical devotion and at least as many years of practice as does the violin. It's all done with words, isn't it? And everyone uses words.

Yes, everyone does use (or misuse) words, but not as a poet does. A buzz saw and a rusty hinge have certain vibrations in common with those of a violin, but the violin properly played puts its vibrations to measured uses, *and it speaks its music not in the vibrations but in the inner relations of those measures.* When a poet uses a word, he is using not only a label for something but a picture, a feeling, an association, a history, a sound, and a rhythmic impulse. The word "Brazil" in a geography book is a simple label. But find a lonesome Brazilian in a 14th Street bar and whisper in his ear "Braz-eel" and you will have awakened the blood of things. We are all lonesome Brazilians where we live most. Poetry is what comes up behind us and whispers the singing name of home in our ears.

The good poet lives to awaken words and phrases in this way, and the principal language of his poem is in the relation of these awakened measures to one another. And he is not only awakening his words, he is eliciting one word from another, his poem giving rise to itself, the individual words answering to their inner measure rather than to the dictionary of prose usage. Nothing is more characteristic of a good poem than the fact that the interplay of those measures *releases* more meaning than could be *stated*.

The work sheets of Keats's "The Eve of Saint Agnes" provide a stunning example of one of the ways in which a poet relates the measures of his words. The passage that describes Madeleine undressing runs:

> Of all its wreathéd-pearls her hair she frees;
> Unclasps her warméd jewels one by one;
> Loosens her fragrant boddice . . .

In the original work sheets, now in the Houghton Library at Harvard, the last line read in first draft "Loosened her *bursting* boddice." Bursting? To be sure there is nothing in nature to keep Madeleine from being as buxom as you please without surrendering any delicacy, but the titanic suggestions of the word were obviously dead wrong for the poem, and Keats stopped right there. He next tried "Loosened her boddice lace-strings and did bare/Her . . ." But there he was at the same impasse. What else could she bare? At all costs he must avoid that overtone of emphatic fleshiness. Finally he solved his problem, triumphantly, with "fragrant." But it must be noted that "fragrant" is the right word not because Madeleine was any more or less buxom as a consequence of Keats's choice, but because "fragrant" is exactly related to "warméd," the measure of each word being to suggest the presence of her body rather than to assert it, and to do so sensuously but at one delicate remove. The two words are brother and sister, and they are first cousins to the lightness and delicacy of "wreathéd." And the speaking marvel of the passage is exactly in those silently established relationships.

But obviously this order of poetry is not something we all have in common. The fact is that the kind of poetry Everyman commits is not poetry at all but a much lesser thing perhaps best labeled "self-expression," not the mortal need to lay our hands to a shapen thing, but the ego's boozier need to let some emotion out of the system in the easiest possible way. Hundreds of poems come to the poetry desk of *The Saturday Review* weekly and scarcely a handful of them even try to be poetry.

The first function of a poetry editor, as I understand it, is to separate the poetry from the self-expression and to return the self-expression in the (please note) accompanying stamped and self-addressed envelope in the custody of a printed rejection slip. When the accompanying note is especially heart-rending one may add a word or two of "criticism" but in the nature of things that scrawl is never criticism and cannot be. The basic answer remains as it must, simply yes or no, and any addition is merely palliative.

At root, of course, that selection and rejection, right or wrong, is a function of taste and no set of principles can systematize it completely. On the day of total principles this magazine will order its Poetry Editor from IBM and plug him in. Until that day the relation between any poetry editor and the poem must remain human, partial, and imperfect. And how can one know wholly why he likes a poem?—the acceptances always have some element of happy surprise in them. It is the rejections that tend to go by familiar pattern. Impossible as it is, therefore, to systematize the goodness of a good poem, one may still fix at least part of the badness of most bad poems, and in the hope that to identify badness is some approach to goodness, I append these first principles of rejection.

Poetry, I believe, is a life-summoning force on the order of a religion. There will, consequently, always be readers who, holding that universe in view, will sneer at all technical discussion. Why not sneer as well at a violinist who worries about slurring his chords? The passion must also be technical. In poetry there is no more immediate nor more conclusive sign of slovenliness than occurs in the abuse of adjectives.

A good English style moves on its nouns and verbs. Now and then for special effect a good poet lays the adjectives on hard, as Chaucer does in "He was a verray parfit gentil knight," and as Keats does with "happy" in "Ode on a Grecian Urn." Yet even as word-whirling a poet as Hopkins uses, by actual count, at least as many verbs as adjectives, and in most good English poetry the verb-to-adjective ratio tends to run at least two to one, and often higher.

A heavily adjectival style is slovenly because it is badly selected. The adjectives tend to be there only because the author failed to select the right noun in the first place. One has no need to say "coarse, abusive, and shrewish vituperation" when the language offers as good a word as "billingsgate," or "a stingy person who hoards wealth for its own sake" when "miser" is available. The good poets tend to nouns that contain within themselves the force that poor poets try to tack on with an adjective. Much the same points can be made, of course, about verbs and adverbs, but it remains the adjectives that most often offend. The possible analogies are as obvious as the rule should be: never send an adjective on a noun's errand.

Many doubly abused adjectives, however, lack any justifiable errand. Some are there simply to pad out the rhyme scheme (wine/azurine). Many are wholly useless, their force being already implicit in the noun (blue sky, salt sea, sad plight, brilliant shining). Still others are hopelessly stereotyped (cold sweat, mortal fear, passing parade). Any editor who respects poetry must stop reading and reject the poem at the first occurrence of any such adjective.

There is, moreover, a class of adjectives to which non-poets are especially drawn, and it is made up of those adjectives that assert a judgment of an object instead of presenting a quality of the object and letting the reader form his own judgment on the sensory evidence so presented. "Beautiful" is certainly queen of this court but "pure, rich, awesome, implacable, bittersweet," etc., are all ladies-in-waiting in high standing. I wish the addicts of this sort of adjectival assertion would ponder Robert Frost's remark to a class at Bread Loaf. "When a man takes out his poetic license," he said, "it is stamped 'entitles bearer to three uses of the word *beautiful*.' After sixty-five years I have all three of my permissions yet to use."

Inevitably, too, the poets who lean hardest on adjectival crutches are the first to sink into the wheelchairs of such exhausted nouns as "threnody," "monody," "replevin," "sarabande (stately)," "surges (cosmic)," and of course, "heart (fierce, proud, resolute, a mother's, or—and a good thing too—beating," but in any case lots of "heart").

These are, of course, not only examples of vapid language, but also of clichés, and perhaps all that need be said of verbal clichés is that the poem almost certainly will not survive them. For though the verbal cliché is bad enough in itself as an aesthetically criminal negligence of the poet's duty to reawaken and to reinvigorate the language, it is even more reprehensible as evidence of the poet's human failure to approach his own sense of his own life. For there are clichés of attitude and of perception as well as of phrase, and the fact is that, as far as the poem is concerned, the poet may be a drunkard, a thief, a wife-beater, and a murderer, but his perceptions and his attitudes cannot afford to be stereotyped.

Nor does it help the case that such clichés are most often put forth in the name of the highest moral "message." Poetry is neither moral nor immoral; it is of life and death and as such it includes but goes beyond good and evil. More poems die of platitudinous decency than of any other cause. The vocabulary of humanism joined by a syntax of oh's and ah's and punctuated exclusively by exclamation points will not produce a language for poetry.

For some reason, the sweet, sincere, and dull people who most often emit this sort of high-frequency exaltation are almost invariably sonnet-addicts. Perhaps to the uncritical the sonnet seems an easy form. Perhaps, lacking rules within themselves, the sweet-singers believe that the sonnet will provide rules for them. The fact remains that there is almost no form harder to manage in our time and that even our best contemporary poets have produced relatively few memorable sonnets. Yet day after day hundreds of otherwise admirable ladies and gentlemen continue to turn out fourteen-line confections that run the same sets of images through the same sets of rhymes, thereby producing a counted and lined quantity of language chiefly remarkable for the way in which every such "sonnet" sounds like every other. Write sonnets if you must but—barring the miracle—do not expect to find them in the pages of this magazine.

There are other grounds on which a poem can and must be rejected at a glance. The word choices, being the most readily visible part of a poem, are simply the most readily describable, and I have therefore stressed them. Even more readily, however, a living poem declares itself in its rhythms: the words stand up and move, they bump heads, they marry and roll. And above all they respond to the cadence of a living language. Nothing is more deadening to a poem than to hear it tick, its metronome clacking through the music.

And, finally, there is always the poem that avoids all these faults and still must be rejected as lifeless. A competent and a tidy exercise, one thinks—that is to say, a nothing. "I see you are literate," I want to say to the author. "When do you become mortal? When do you break through?"

For above all a poem is not an echo but an originating sound. It echoes in us because it has dared to throw itself against the wall of some ultimately real feeling. It does not always seem to make sense; it tries rather to be of life.

I hope the readers of *The Saturday Review* will join me in entertaining poems that are sometimes more venturesome than tidy, poems that dare to take a mortal chance. The fragments of a true failure can be far more moving than the neat measures of a false success, and I must believe it to be a service to poetry to select such true failures in preference to such false successes.

THE ACT OF LANGUAGE*

At the beginning of *The Divine Comedy*, Dante finds himself in a Dark Wood, lost from the light of God. It was no single, specific evil act that led Dante into the darkness but, rather, the sin of omission. Its name is Acedia, the fourth of the Seven Deadly Sins, and by us generally translated "Sloth."

In American-English, however, Sloth may seem to imply mere physical laziness and untidiness. The torpor of Acedia, it must be understood, is spiritual rather than physical. It is to know the good, but to be lax in its pursuit.

Whether one thinks of it as a sin or as a behavioral failure, Acedia is also the one fault for which no artist can be forgiven. Time, as W. H. Auden wrote in his poem titled "In Memory of W. B. Yeats":

> Worships language and forgives
> Everyone by whom it lives;
> Pardons cowardice, conceit,
> Lays its honors at their feet.

In place of cowardice and conceit, Auden might have cited any catalogue of pride, envy, wrath, avarice, gluttony or carnality, and he could still have said that time forgives. The poet may cheat anything else and still win honor from time, but he may not cheat the poem and live.

For a man is finally defined by what he does with his attention.

* Published in *The Saturday Evening Post* as part of its "Adventures of the Mind" series.

It was Simone Weil who said, "Absolute attention is absolute prayer." I do not, of course, know what an absolute attention is, except as an absolutely unattainable goal. But certainly to seek that increasing purity and concentration of one's attention that will lead to more and more meaningful perception, is not only possible but is the basic human exercise of any art. It must be added, however, that *in art it does not matter what one pays attention to; the quality of the attention is what counts.*

I have just made a dangerous statement; one that will probably breed protest, that will be difficult to explain, and that will turn out in the end to be only partly true. It is still necessary to make the statement first, and then to go the long way round to explaining why it is necessary, and in what way it is true.

The need to go the long way round brings matters back to another parable of poetry that one may read in Dante's opening situation. The language of parables is always likely to be apt to the discussion of poetry.

As soon as Dante realizes that he is in darkness, he looks up and sees the first light of the dawn shawling the shoulders of a little hill. (In Dante, the Sun is always a symbol of God as Divine Illumination.) The allegory should be clear enough: the very realization that one is lost is the beginning of finding oneself.

What happens next is the heart of the matter. His goal in sight, Dante tries to race straight up the hill—to reach the light, as it were, by direct assault. Note that common sense would certainly be on Dante's side. There is the light and there is the hill: go to it. Nothing could be simpler. Nor, as Dante discovers, could anything be more false. Almost immediately his way is blocked by three beasts. These beasts—a Leopard, a Lion, and a She-wolf—represent all the sins of the world. They represent, therefore, the world's total becloudment of any man's best attention, for all that has ever lured any man away from his own good is contained within them.

The three beasts drive Dante back into the darkness. There Dante comes on the soul of Virgil, who symbolizes Human Reason. In that role Virgil explains that a man may reach the light only by going the long way round. Dante must risk the dangerous descent into Hell —to the recognition of sin. And he must make the arduous ascent of

Purgatory—to the renunciation of sin. Only then may he enter, bit by bit, the final presence of the light, which is to say, Heaven.

The point of the parable is that in art as in theology—as in all things that concern a man in his profoundest being—the long way round is the only way home. Short cuts are useful only in mechanics. The man who seeks mortal understanding must go the long, encompassing way of his deepest involvement.

Americans, susceptible as they are to the legend of mechanical know-how and get-it-done, may especially need to be told that there is no easy digest of understanding and no gift package of insight. May they learn, too, that "common sense," useful as it can be in its own sphere, cannot lead a man as deeply into himself as he must be led if he is to enter a meaningful experience of art or of life. Every man who looks long enough at the stars must come to feel their other-reality engulfing his mortal state, and nothing from the world's efficiencies and practicalities is specific to that awareness in him.

Poetry is written of that man under the stars in trouble and in joy, and the truth of poetry cannot be spoken meaningfully in simple common-sense assertions. In poetry, as in all our deepest emotions, many feelings and many thoughts and half-thoughts happen at once. Often these feelings and thoughts are in conflict:

We love and hate the same thing, desire it and dread it, need it and are destroyed by it. Always, too, there are more thoughts and feelings in a profound experience than we can put a finger on. What has common sense to say to such states of man? Common sense tends always to the easier assumption that only one thing is "really" happening in a man at one time, and that a simple, straightforward course of action will take care of it.

Such an assumption can only blind one to poetry. To read a poem with no thought in mind but to paraphrase it into a single, simple, and usually high-minded, prose statement is the destruction of poetry. Nor does it make much difference that one can quote poetry, and good poetry, in defense of such destruction. At the end of "Ode on a Grecian Urn," John Keats wrote:

"Beauty is truth, truth beauty,"—that is all
Ye know on earth, and all ye need to know.

Heaven knows how many enthusiasts have used these lines as evidence that poetry is somehow an act of inspiration not to be measured by any criteria but an undefined devotion to "beauty," "truth," and "inspiring message."

But if beauty and truth are all that Grecian urns and men need know on earth, Keats makes evident by his own practice that a poet also needs to know a great deal about his trade, and that he must be passionately concerned for its basic elements.

Those basic elements are not beauty and truth but *rhythm, diction, image,* and *form.* Certainly Keats cared about beauty and truth. Any sensitive man must care. No matter that one must forever fumble at the definition of such ideas; they are still matters of ultimate concern. But so was Dante's yearning for the light, and he discovered at once that it can be reached only by the long way round.

The poet's way round is by way of rhythm, diction, image, and form. It is the right, the duty, and the joy of his trade to be passionate about these things. To be passionate about them in the minutest and even the most frivolous detail. To be passionate about them, if need be, to the exclusion of what is generally understood by "sincerity" and "meaning." To be more passionate about them than he is about the cold war, the Gunpowder Plot, the next election, abolition, the H-bomb, the Inquisition, juvenile delinquency, the Spanish Armada, or his own survival.

The good poets have not generally sneered at the world of affairs. Some have, but many others have functioned well within that world. Yet the need and the right of all poets to detach themselves from the things of the world in order to pursue the things of the poetic trade have always been inseparable from their success as poets.

The poet must be passionate about the four elements of his trade for the most fundamental of reasons. He must be so because those passions are both a joy and an addiction within him. Because they are the life of the poem, without which nothing of value can happen either in the poem or to the reader. Because writing a poem is a more sentient way of living than not writing it, because no poem can be written well except as these passions inform it, and because only when the poem is so written can the beauty and truth of that more sentient way of living be brought to mortal consequence.

The act of poetry may seem to have very simple surfaces, but it is always compounded of many things at once. As Robert Frost wrote in "Two Tramps in Mud Time":

> Only where love and need are one,
> And the work is play for mortal stakes,
> Is the deed ever really done
> For Heaven and the future's sakes.

The voice of common sense rises immediately in protest. "Mystification!" it cries. "A poem still has to *mean* something. What does it *mean*?" And the poet must answer, "Never what you think. Not when you ask the question in that way."

But how shall the question be asked? Let the questioner listen first to a kind of statement he has probably passed over without enough attention. He can find one such in Walter Pater's essay on Winckelmann. "Let us understand by poetry," wrote Pater, "all literary production which attains the power of giving pleasure by its form as distinct from its matter."

He can find another in a book titled *The Fire and the Fountain* by the English poet and critic John Press. "The essence of the poet," wrote Press, "is to be found less in his opinions than in his idiom." He may even find one in a textbook titled *Reading Poems*, in which Prof. Wright Thomas says, "The *subject* is a very poor indication of what the *poem* is"—to which I should add only that it is no indication whatever.

But if the meaning is not in the subject, what then does a poem mean? It means always and above all else the poet's deep involvement in the four basic elements of his trade. It means not the subject but the way the poetic involvement transfigures the subject. It means, that is to say—the very act of language by which it comes into existence. The poem may purport to be about anything from pussy willows to battleships, but the meaning of any good poem is its act of language.

Because it is an act of language, a good poem is deeply connected with everything men are and do. For language is certainly one of the most fundamental activities in which human beings engage. Take away a man's language, and you take most of his ability to think and to experience. Enrich his language, and you cannot fail to enrich his experience. Any man who has let great language into his head is the richer for it.

He is not made richer by what is being said. It is the language itself that brings his enrichment. Could poetry be meaningful aside from its act of language, it would have no reason for being, and the whole history of poetry could be reduced to a series of simple paraphrases.

Consider as simple a passage as the beginning of Herrick's "Upon Julia's Clothes":

> Whenas in silks my Julia goes,
> Then, then, methinks, how sweetly flows
> The liquefaction of her clothes.

Who can read those lines without a thrill of pleasure? But now consider the paraphrase: "I like the rustle of Julia's silks when she walks." The poetry and the paraphrase are certainly about equal in subject matter. The difference is that the poetry is a full and rich act of language, whereas the paraphrase, though faultless, lacks, among other things, measure, pause, stress, rhyme, and the pleasure of lingering over the word "liquefaction."

"But what is Julia doing there?" cries that voice of common sense. "She must have something to do with the poem or she wouldn't be in it!"

The owner of that voice would do well to ponder the relation between a good portrait and its subject. The subject is there, to be sure —at least in most cases. But the instant the painter puts one brush stroke on the canvas and then another, the two brush strokes take on a relation to each other and to the space around them. The two then take on a relation to the third, and it to them. And so forth. The painting immediately begins to exert its own demands upon the painter, its own way of going. Immediately the subject begins to disappear.

All too soon, for that matter, the subject will have changed with age or will have died. After a while no living person will have any recollection of what the subject looked like. All that will remain then is a portrait head which must be either self-validating or worthless. Because the subject cannot validate the painting, he or she will have become irrelevant. All that can finally validate the portrait is the way in which the painter engaged the act of painting.

And one more thing—the good artist always thinks in long terms. He knows, even at the moment of the painting, that both he and the subject will disappear. Any good painter will be painting for the painting—for the time when the subject will have blown away into time.

So with poetry. The one final and enduring meaning of any poem lies not in what it seems to have set out to say, but in its act of language.

The only test of that act of language is the memory of the race. Bad poetry is by nature forgettable; it is, therefore, soon forgotten. But good poetry, like any good act of language, hooks onto human memory and stays there. Write well, and there will always be someone somewhere who carries in his mind what you have written. It will stay in memory because man is the language animal, and because his need of language is from the roots of his consciousness. That need in him is not a need for meaning. Rather, good language in him takes possession of meaning; it fills him with a resonance that the best of men understand only dimly, but without which no man is entirely alive. Poetry is that presence and that resonance. As Archibald MacLeish put it in his much-discussed "Ars Poetica":

A poem should not mean
But be.

If the reader truly wishes to engage poetry, let him forget meaning. Let him think rather: "I shall summon great language to mind. I shall summon language so fully, so resonantly and so precisely used that it will bring all my meanings to me." Then let him turn to poetry, and let him listen to the passions of the poet's trade.

Listen to great rhythms. Here is the opening stanza of John Donne's "The Anniversarie":

> All Kings, and all their favourites,
> All glory of honours, beauties, wits,
> The Sun it selfe, which makes times as they passe,
> Is elder by a yeare, now, than it was
> When thou and I first one another saw:
> All other things, to their destruction draw,
>   Only our love hath no decay:
> This, no to morrow hath, nor yesterday.
> Running, it never runs from us away,
> But truly keeps his first, last, everlasting day.

Worldly things pass away, but true love is constant, says the subject matter. All true enough and tried enough. But listen to the rhythm enforce itself upon the saying, especially in the last four lines. For present purposes, let the voice ignore the lesser accents. Let it stress only those syllables printed in capital letters below, while observing the pauses as indicated by the slash marks. And forget the meaning. Read for the voice emphasis and the voice pauses:

> Only OUR LOVE hath no deCAY //
> THIS // no to MOrrow hath // nor YESterday //
> RUNning // it never runs from us aWAY //
> But truly keeps his FIRST // LAST // EVerlasting DAY.

Not all rhythms are so percussive, so measured out by pauses, and so metrically irregular. Listen to this smoother rhythm from Poe's "Israfel":

> If I could dwell
> Where Israfel
>   Hath dwelt, and he where I,
> He might not sing so wildly well
>   A mortal melody,
> While a bolder note than his might swell
>   From my lyre within the sky.

Or the rhythm may be percussive, but without substantial pauses, as in the last line of this passage from the end of Gerard Manley Hopkins's "Felix Randal," an elegy for a blacksmith:

> How far from then forethought of, all thy more boisterous years,
> When thou at the random grim forge, powerful amidst peers,
> Didst fettle for the great gray drayhorse his bright and battering
>   sandal.

Listen to the hammerfall of that last line: "Didst FEttle for the GREAT GRAY DRAYhorse his BRIGHT and BAttering SANdal."

Or listen to the spacing of the "ah" sounds as a rhythmic emphasis in the last line of this final passage from Meredith's "Lucifer in Starlight":

> Around the ancient track marched, rank on rank,
> The ARmy of unALterable LAW.

Percussive, smooth, flowing, or studded with pauses—there is no end to the variety and delight of great language rhythms. For the poet, his rhythms are forever more than a matter of making a "meaningful" statement; they are a joy in their own right. No poet hates meaning. But the poet's passion is for the triumph of language. No reader can come to real contact with a poem until he comes to it through the joy of that rhythmic act of language.

As for rhythm, so for diction. The poet goes to language—or it comes to him and he receives it—for his joy in the precision of great word choices. Give him such a line as Whitman's "I witness the corpse with the dabbled hair," and he will register the corpse, to be sure, but it will be "dabbled" he seizes upon with the joy of a botanist coming on a rare specimen. So when Keats speaks of Ruth amid "the alien corn" or when Theodore Roethke speaks of sheep "strewn" on a field, the good reader will certainly care about the dramatic situation of the poem, but he cannot fail to answer with a special joy to "alien" and to "strewn."

What, after all, is the subject as compared to his joy in such rich precision? Thousands of English poems have described the passing of

winter and the coming of spring. Certainly there is little in that subject as a subject to attract him. But listen to the pure flutefall of the
word choices I have italicized in the following passage from Stanley
Kunitz's "Deciduous Bough," and note how the self-delight in language makes everything immediate and new again:

Winter that *coils* in the thicket now
Will *glide* from the field, the *swinging* rain
Be *knotted* with flowers, on every bough
A bird will *meditate* again.

"Poetry," said Coleridge, "is the best words in the best order." How
can anyone reading the Kunitz passage escape a sense that the language is being ultimately and unimprovably selected? The delight
one feels in coming on such language is not only in the experience of
perfection but also in the fact that perfection has been made to seem
not only effortless but inevitable.

And let this much more be added to the idea of poetic meaning:
nothing in a good poem happens by accident; every word, every
comma, every variant spelling must enter as an act of the poet's
choice. A poem is a machine for making choices. The mark of the
good poet is his refusal to make easy or cheap choices. The better the
poet, the greater the demands he makes upon himself, and the higher
he sets his level of choice. Thus, a good poem is not only an act of
mind but an act of devotion to mind. The poet who chooses cheaply
or lazily is guilty of aesthetic Acedia, and he is lost thereby. The poet
who spares himself nothing in his search for the most demanding
choices is shaping a human attention that offers itself as a high—and
joyful—example to all men of mind and devotion. Every act of great
language, whatever its subject matter, illustrates an idea of order and
a resonance of human possibility without which no man's mind can
sense its own fullest dimensions.

As for rhythm and diction, so for imagery. To be sure, every word
is at root an image, and poetic images must be made of words. Yet certainly there is in a well-constructed image an effect that cannot be
said to rise from any one word choice, but from the total phrasing.

So for the sensory shiver of Keats's "The silver snarling trumpets 'gan to chide." So for the wonderfully woozy effect of John Frederick Nims's "The drunk clambering on his undulant floor." So for the grand hyperbole of Howard Nemerov saying that the way a young girl looks at him "sets his knees to splashing like two waves."

We learn both imagination and precision from the poet's eye. And we learn correspondences. Consider the following image from "Areopagus" by Louis MacNeice, a poem as playful as it is serious, in which MacNeice describes Athens as a cradle of the Western mind. Cradles, he makes clear, generally contain children, and all those boy-gods and girl-goddesses had their childish side:

> . . . you still may glimpse
> The child-eyed Fury tossing her shock of snakes,
> Careering over the Parthenon's ruined playpen.

It is a bit shocking to have the Parthenon spoken of as a playpen, but once the shock has passed, what a triumph there is in the figure: everything corresponds! Think how much would have been lost had the Parthenon a surviving roof, or had its general proportions or the placement of the pillars—slats—resisted the comparison. The joy of it is that, despite the first shock, nothing resists the comparison; and we find that the surprise turns out to be a true correspondence.

One of the poet's happiest—and most mortal—games is in seeking such correspondences. But what flows from them is more than a game. Every discovery of a true correspondence is an act of reason and an instruction to the mind. For intelligence does not consist of masses of factual detail. It consists of seeing essential likenesses and essential differences and of relating them, allowing for differences within the likeness and for likenesses within the differences. Mentality is born of analogy.

Note, too, that the image-idea of "ruined playpen" does not simply happen, but is prepared for in "child-eyed." And note, further, the nice double meaning of "careering" as both "a wild rush" and "to make a career of."

A good extended image, that is to say, is made of various elements and is marked by both sequence and structure. Thus we have already touched upon the essence of the fourth element of the poet's trade: form.

There are many kinds of poetic form, but since all are based on pattern and sequence, let a tightly patterned poem illustrate. Here is Emily Dickinson's "The Soul Selects":

> The soul selects her own society,
> Then shuts the door;
> On her divine majority
> Obtrude no more.
>
> Unmoved, she notes the chariot's pausing
> At her low gate;
> Unmoved, an emperor is kneeling
> Upon her mat.
> I've known her from an ample nation
> Choose one;
> Then close the valves of her attention
> Like stone.

Whatever the hunters of beauty and truth find for their pleasure in such a poem, the poet's joy will be in its form and management. He responds to the passion of the language for its own sparseness, to the pattern of rhyme and half-rhyme, to the flavor of the images (connotation), and to the way those flavors relate to one another. He responds to the interplay of the four-foot feminine lines (feminine lines end on an unaccented syllable) and the two-foot masculine lines (which end on an accented syllable).

And he responds, above all, to the way those two-foot lines develop in the last stanza into two boldly stroked syllables apiece (monosyllabic feet) so that the emotion held down throughout the poem by the sparseness of the language is hammered into sensation by the beat of those last two words: "Like stone"—thud! thud!

Beauty and truth are no irrelevancies, but they are abstractions that must remain meaningless to poetry until they are brought to being in the management of a specific form. It is that management the poet must love: the joy of sensing the poem falls into inescapable form, and therefore into inescapable experience. For the poet's trade is not to talk about experience, but to make it happen. His act of making is all he knows of beauty and truth. It is, in fact, his way of knowing them. His only way of knowing them.

As I. A. Richards, poet and scholar of the language, put it in a recent poem titled "The Ruins":

> Sometimes a word is wiser much than men:
> "Faithful" e.g., "responsible" and "true."
> And words it is, not poets, make up poems.
> *Our* words, we say, but we are theirs, too,
> For words made men and may unmake again.

And now, at last, it is time to repeat the statement from which this long way round began. "In art," I said, "it does not matter what one pays attention to; the quality of the attention is what counts." It is time to amend that necessary false statement.

For it does matter where the poet fixes his attention. Attention must be to *something*. That something, however, is so casually connected with the subject of the poem that any reader will do well to dismiss the subject as no more than a point of departure. Any impassioning point of departure will do. The poet, being a man, must believe something, but what that something is does not matter so long as he believes it strongly enough to be passionate about it. What he believes, moreover, may be touched off by an image, a rhythm, or the quality of a word *in pursuit of which the subject is invented.*

The poem, in any case, is not in its point of departure, but in its journey to itself. That journey, the act of the poem, is its act of language. That act is the true final subject and meaning of any poem. It is to that act of language the poet shapes his most devoted attention—to the fullness of rhythm, diction, image, and form. Only in that devotion can he seize the world and make it evident.

THE SHOCK REACTION
TO POETRY

Shortly after my return from the war I found myself on a Missouri farm in an endless rainy flood-season. It seemed for a while that the world was being washed away, both from above and from below, and I found myself recalling a boyhood best-friend who had drowned all those worlds ago. I recalled an incident from his funeral, and its ritual brought back to mind what a great deal of religious turmoil I had gone through in mad adolescence and forgotten since. Another long world ago and gone. As—to my surprise—the war that had seemed eternal on last year's island was gone, too. I had the feeling for the moment of the poem I then sat down to write that the one thing that went on and that I could live and die to forever was the rain—how long it was. I concluded the poem:

> Having survived a theology and a war,
> I am beginning to understand
> The rain.

I have no thought of arguing the merits of the poem as written. It may be a bad poem. My only point here is that a critic once offered those lines to me as an example of the incomprehensible. I was forced to reply that I did not see how they could be clearer. My critic shot me a look: "How can you dare say you understand the rain?" Had I said that? I denied it and pointed out that I had used the word "beginning" in the second of the three lines, and used it on the assumption that it still had meaning in the American language. Inevitably, I was accused of being evasive.

Self-defense aside, I see that objection as a case of simple shock reaction. Some preformed belief made my critic recoil from the statement of the poem. In so recoiling, he closed his mind not only to all
further consideration but to the essential qualification within the
statement itself. The passage was jargon, not because he failed to
understand it, but because he refused to grant me a right to that idea.

On another occasion the president of a tea-and-poetry group offered
me an example of a slightly different kind of shock reaction. Here,
too, the charge was "meaningless jargon," but basically Mr. President
was refusing to believe that the poet could possibly be saying what he
was very clearly saying. The passage was the last stanza of Richard
Wilbur's "Museum Piece." The preceding poem describes a Degas
dancer in a museum—those chill stone vaults of the Beautiful pa-
trolled by "the good grey guardians of art." So wrenched from life,
the dancer pirouettes on in her maker's dream of life. The poem concludes:

> Edgar Degas purchased once
> A fine El Greco which he kept
> Against the wall beside his bed
> To hang his pants on while he slept.

One cannot help knowing that the tone of mixed playfulness-and-
seriousness confuses many readers, but are those lines meaningless? I
do not know whether or not the incident described is a true one, but
I certainly hope it is. Mr. President flatly refused to believe that either
Degas or Wilbur could possibly intend such irreverence to El Greco.
Wilbur must mean something else. But what? Nothing. The passage
was, "Just meaningless jargon. A way of being smarty."

These were the president's terms and obviously they exclude rather
than invite discussion. "Here is my two-cubic-inch box of common
sense," says the defender: "Put all your spirals of meaning into it
without mashing or distorting them. Or else admit that you are equivocating." It simply cannot be done that way. Wilbur is writing a kind
of dramatic parable, and the power of such parable is in its many possibilities of meaning around the center. It is the center that one can
identify, and, at a risk, I tried to locate it for the president in terms

of the artist's relation to his art. An unmistakable theme of the poem is that art is not something to be put apart from daily life (as, for example, in a guarded museum). There comes a time when the artist must marry his muse, and then—like all husbands—he will have pork chops and pants hooks to think about as well as moonlight and adoration. Mr. President, however, would have nothing to do with such possibilities.

On yet another occasion I heard a professor of some distinction lecture on "The Virtue of Poetry." Among other things, he cited two lines from Auden's elegy for Yeats:

> The words of a dead man
> Are modified in the guts of the living.

These lines, he informed his audience, are not only meaningless but coarse, offensive, and vulgar. I had no opportunity to press the professor further, but certainly the lines are so clear that, in the face of such a charge, I can only conclude that something other than lack of clarity had brought on the shock reaction in the professor.

I speculate that one source of shock was the word "guts," and that the professor's charge—too obviously random to do him credit—was really a result of his discomfort at finding such a word in a serious poem. Before he is seriously tempted to defend that attitude, however, he would do well (after rereading a little Chaucer and Shakespeare for flavor) to take a long reflective look at the tradition of the literary select tongue in France and Italy, and to consider carefully how systematic academic Comstockery has worked in the past (and still exerts a force despite valuable poetic rebellions) to smother the life of poetry in those traditions.

Speculating further, I sense a second, though related, source of the professor's shock reaction. I suspect that his previous contact with poetry had determined him *a priori* in favor of the poetry of high-seriousness, and that such preparation has left him unable to respond to the emotional force of what may be called "flatting"—the poetic device by which the poet meets the spiritual climaxes of his poem in terms of *the least language* (colloquial understatement or sometimes even "throwaway" slang) rather than in terms of *the most* ("purple-passage" rhetoric). If any man can still believe that "flatting" is not a basic idiom of great emotional experience in our times, then tens of thousands of G.I.'s have died wisecracking without having been listened to, and a number of good and great novelists have labored to portray twentieth-century man's response to his fate in a lying tongue. The language of good poetry always shapes itself from the idiom and speech rhythms of its times. To insist on nineteenth-century idiom and rhythms in twentieth-century poetry is to insist on a death in poetry.

The trouble with such shock reactions is that under their impulsion the reader leaps to a high moral position, slamming his mind shut as he goes. "Coarse, vulgar, and offensive," said the professor. But can he really believe, with his best mind, that a man of Auden's passion and gift could slyly dedicate himself to such ends? Every poet has his vision of beauty: how else could he be a poet? His devotion, however, must be not only to an ideal beauty, but to the perception of life itself in all its aspects. At some stage, the poet—especially the young poet—may even become fascinated by ugliness. Are there not enough reasons, today as always, for a sensitive young man to feel that his elders have betrayed him into empty ideals of conduct and that his contemporaries are thieves and hypocrites? I do not advocate that position, but it is certainly not a rare one in which to find our best young men, and not at all a hard one to understand. What is more natural for the young poet—shocked by the inadequacy of what he has been taught as truth—than to reply by seeking to shock in his turn?

Given sufficient talent, humanity and dedication, he will survive that adolescence. He will begin to see the world's multiplicity as its own endearing fact, and various enough to include the whole range of human existence, all of it fused (if only ideally) into the subliming act of a perception grand enough to dedicate itself neither to the Tea Shoppe of Life nor to the Slaughterhouse of Life but to the total City of Life—to the transcendent idea of what it is to be a human being.

No Western writers have achieved that idea as sublimely as have Dante and Shakespeare. No Western man is half-prepared to discuss the idea of the beautiful without having read carefully some substantial part of the work of these masters. Yet where could one find two writers with a better-developed perception of "the coarse, the vulgar, and the offensive"? But the labels themselves exist only as part of the shock reaction of the Genteel. The masters do not shock: they perceive. Their perceptions include the bawdy and the bitter detail, but as an act of encompassment. The aristocrat, as has been well said, is never genteel.

If Longfellow, in translating Dante, felt that he must "correct" many of Dante's details into something more acceptable to Cambridge conversation, such defacement must speak not Dante's limitation, but Longfellow's and Cambridge's. It must go down, even, as an act of arrogance—for certainly it is an arrogance in any man to conceive himself as possessing better taste and nicer moral scruples than Dante managed to achieve. Gentility always reduces the range of life.

Conversely, to include is to be multiple, and multiplicity leads to complexity. As the world of modern man is multiple, so must it follow that the poet who seeks truly to express it must be, at times, complex. Complexities are often obscure. To call a poem obscure is in no way to damn it. The deepest in all of us is obscure. Hamlet is obscure. Freud is obscure. Every man's life is motivated, at depth, in obscure ways. What, for that matter, is more obscure than the Bible? Its obscurity, *together with its unmistakable sense of pertinence-in-depth,* is of the essence of its greatness. Though centuries of scholarship, piety, and exhortation have labored to make it clear, it still remains unfathomed, unsummed, and alive; still open to interpretation and to the self-rewarding labor of understanding.

For though the terms are often confused, obscurity is not at all the same thing as unintelligibility. *Obscurity is what happens when a writer undertakes a theme and method for which the reader is not sufficiently prepared. Unintelligibility is what happens when the writer undertakes a theme and method for which he himself is not sufficiently prepared.*

A good creation is an enlarging experience, and the act of enlargement must require the reader to extend himself. Only the thoroughly familiar—which is to say, the already encompassed—may reasonably be expected to be immediately clear. True, the surface of a poem may seem deceptively clear, thus leading the careless reader to settle for an easy first response as the true total. But even in work of such surface clarity as Frost's, it will be a foolish reader indeed who permits himself the illusion that one easy reading will reveal all of the poem. In this sense, indeed, there can be no great poetry without obscurity. Had the Bible been clear at a glance, what reasons would there have been for rereading it?

If, on the other hand, the issue is to be not obscurity but unintelligibility, one may yet reasonably ask, "Unintelligible to whom?" I have grown tired, for example, of being told that e. e. cummings writes unintelligible stuff. Now and then I do find a poem of his that gets so involved in its own trick that I lose interest. But aside from such rare instances, and aside from some simply enough deciphered typographical scrambles (which are there for a reason), cummings is a simple poet. What triumphs in the cummings poem is the aliveness of the poet's five senses, and the gift with which he makes of the poem a word-machine full of the sparks of an inner motion and coherence, rich with a constant release of the seeds of language.

One may be wrong in the thousandth case, but he is still justified in suspecting that when X insists that a cummings poem is unintelligible, X has not read much cummings. When it turns out further that X has not read much contemporary poetry of any sort with real care —then, I must confess, I wonder on what basis X thinks of himself as qualified to issue verdicts, or even to have his opinion seriously regarded. Though we live in the Age of the Pollster, it must still be defended that, in art, simply to have an opinion is nothing: to have earned it by the happy involvement of one's attention is all.

But, pretentiousness aside, let me assume that the self-declared reader is, in fact, one who reads, and that he is willing to indulge an open-minded speculation. Then let me assume that we have located some lines we can both agree are unintelligible. These, for instance:

> Prurient heliotropes nibbled the moon.
> A sky Sylvester-blue held up the day.
> Truth broke its plate and threw away the spoon.
> "Starvation!" cried the landmarks in the bay.

Sad stuff, agreed. But is there no possibility of sensing what the poet is about? Is it not possible that, though we cannot make out *what the lines are saying,* we may yet end up with a fairly sound sense of *why the poet wrote them that way?* If one can avoid the legislations of moral indignation, it is at least conceivable that an uncommitted speculation on badness may teach something about goodness.

Quite clearly, I submit, this poet has overreached for originality and fallen into eccentricity. He ends up with simply a blob of language, confusion tangled with confusion within it. How can a heliotrope be prurient? How can it nibble? Heliotropes are the sun's flower: why do they now move to the moon? How is moon related to day? What is Sylvester-blue?—is it gibberish or a missed allusion? How can the sky be said to hold up the day?

Conceivably, to be sure, the poem might have established the fact that the poet is lying on the ground in such a way that the heliotropes fall in a line between his eye and the moon and conceivably, in that case, they might (conceivably) give rise to a fantasy that they are nibbling the moon. A wily arguer could throw up a screen of such defenses, point by point. But the conclusion would still be forgone. There is obviously too much more to defend here than there is to experience. Anything can be made workable in a poem, with proper management. It is precisely the fact that the poem requires more management than the poet has talent to give it that makes it unintelligible. He is not *making:* he is simply *giving out.*

Very well, then—who has been offended? We have observed and understood a poetic mistake. Yet suppose yourself to be looking for possibility, as a teacher must, rather than for performance, as an editor must, and suppose you are asked to make a choice between prurient heliotropes and the following:

> Be cheerful on the road of life, be gay.
> A smile will cost you nothing on the way.
> Be a neighbor to your neighbor and a husband to your wife.
> And smile away your troubles on the rocky road of life.

Hallmark-clear though they may be, I submit that these lines are as utterly unintelligible as whole hothouses full of prurient heliotropes. What this poet offers, in a pastiche of clichés, is the ridiculous affirmation that the simple act of smiling while being neighborly and a good husband will counteract all the ills that flesh is heir to. The words are clear enough, but as I hope to breathe I cannot find the sentiment intelligible. To be sure, the prurient heliotropes thing is a pastiche, too. I cannot see, however, that one sort of nonsense makes any better sense than the other.

But back to the original suggestion: suppose you were given these two examples and had to decide which writer was more potentially a poet. Is it not clear that within the great deficiencies of the first, something like poetry is at work? The total is as out of kilter as the second man's foolish smiles, but what is out of kilter is at least a poetic sensibility. What is out of kilter in the second passage is not poetry at all, but an unimaged, unrhythmic, and dictionless moral sense. There is at least some self-relation, if only as paradox, in the sequence heliotrope-moon-day. Truth, presented as a child (my guess), throws a tantrum in which the tools of eating are broken and thrown away; and the next image is of the physical world crying "starvation!" The writer has not clarified the relation of the two images (lack of management again), but the fact that they are in some way related is self-evident. The writer is at least thinking in terms of his material; and though both poems are mistakes, the first is at least a poetic mistake.

I submit that to have derived even that much from a speculation on two passages of "meaningless jargon" is to have made a reasonable profit. More profit, certainly, than could have resulted from the indignant refusals of the shock reaction. What shall be the joy of the world, if not to keep its possibilities open? The praise that poetry can speak must be for the supple and the open mind.

A POEM TALKS TO ITSELF
ONE THING CALLS
ANOTHER INTO BEING

So spake the enemy of mankind, enclosed
In serpent, inmate bad, and toward Eve
Addressed his way, not with indented wave,
Prone on the ground, as since, but on his rear
Circular base of rising folds, that towered
Fold above fold a surging maze; his head
Crested aloft, and carbuncle his eyes;
With burnished neck of verdant gold, erect
Against his circling spires that on the grass
Floated redundant.
JOHN MILTON, *Paradise Lost.*

John Milton had a peculiar problem in the forgoing passage in which he described the serpent's approach to Eve. Milton's theology demanded the belief that the serpent was condemned to crawl on its belly for its crime in tempting Eve. It follows, then, that serpents originally moved in some other way. That theological point forces Milton to invent a rather fanciful rear-wheel drive, the details of which he well-advisedly keeps a bit vague.

An assiduous digger through European archives could turn up a number of ponderous treatises on snake locomotion before and after. By the world's evidence, then, as well as his own conviction, Milton was dealing with facts. There was a time not too long since when the study of such facts was very nearly all there was to the study of poetry in our universities, and there is still a marked tendency among many readers to think they have made a sufficient contact with the poem when they have identified and placed such central facts.

Because the natural form for the exposition of facts seems to be the essay, such a fact-centered reading of poetry may be thought of as "the essay approach." The true nature of a poem's performance of itself, however, is so lightly concerned with its essay-content that it may reasonably serve the purposes of good reading to pretend that there are no facts in the poem. A poet must believe *something* passionately enough to have strong feelings about it, but what that *something* is in actual fact is the item of least consequence as far as the poetic performance is concerned.

The essay has satisfied its essential requirements when it has followed the facts—facts, opinions, arguments, all in general that it "has to say."

Poetry does, as noted, involve itself with facts, but the poetic essence is so much nearer that of music than it is that of the essay that to stress factual content is often the quickest way to lose sight of the poem. *The essence of a poem is that one thing in it requires another.* As far as the words of poetry are concerned, that inner requirement is so little a matter of external meaning (denotation) and so much an inner dialogue of connotations (feelings, sounds, and historical and pictorial roots) that it will at least serve to redress the balance to pretend that denotation has no function, and to practice the experience of a poem in something like pure musical terms.

The French critic Boileau called the essence of poetry a *je-ne-sais-quoi*, an "I-don't-know-what." Line by line and passage by passage the poem comes to the poet from sources he feels strongly but does not pretend to understand. At least at the beginning of the poem. Very soon, however, whatever comes to him from the *je-ne-sais-quoi* had better start coming in response to what he has already written down or he is not going to have a poem. Maybe the first line comes from nowhere. And maybe the second comes from a second theme nowhere. But wherever the third line comes from, it has to come from those first lines as well. The poem, that is, is forever generating its own context. Like a piece of music, it follows itself into itself.

To answer to that musicality within the structure of the poem is to answer to the poem itself. Milton's rear-wheel-snake passage, ridiculous as its essay-content is bound to seem, is an example of poetry elevated to sublimity by the rich and powerful development of its diction into musiclike themes.

The first characteristic of Milton's diction here is precision. Note especially the rightness of "indented." Milton wished to ascribe to the post-Paradisal snake a wavelike motion. Now a wave may be conceived in many ways—as a single peak, as a trough-and-crest, or as a long roller. But the clear historical meaning of "indented" is "cut into toothlike points." For Milton—so passionate a Latinist that he could speak of "elephants endorsed with towers"—that root image of "indented" establishes a whole series of waves. For clearly a single wave cannot be indented. At least two are required to make an indentation. In poetry, the force of any given sense is readily extended; as soon as the pluralness of the wave is established, the suggested picture at once becomes not two waves, but many.

Parenthetically, it must be noted that the process of selection going on in the poet's mind (or the recognition of that process in the mind of a good reader) is not spread out across a paragraph of description. It is most likely to happen as an instantaneous, surprising, and happy discovery.

The rightness of the choice is felt in many ways at once. It is the explanation that labors, not the poem. The one point of the explanation is to guide the reader back to the poem with a sharper awareness of what he must learn to experience instantaneously.

Now note the last phrase, "floated redundant." As the snake rears its jeweled head, the remaining coils lie on the grass as if they floated. "Floated," of course, once more suggests the wave-image, and in combination with "redundant" it urges a picture of many slow coils lying at ease on the waters, resting but still keeping a slow, endless, easy motion.

But why "redundant"? Why not "superfluous"? "remaining"? "excessive"? Milton's choice was partly determined by the sound of the word, to be sure, but much more urgently because of the picture hidden in the Latin roots of the word (*redundare*, to overflow; from *unda*, a wave). "Superfluous" also means "to overflow" but with a single, continuous outward motion, as of a river, rather than with the better-related suggestion of a wave's surging-and-receding motion.

Quite clearly Milton has chosen his words not only, nor even primarily, for the rightness of their denotation (essay-wise) but for the interconnection of their connotations (musically); not for their exactness to the "facts" but for the way they follow from other words in the passage. "Floated redundant," for example, might factually have been expressed "sprawled out in excess loops and coils"; but then the interplay of one wave of suggestion with another would have been lost. The point cannot be made often enough that it is exactly such interplays that determine the poem as a poem, and that such interplays, far from being ornamental, are inseparable from the poem's "meaning." They *are* the meaning, and if they are not, there is no defense for poetry, nor any meaningful way of preferring it to embroidery, crossword puzzles, or the day's prose from Washington.

Having located "indented wave" and "floated redundant" as specific kinds of watery motion, one may now look back and see that "surging," too, is at root a watery motion. Its base picture is of a spring bubbling up, its waters agitated in all directions around it. Thus in nine-and-a-fraction lines, that suggestion of watery motion has been three times urged upon the reader. What could be more like the way in which the fragments of a musical theme are picked up, dropped, and picked up again? If the jargon is not objectionable, this sort of poetic development may reasonably be called an "overtone theme." Just as certain characters in opera are identifiable by a musical theme that accompanies them through the action, so the serpent is carried through this description to the theme of a constant wavering watery motion.

And having noted one theme, the reader can hardly fail to note another: the snake also moves like an oriental monarch. His elevation is regal: ("Towered," "crested-aloft," "spires"). His ornaments are all magnificence: ("crested"—*i.e.,* crowned, "carbuncled"—*i.e.,* diamonded, and "gold"). Thus the theme of watery motion is accompanied by a theme of regal splendor. Again the poem performs itself much as does a piece of music.

And much as in a piece of music, the two themes join. Waves "tower" and kings may be said to "tower" above men. "Crested aloft" suggests a wave at peak, and it also means "crowned on high."

Now if one rereads the passage he can note three groupings of overtone themes: watery-motion, regal-splendor, and the two together. Arranged in three columns the words and phrases that might be related to each of these themes would appear so:

Watery motion	*Regal splendor*
indented wave	carbuncle
circular base	burnished
rising folds	gold
fold upon fold	circling spires
surging maze	
floated redundant	

Regal splendor
and
Watery motion

towered
crested aloft

Whatever the value of such a tabulation, it cannot fail to make clear, first, that a unified principle of selection is at work in this diction, and, second, that the words are being selected from inside their connotations and in answer to one another's connotations, rather than from inside their denotation.

For poetry, it must be understood, is a made thing. It does not *record* reality or even imagination; it *selects* from them. The ideal newspaper account of an incident, for example, aims at recording what happened; a good short story selects and shapes. Whatever the short story's take-off from fact, it must end by shaping itself to itself. The fact that a given event happened in "real life" does not make it happen in an art form; it must be made to happen *in terms of what has previously been established.* A good painting is neither a photograph nor a blueprint but an interpretation and an intensification achieved by emphasizing some things, subordinating others, and by following the inner-requiredness of the composition. Put a dab of paint on an endless surface and it does not matter where it falls. But put a frame around it, and immediately the one dab requires another, and the two a third, until some sort of composition has been achieved.

These scattering examples are all to the point that every art form presents its material within a convention and a limitation, and that the material does not exist meaningfully in that art form until it has become involved in the inner-requiredness of its formal limitations. Until the perception of a poem becomes a perception of that inner-requiredness, the poem has not come into view. To paraphrase a statement by I. A. Richards, "One talks about the subject of a poem when he does not know what to do with the poemness of the poem." That "poemness" exists nowhere but in the poem's performance of itself from itself into itself.

POETRY IS FOR PLEASURE*

The function of poetry, as Horace wrote centuries ago, is "to teach while delighting." Poetry can, and does, utter matters of great moral consequence: that is its teaching, its meaning. But unless the pleasure and delight of poetry come first no real meaning can follow.

Pleasure is, of course, in some way connected with the subject matter of the poem; but those ways can be so misleading that it is better to forget meaning. Or at least not to worry about it. Learn to respond to the pleasure of poetry and the meaning will take care of itself. Sail into a poem, on the other hand, with no aim but to hunt out a paraphrase, and all will be lost.

For the meaning of a true poem is not contained in a prose statement but in a poetic performance. What a poem always means most deeply is, as in music, its own performance of itself. Itself gives rise to itself. Itself must evolve the terms of its own conclusion.

The true sources of poetic pleasure, that is to say, lie in the formal elements of the poem, and it is exactly those elements that disappear when the poem is reduced to a paraphrase. It is for this reason that poetry so often seems so dull to students. Almost all academic work in poetry today hammers away at paraphrasing "the meaning" of the poem while ignoring its joyful existence as a form.

The pleasure of form may be a very simple thing, as in a jingle, or it may be very complicated. Complexity is no charge against poetry. The pleasure of listening to Bach can be a very complicated thing; but music-lovers, when they have learned to listen in a subtle way,

* First published in *Glamour*.

come to relish that complexity-within-form as part of their essential pleasure. It is just so with poetry. Once one has begun to respond to form, his own excitement will carry him pleasurably to more and more complex sorts of form, and he will care less and less for paraphrasing.

Certainly no good poet ever wrote in order to have his poems paraphrased. The poet writes in pursuit of form. He can be engaged only within his form. Capturing that form is his pleasure; responding to it is the reader's. For all men find delight in the form of a well-done thing, whether it be a Grecian urn, a home run, or a graceful dance. That pleasure in form springs from the deepest sources of human behavior.

There is no end to the possible variations and subtleties of good poetic form, but fundamental to all else is the principle that *one thing in a poem calls another into being*. It may be hard to understand this principle if one thinks of a poem as some sort of essay made up of logical propositions whose order is dictated by the subject matter. The principle should be clear at once, however, if one thinks of the poem as more nearly a musical sequence—a self-entering, self-developing, self-complicating, self-resolving form.

What starts a poet off? Usually nothing more elaborate than what we might call a "sense of possibility," analogous to the theme that first floats through a composer's head and that prompts all subsequent harmonic, melodic, and rhythmic development in a musical piece. This "sense of possibility" could be an idea, a phrase, a metaphor, a dramatic situation, an image plucked from the air. Whatever it is, it bothers the poet. He wants to write about it. But no good poet knows exactly *how* he is going to develop the initial possibility until his poem requires it of him. As in a symphony or a fugue (that elegant polyphonic concoction in which one initial theme calls into being and is inexplicably welded to a series of counterthemes), one poetic image unfolds into another and then another and then another.

But enough generalizations. There is, after all, no way to read poetry except one poem at a time. Let the living bird illustrate the theory of flight. One of my favorite poems is "A Valediction Forbidding Mourning" by the seventeenth-century Metaphysical poet John Donne, and it will serve admirably to illustrate how one element in a poem evolves from another in a musical rather than in an essay way.

As far as such analogies can be pushed within reason, the form of this particular poem may be thought of as a fugue with a coda (*i.e.,* an elaborate musical epilogue). Some other poem—say, Eliot's "Love Song of J. Alfred Prufrock"—could be argued to correspond to something more nearly like a Debussy suite resolving on a dying fall. Still other poems suggest jazz structures. There is no end to the possible musical analogies one might develop, but it will still be necessary to develop them one poem at a time.

A VALEDICTION FORBIDDING MOURNING

John Donne

As virtuous men pass mildly away,
    And whisper to their souls to go,
Whilst some of their sad friends do say,
    The breath goes now, and some say, No;

So let us melt, and make no noise,
    No tear-floods, nor sigh-tempests move,
'Twere profanation of our joys
    To tell the laity our love.

Moving of th'earth brings harms and fears,
    Men reckon what it did and meant,
But trepidation of the spheres,
    Though greater far, is innocent.

Dull sublunary lovers' love
    (Whose soul is sense) cannot admit
Absence, because it doth remove
    Those things which elemented it.

But we by a love, so much refined
    That ourselves know not what it is,
Inter-assured of the mind,
    Care less eyes, lips, and hands to miss.

Our two souls therefore, which are one,
  Though I must go, endure not yet
A breach, but an expansion,
  Like gold to airy thinness beat.

If they be two, they are two so
  As stiff twin compasses are two,
Thy soul, the fixed foot, makes no show
  To move, but doth, if th'other do.

And though it in the center sit,
  Yet when the other far doth roam,
It leans, and harkens after it,
  And grows erect, as that comes home.

Such wilt thou be to me, who must
  Like th'other foot, obliquely run;
Thy firmness makes my circle just,
  And makes me end, where I begun.

The subject matter of "Valediction" may be disposed of readily enough. Donne, as his other poems make clear, held passionately to an idea of Platonic love as a union of souls. Two souls so joined by true love can never be truly separated. For the soul, Donne believed, is an immaterial essence, and as such it is not subject to time and space. Donne, having been called away to the Continent on affairs of state, addressed this poem to his wife, forbidding her to show any signs of violent grief at parting because to do so would deny the perfection of their union of souls.

Such a summary, though imperfect as all paraphrase must be, will do well enough as a standard examination answer. It is essential, however, to understand that when one has so disposed of the subject matter, he has said *nothing whatever about the poem as a poem.*

"But," one may ask, "what is there to say?"

Look first at the word "melt" in line five. It seems an odd word choice. Donne might, for example, have said, "So let us part." Why instead did he say, "So let us melt?"

"Part," to be sure, would have been acceptable. But "melt" goes beyond the acceptable to the superb. Donne wanted to express not simply parting, but a parting that involved the least violent transition from one state to another. "Let us not break apart in violent grief," he is saying, "but melt away almost imperceptibly."

Taken simply by itself, "melt" is one of those master word-choices that all men associate with the true art of poetry. It is still necessary to see, however, that "melt" does not exist by itself but in response to everything that has gone before it in the poem.

Look back to the first stanza. "As *virtuous* men pass *mildly* away," the poet says. Virtuous men pass away without violent emotion (mildly) because they are assured within themselves; their souls are at rest. It is exactly this sense of holy assurance Donne wishes to convey to his wife, for he sees their love as a sacred and eternal thing. When such virtuous men pass away they make no loud protestations; they do no more than "whisper to their souls to go."

Virtuous, mildly, and *whispers,* one must see, are all chosen because of their common quality of tone; all of them suggest the calm of the self-assured soul. This suggestion (overtone) is again released in the image of the death-bed scene (lines three and four) in which the soul hangs so delicately balanced that the watching friends remain unsure whether or not the man has really died. Note, too, that the friends make no violent outcry. All is serene and still.

Thus in four lines the poet has four times released the same overtone. What makes "melt" so musically superb a choice is the fact that it expresses the idea of parting in perfect response to the other tones Donne has established in the first stanza. Had Donne said "part" instead of "melt" he would have expressed his essay idea but he would have fudged his musical idea.

Now let us assume that Donne began his poem with a wish to put into the best possible formal language a sense of what an ideal parting between man and woman should be. This was his initial "sense of possibility," the fragmentary theme dancing around in his mind. As in music, opposites suggest one another—a violent opening theme is balanced with a soft second theme, or vice versa. In "Valediction" the idea of melting serenity develops itself into a countertheme: "So let us melt and make no noise."

"Noise" is not only the violent opposite of melt but the signature of the second theme. The first theme (it might be called the "melt theme") develops those overtones that Donne approves. The second (the "noise theme") develops those overtones of which Donne disapproves. Thus from "noise" there follow "tear-floods" and "sigh-tempests"—noisy, violent, and excessive shows of emotion.

At this point Donne has completed his first statement of theme and countertheme. He now begins to develop their counterplay, changing the relation from serene-violent to sacred-profane. It would be a profanation of our joys, he says, to tell the laity (the noisy unordained) of our (serene, sacred) love.

Obviously this shift of terms to sacred-profane is not a random change but a development of the idea of religious faith implicit in the death of the virtuous man. As in music, everything in a good poem arises from what has already been established.

And with the establishment of high-low in terms of sacred-profane, it is a natural extension to carry the theme next to high and low in terms of heaven and earth. "Moving of th'earth" (earthquake) is a relatively small motion as compared to the vast distances through which the heavenly spheres vibrate. Yet that relatively insignificant earthly motion produces all sorts of violent disturbances, whereas the much greater (and higher) motion is not only innocent (*i.e.*, harmless), but produces the serene music of the spheres. Donne does not himself mention the music of the spheres, but only because he knows very well that it will inevitably suggest itself to his reader if the reader is at all aware of poetic convention.

Any reader acquainted with the background of Donne's mind will also have realized that when he speaks of "trepidation of the spheres" he is referring to the Ptolemaic Universe, which was conceived to be made up of nine concentric spheres with the earth as their center. In such a universe there is a built-in scale of holiness: the further one goes from the earth-center, the closer he draws to God. High-and-low are not simply up-and-down, but nearer-to-God and further-from-God.

Mind you, this little excursion into the Ptolemaic system is not necessary to one's enjoyment of the poem. A poem can still give pleasure even if you don't understand every specialized reference in it. But such knowledge of the times in which a poem was written, whether Roman, Medieval, Elizabethan, or Victorian, adds another dimension to poetry reading, just as, say, identifying the dance in a symphony's dance movement can add another dimension to one's pleasure in the music.

Thus Donne has developed the opposition of his themes as melt *versus* noise, as sacred *versus* profane, and as heaven *versus* earth. The same oppositions might be called high *versus* low in terms of the conduct of the soul, of church hierarchy, and of the structure of the universe.

Having brought the high-low opposition thus far, Donne equates it in very specific terms to spiritual *versus* merely physical love. "Dull sublunary lovers" are those who live beneath the sphere of the moon, which is to say, on earth. They are the earth-bound, who can deal only in material things. And tied as they are forever to the center of the Ptolemaic Universe, they are forever furthest from God and the things of the spirit.

With the kind of wittily exaggerated logic that has become the hallmark of the Metaphysical poets, Donne then dismisses such merely physical lovers. They cannot experience absence because their love consists only of bodily contact. Once that contact is broken, therefore, the love ceases, since its entire reason for being disappears. He and his wife, on the other hand, by a love so much refined (*i.e.*, purified of the dross of the material) are not confined by the physical.

But what is refined (as gold) is still material. And Donne certainly was no man to deny physical love. He has said merely that two who love with all their souls "care less" about missing one another's physical presence. Yet there is a moment of confusion here. Through the first four stanzas the two themes were treated as clean opposites. By the end of the fifth, some element of the physical-love theme has been admitted into the spiritual-love theme. Something must be done if the two themes are not to lose their definition. They must be brought to some sort of clarifying resolution.

That resolution is in stanza six. Picking up the image he has suggested in his use of "refined," Donne carries it forward in terms of gold-beating. Gold is a material thing, to be sure, but it is, to begin with, refined and it is then beaten to an "airy thinness." It becomes, therefore, not only the most worthy but also the least material of all material things.

It was, moreover, a common belief of Donne's time that the universe consisted of four basic elements, which were earth, water, fire, and air. Earth and water were held to be the heavy, or falling, elements. Fire and air were the light, or rising, elements. Thus, though true lovers are creatures of the earth, as all men and women are, their lesser elements are purified from them and their souls expand into the lightest, least material, and most valuable of earthly elements. Being so wrought to airy thinness, moreover, their souls must tend to rise from earth toward God. And thus once more the theme has turned out to be a development of the sacred *versus* the profane.

Then to bring his fugue back to its first point, Donne phrases the opposition in terms that cannot fail to suggest melt-noise: he and his wife must part not as a "breach" (a violent and noisy rupture) but as an "expansion" (like "melt," the least perceptible transition from one state to another, but now with the added sense of "growing larger"). And with that resolution the conflicting themes have been brought to rest. That trace of beaten gold has been accepted from the earthly theme but only that.

Note that the fuguelike development of the first six stanzas is carried through many different images—a death-bed scene, such physical phenomena as melting and noise, church hierarchy, and so on. In the final three stanzas Donne develops a magnificent coda clearly distinguished from the first fugal figure by the fact that it develops a single image (dominant metaphor) for three stanzas. That sustained compass-image is certainly one of the master metaphoric structures of English poetry.

The two souls of the spiritual lovers are compared to the two legs of the compass joined at the top (at the highest level) in such a way that one cannot move without a responsive motion in the other. Being so joined, they create the perfect circle. The circle, of course, is a natural symbol of unity. Note also that the line of the circle is endless (as true love is everlasting).

Thus, through everlasting union the soul returns to its beginning—"And makes me end, where I begun." The line is a superb tonic chord, bringing both the final image and the total poem to rest upon itself, just as the life of that good man in stanza one comes to rest in the everlasting assurance of the perfect spiritual cycle that returns him to God.

What has happened—exactly as in a piece of good music—is that the development has put to rest every expectation it gave birth to, and every conflict of its elements. It has made itself and answered itself, and nothing has been left over. The material of the theme and countertheme has been entirely consumed because every formal element in the poem has been related to every other. This is the idea of organic form in which nothing is out of place.

Feeling the poem come to rest upon itself produces the same joy one experiences in hearing the last perfect chord of the music sink into silence. Until one learns to listen to the poem hearkening to itself and answering itself in this way, he may be parsing out the subject matter, but he is not responding to the pleasure, and, therefore, to the essence of the poetry.

WHAT EVERY WRITER MUST LEARN*

The teaching of writing has become practically a profession by now. There is hardly a college in the land that does not offer at least one course in "creative writing" (whatever that is) by some "teacher of writing" (whoever he is). There are, moreover, at least fifty annual writers' conferences now functioning among us with something like fifty degrees of competence. And there seems to be no way of counting the number of literary counselors, good and bad, who are prepared to promise that they can teach a writer what he needs to know.

I am myself a "teacher of writing," but though it be taken as a confession of fraud I must insist, in the face of all this "teaching" apparatus, that writing cannot in fact be taught. What a writer must have above all else is inventiveness. Dedication, commitment, passion —whatever one chooses to call the writer's human motivation—must be there, to be sure. But to require human motivation is only to assume that the writer is a human being—certainly not a very hard assumption to make. Art, however, is not humanity but the *expression* of humanity, and for enduring expression the one gift above all is inventiveness.

But where, in what curriculum ever, has there been, or can there be, a course in inventiveness—which is to say, in creativity? The truly creative—whether in art, in science, or in philosophy—is always, and precisely, that which cannot be taught. And yet, though it seem paradoxical, creativity cannot spring from the untaught. Creativity is the

* Delivered as the opening lecture of the Bread Loaf Writers' Conference, 1956.

imaginatively gifted recombination of known elements into something new.

And so, it may seem, there is no real paradox. The elements of an invention or of a creation can be taught, but the creativity must be self-discovered and self-disciplined. A good teacher—whether in a college classroom, a Parisian café, or a Greek market place—can marvelously assist the learning. But in writing, as in all creativity, it is the gift that must learn itself.

The good teacher will be able to itemize a tremendous amount of essential lore. He can tell a would-be novelist that if an incidental character is given a name that character had best reappear in the later action, and that if he is not going to reappear he should be identified simply as "the supply sergeant," "the big blond," "the man in the red waistcoat," or whatever. He can point out that good dialogue avoids "he averred," "he bellowed," "he boomed," "he interpolated," and that it is wise to write simply "he said," indicating any important direction for the tone of voice in a separate sentence. He can demonstrate that in all fiction the action must be perceived by someone, and he can defend in theory and support by endless instances that in effective fiction one does not allow more than one means of perception within a single scene. He can point out to would-be poets that traditional rhyme and traditional metrics are not indispensable, but that once a pattern has been established the writer must respect it. And he can then point out that within the pattern established at the start of the student's poem certain lines are metrically deficient and certain rhymes forced.

He may "teach" (or preach) any number of such particulars. And if he is a good man for the job he will never forget that these particulars are simply rules of thumb, any one of which may be violated by a master, but none of which may be safely ignored by a writer who has not yet learned they exist.

Belaboring such particulars is a useful device to the would-be writer, who under a competent teacher may save himself years of floundering trial-and-error. Writers are forever being produced by literary groups of one sort or another, and one of the most important things a writer acquires in the give-and-take of a good literary group is a headful of precisely such particulars. The most important thing a teacher of writing can do is to create a literary group in which he teaches minimums while the most talented of his students learn maximums—very largely from fighting with one another (rarely, if ever, from mutual admiration).

But if writing requires a starting talent that a man either has or has not and which he cannot learn, and if the teachable elements are not enough to make a writer of him, what is it he must learn? What are the measures by which his gift comes to know itself?

The answers to that question must be given separately, and if they are so given they must be put down one after the other with some sort of natural implication that the order in which they are given is keyed to their importance. Such mechanical necessity (and it is one of the most constant seductions of the classroom) must not be allowed to obscure the far greater likelihood that the answers all exist at the same time in the behavior of a good writer, and that all are equally important. That, too, is part of what must be learned. As is the fact that no one set of generalizations will ever suffice. But one must begin somewhere. I offer the following six points as the most meaningful and the most central I have been able to locate.

1. SOMETHING TO WRITE ABOUT

"You have to give them something to write about," Robert Frost once said in discussing his classroom principles. His own poems are full of stunning examples of the central truth that good writers deal in information, and that even the lofty (if they are lofty) acreages of poetry are sown to fact. Consider the opening lines of "Mending Wall":

> Something there is that doesn't love a wall,
> That sends the frozen-groundswell under it,
> And spills the upper boulders in the sun;
> And makes gaps even two can pass abreast.
> The work of hunters is another thing:
> I have come after them and made repair
> Where they have left not one stone on a stone,
> But they would have the rabbit out of hiding,

To please the yelping dogs. The gaps I mean,
No one has seen them made or heard them made,
But at spring mending-time we find them there . . .

I intend no elaborate critique of this passage. I want simply to make the point that it contains as much specific information about stone walls as one could hope to find in a Department of Agriculture pamphlet.

Frost states his passion for the *things* of the world both in example and in precept. "The fact is the sweetest dream the labor knows," he writes in "The Mowing." One has only to compare that line with R. P. T. Coffin's "Nothing so crude as fact could enter here" to understand an important part of the difference between a poet and something less than a poet.

Even so mystical a poet as Gerard Manley Hopkins (I misuse the word "mystical" in order to save three paragraphs, but let me at least file an apology) is gorgeously given to the fact of the thing. Consider: "And blue bleak embers, ah my dear, / Fall, gall themselves, and gash gold-vermilion." (I.e., "Coal embers in a grate, their outside surfaces burned out and blue-bleak, sift down, fall through the grate, strike the surface below, and are gashed open to reveal the gold-vermilion fire still glowing at their core.")

The writer of fiction deals his facts in a different way, but it will not do to say that he is more bound to fact than is the poet: he simply is not required to keep his facts under poetic compression; keep hard to them he still must. Consider Melville's passion for the details of whaling; or Defoe's for the details of criminality, of ransoming an English merchant captured by a French ship, or of Robinson Crusoe's carpentry. The passion for fact was powerful enough in these masters to lure them into shattering the pace of their own best fiction, and to do so time and time again. And who is to say that a man reading for more than amusement, a man passionate to touch the writer's mind in his writing, has any real objection to having the pace so shattered? All those self-blooming, lovingly managed, chunky, touchable facts!

For a writer is a man who must know something better than anyone else does, be it so little as his own goldfish or so much as himself. True, he is not required to know any one specific thing. Not at least until he begins to write about it. But once he has chosen to write about X then he is responsible for knowing everything the writing needs to know about X. I know of no writer of any consequence whatever who did not treasure the world enough to gather to himself a strange and wonderful headful and soulful of facts about its going and coming.

2. AN OUTSIDE EYE

Nothing is more difficult than for the writer to ride his passion while still managing to observe it critically. The memoirs of good writers of every sort are studded with long thoughts on this essential duplicity, this sense of aesthetic detachment, of a second attention lurking in the mind at the very moment they have felt the need to be most indivisibly absorbed in what they are doing.

The writer absolutely must learn to develop that eye outside himself, for the last action every writer must perform for his writing is to become its reader. It is not easy to approach one's own output as if he were coming on it fresh. Yet unless the writer turns that trick any communication that happens will either be by accident or by such genius as transcends the possibility of discussion.

For the writer's relation to his writing is a developing relation. The writing starts as a conceptual buzz. Approaching the writing thus with the buzz loud in the head, one may easily believe that anything he sets down is actually full of that starting buzz. But one must remember that the buzz is there before the writing, and that should some accident interfere with the actual writing the buzz would still be there. A writer in a really heightened state could jot down telephone numbers and actually believe that he has set down a piece of writing that accurately conveys his original impulse.

The reader, however, is in a very different situation. He comes to the writing committed to no prior emotion. There is no starting buzz in his head, except by irrelevant accident. It is the writer's job to make that reader buzz. Not, to be sure, to make every reader buzz—the world is full of the practically unbuzzable—but to make the competent reader buzz. Simply to say, "I buzz," is not enough. To make the reader experience the original buzz with nothing but the writing to create the buzz within him—that is the function of every sort of literature, the communication of experience in experienceable terms. The disciplines of any art form are among other things ways of estimating the amount of buzz the form is transmitting.

3. FLUENCY

As noted, one does not hope to reach all readers, but only the competent. In one way the qualifications of a good reader are the same as those of a competent writer. Both must achieve fluency. By fluency I mean the ability to receive more than one impression at the same time. To create or to experience art one must be both technically and emotionally fluent.

A pun is a simple example of the necessity for technical fluency. The two or more faces of a pun must be received at the same instant or all is lost. The news comes over the radio that the Communist leader of Pisa has been chastised by Moscow for making overtures to the left-center parties for a united front, and the happy punster says, "Aha, a Lenin tower of a-Pisa-ment!" then settles back in his moment of personal splendor. This golden instant from my autobiography—but what good is even glory if it has to be explained? "I don't get it," says the guest who will never be invited again, and the evening is ruined.

The pun, of course, is only the simplest example of the need for technical fluency. Unless the writer and the reader have in common the necessary language of simultaneity in its millions of shadings, the best will die en route.

The need for emotional fluency is analogous. Good writing constantly requires the writer to perceive and the reader to receive different sets of feelings at the same instant. Both the writer and the reader must be equal to the emotion of the subject dealt with. Shakespeare can put a world into *Hamlet*, but where is that world when a five-year-old child or an emotionally-five-year-old adult attempts to read or to see the play? Whatever he may see, it is certainly not Shakespeare. A reader who is emotionally immature, or who is too psychically rigid (the same thing really) to enter into the simultaneity of the human experiences commonly portrayed in literature, is simply not capable of any sort of writing with the possible exception of the technical report, the statistical summary, or that semi-literate combination, the Ph.D. thesis.

4. A SENSE OF THE PAST

No painter can produce a good canvas without a broad knowledge of what has been painted before him, no architect can plan a meaningful building except as he has pondered the architecture of the past, and no writer can produce good writing without a sure sense of what has been accomplished in the past within his form.

There are legions of poets today who are trying belatedly to be Wordsworth, and legions of fictioneers who are trying to be Louisa May Alcott. I imply no attack here on either Wordsworth or Alcott. I simply make the point that it is too late to be either of them again. Both of them, moreover, did a better job of being themselves than any of their imitators can aspire to. As the Kitty-cat bird in Theodore Roethke's poem said: "Whoever you are, be sure it's you."

Nor does one learn the past of his form only to adhere to it. Such an adherence, if overdedicated, would be a death in itself. I mean, rather, that it is impossible to venture meaningful innovation unless one knows what he is *innovating from.* With no exception I am able to think of, the best innovators in our literature have been those who best knew their past tradition.

I am saying simply that a writer must learn to read. He must read widely and thoughtfully, and he must learn to read not as an amateur spectator but as an engaged professional. Just as the football coach sees more of the play than do the coeds, so the writer must learn to see more of what is happening under the surface of the illusion than does the reader who simply yields to the illusion. William Dean Howells, then editor of *The Atlantic,* paid what he intended as a supreme compliment to one of Mark Twain's books when he reported that he had begun the book and for the first time in many years had found himself reading as a reader rather than as an editor. A happy indulgence and a gracious compliment, but once the writer has allowed himself that much it becomes his duty to reread the book with his glasses on—not only to enter into the illusion of the writing, but to identify the devices (*i.e.*, the inventions) by which the illusion was created and made to work upon him. And here, too, he must experience his essential duplicity, for the best reading is exactly that reading in which the passion of the illusion and the awareness of its technical management arrive at the same time.

5. A SENSE OF THE AGE

The true writer, that is to say the writer who is something more than a competent technician, has a yet more difficult thing to learn. He must not only know his human and artistic past; he must learn to read the mood of his world under its own names for itself. He must become an instrument, tuned by devices he can never wholly understand, to the reception of a sense of his age, its mood, its climate of ideas, its human position, and its potential of action. And he must not let himself be deceived into thinking that the world answers to the names it gives itself. Hitler's agencies once gave a great deal of attention to what they called "Strength-through-Joy." It was the product of this Strength-through-Joy that Lord Beaverbrook called at the time "the stalwart young Nazis of Germany." The names were "strength," "joy," and "stalwarts." Yet any man today can see that those who answered to these shining names contained within themselves possibilities for action that must answer to much darker names. Any man can see it—now. I think it is very much to the point that all of the best writers sensed it then, and that the better the German writers were, the earlier they left Germany. Good writing must be of its times and must contain within itself—God knows how but the writer must learn for himself—a sense of what Hippolyte Taine called "the moral temperature of the times," what the Germans call "der Zeitgeist," and what English and American writers have come to call "the climate."

6. ART IS ARTIFICE

And along with all else, as an essential part of his duplicity, his commitment, his fluency, and his sense of past and present, the writer must learn beyond any flicker of doubt within himself that art is not life itself but a made representation of life. He must learn that it is no defense of a piece of fiction, for example, to argue. "But that's the way it happened." The fact that it happened that way in the world of the *Daily News* does not make it happen to the reader within the world of the writing.

The writer's subject is reality but his medium is illusion. Only by illusory means can the sense of reality be transmitted in an art form. That complex of pigment-on-canvas is not four maidens dancing, but it is the managed illusion whereby Botticelli transmits his real vision of the four seasons. Those words on paper are not Emma Bovary, but they are the elements of the illusion whereby we experience her as a living creation. The writer, like every artist, deals in what I have come to call the AS-IF. AS-IF is the mode of all poetry and of all imaginative writing. IS is the mode of what passes for reality and of all information-prose. Is IS more real than AS-IF? One must ask: "More real for what purposes?" I have no argument with, for example, the research chemists. I mean rather to hold them in considerable admiration. But though many of them think of themselves as the IS-iest men in the world, which of them has ever determined a piece of truth except by setting up and pursuing a starting hypothesis (let me leave accident out of consideration)? And what is a starting hypothesis but an AS-IF? "Let us act AS-IF this hypothesis were true," says the researcher, "and then see how it checks out." At the end of ten, or a hundred, or ten thousand starting AS-IF's lurks the nailed-down IS of valence, or quanta, or transmutation of elements. Maybe. And then only until the next revolution in IS outdates the researcher's results.

At the far end of all the AS-IF's a man, and particularly a writer, can summon from himself, there lurks that final IS (maybe) that will be a truth for him. But not all of the truth will be told at one time. Part of the truth, I think the most truth, a writer must learn is that writing is not a decorative act, but a specific, disciplined, and infinitely viable means of knowledge. Poetry and fiction, like all the arts, are ways of perceiving and of understanding the world. Good writing is as positive a search for truth as is any part of science, and it deals with kinds of truth that must forever be beyond science. The writer must learn, necessarily of himself and within himself, that his subject is the nature of reality, that good writing always increases the amount of human knowledge available, and that the one key to that knowledge of reality is AS-IF. His breadth and depth as a human being are measured by the number of AS-IF's he has managed to experience; his stature as a writer, by the number he has managed to bring to life in his work.

For no man in any one lifetime can hope to learn by physical experience (IS) all that he must know and all that he must have experienced in order to be an adequate human being. No writer can hope to engage physically enough worlds of IS to make his imagination and his humanity pertinent. Only by his vicarious assumptions of AS-IF can the writer learn his real human dimension, and only as he dedicates his writing to the creation of a meaningful and experienceable new AS-IF can he hope to write well—to write as no school can teach him to write, but as he must learn for himself if he cares enough, and if he has gift enough.

ON WRITING
AND BAD WRITING*

Every writer sooner or later is tempted into some sort of generalization about his art, craft, business, or whatever he chooses to call the act that takes place between him and his supply of blank paper. Those writers who have been tempted into trying to teach writing classes are not so much tempted as forced.

"How do I learn to write?" says the novice. No question could be more useless. It is almost certain (perhaps not quite) that anyone who insists upon asking it that way will never find the answer. It is a naïve question. It is a stupid one. Yet it is uncomfortably central to the man who has let himself be talked into making his living by hoping that he can help another human being to become a writer.

Perhaps it is good for honest men to be badgered by the innocent, ignorant, and yet primary question. If confusion is bound to follow, praise all that sends honest men honestly to their confusions. Some things—perhaps all matters of ultimate meaning—have to live outside of ironclad conviction. Writing, as I understand it, is a mortal seeking. I no longer try to teach it, but certainly any student who ever brought full-blown certainties into my classroom was invited to leave.

I think it was Bernard DeVoto who pointed out that the best reason for putting anything down on paper is that one may then change it. His remark not only suggests one sound theory of writing but identifies the writing process as a groping one. There is no end to that groping process, but in time the good writer will acquire not only a sense of *groping* for but a sense of having *groped to:* he

* Delivered as the opening lecture of the Bread Loaf Writers' Conference, 1962.

begins to know when he has finally reached whatever he was reaching for.

Ideally, there can be no real end to that groping. To reread is to revise. In the world as it is, however, one has to leave the writing at some point: either that or stay with it forever and never get on to anything else. One gropes *for*, and then in hope and despair, lets himself believe that he has groped *to* it as well as he will ever be able to. But however it goes, it goes by feel, and it is up to every writer to learn his own feel for it. Only he can guess out, finally, his own sense of it.

For no man who writes seriously, and by seriously I mean as a way of life, will write in any but his own way. His way of life is, in fact, to find just his own way of writing—whatever way most nearly informs for him the emotions of experiencing this world.

A good teacher of writing ("writing coach" might be a better title) should be able to teach a bright student to write almost like Dickens, or almost like John Donne, or almost like Emerson. But it would be only almost; the same "almost" that unkindled wood is to the fire it could release if ignited. Any number of semipolished surfaces, and even plain brick, can reflect fire. The starting need of the writer is to be himself the tinder.

If he is that tinder, any library is full of sparks, and almost any teacher could be his Prometheus. The hopeful beginner can burst into flame at the touch of any admired piece of writing. The good writer can blaze at the touch of any mortally glowing experience. But they must first be flammable. No amount of instruction will teach damp souls to dry themselves and to burn. And it seems also to be true that no writer really blazes until he has learned—which is to say, until he has found for himself—how to write as no one else does, to write in his own way.

But where does the would-be writer begin?

The first answer is easy: Because he is a human being and because he is sensitive to the joy and distress of that condition, he is moved to speak his feelings.

But if that is all he has to move him, it is not enough. If the human passion is first, it must yet be joined by an equal passion for the medium before good writing can happen. The writer is a man overpowered by words, sentences, rhythms, ideas, the drama of ideas when there are lives moving in them, and the forms he can shape from his medium. Language haunts him. Words, sentences, rhythms are not things to him; they are presences. The presence of his medium makes him feel more than he really knows how to think or say. He knows that he is wiser, richer, more perceptive, more sentient when he is immersed in his medium than he can hope to be when he is high and dry in ideas and presences that he can identify and talk about with clear and pedagogical coherence. His medium is a gorgeous confusion upon him and a gorgeous flowering of all possibility. It is his house of great ghosts.

No teacher can hope to build for the student that haunted house of the mortally excited talent and self. The good teacher recognizes the real excitement when he sees it. He can encourage it as one encourages a fire by poking, prodding, and blowing on it. But it is dangerous for any teacher to let himself think that the fire is his doing. At best, the teacher may strike the match. But the match must then fall into the all-blazing possibility of soul-tinder.

One of the troubles with beginning writers is that they are almost certain to blaze out of control. Often it is the teacher's job to squirt a little water here and there. For the object is to heat and to illuminate the house, not to burn it down. And the only way to achieve that object is to keep the fire where it belongs—in the fireplace. The act of distinguishing between the logs of the fireplace and the walls of the house is called criticism, and I am tempted to claim that any fires that have been put out as a result of the act of criticism should never have been started.

For writing involves containment. Like all art, it takes place within limits. If writing is thought of as the fire of the soul—and let this be the end of the incendiary metaphor—it must remain within the iron limits of the grate. If it is thought of as happening within a frame, the frame may be hacked at by a true genius (and only by a true genius) but it must not be broken by any man. Writing, like all art, is a formality. The writing cannot be made to take the place of the world. The world will remain in its own sprawl.

Whatever you mean by reality, writing is not it. Writing selects from the unknown reality of things, and, by selecting, it makes known. Writing is a heightening, an excerption, an organic digression from its own beginning, an ordering, perhaps only a moment's ordering; whatever it is, it remains that glimpse through a frame that no man may live in but that the best of men must live toward. What else did Omar mean by citing to Love "this sorry scheme of things" in the dream that he and Love might "shatter it to bits—and then/ Remold it nearer to the heart's desire"? Art has no other function.

What then? What does one tell would-be writers—as if he himself knew? Granting that there are no certainties, that all must be groped for, that there is no teaching of writing but only the coaching one can give to self-learners—is there no useful generalization?

I am inclined to offer one above all others and that is *that the badness of bad writing is never visible to the writer*. I offer that as a generalization and not as a truth, for it is not always but only some-times true. Nevertheless it is usually true. And it seems always to be true of bad writers on their way to being hopeless writers.

Conceivably a man could try to write with all his mortal passion, and write badly, and still retain enough taste and detachment to *know* that he is writing badly. In the exhaustions of honesty, such a man invariably gives up the effort, finds some way of making a living and, having found his living, probably becomes an excellent reader, made the more sensitive to the writing by his own sad sense of failure; as perhaps a man of exquisite ear but badly co-ordinated muscles may have dreamed of playing the cello but could never make his arms and fingers produce what his ear dreamed of hearing. Such men, how-ever, are rare, for it takes a man of rare taste to recognize his failure against all the promptings of the ego that allow the tasteless to go on producing—and cherishing—miserable stuff.

My generalization is once more likely to be untrue of hopeful writers on their way to being good writers. A *writer can, in fact, de-velop only as rapidly as he learns to recognize what is bad in his writing*. If a man means his writing seriously he must mean to write well. But how can he write well until he learns to see what he has written badly? His progress toward good writing and his recognition of bad writing are bound to unfold at something like the same rate.

Give me the young writer who is ashamed this week—really and perceptively ashamed—of what he wrote last week, and I will take him as my example of hope. Not all hopes can be realized, but the young writer's ardent dissatisfaction with his best efforts of a while back is certainly the most hopeful sign I can think to look for.

Any man can write a bad story or a bad poem. Having written it, one man may stay in love with it forever, and another man burn it in anguish when he rereads it. Where can hope be, in this case, but with the arsonist? Whether or not he can itemize the causes of the badness, he has learned that it is bad. All human chance is that he will not fall back into that particular kind of badness, or not, at least, for long.

Conversely, how can the man who goes on cherishing his bad writing hope to write better? How can he refuse badness until he grows to recognize it? What can anyone teach him, or help him to learn? There are plenty of writing coaches who can read a manuscript and identify and analyze specific kinds of badness and point them out to the writer. Hundreds of such writing coaches are built into our college faculties these days. Many such are themselves good writers. But even the best of them can only point out what is bad. If the would-be writer cannot see, nothing follows.

As Poetry Editor of SR I have systematically refused to enter into personal criticisms of manuscripts submitted to us, unless, that is, I was seriously considering them for publication. I have refused for many reasons, including the statistical one that I receive more such requests in a week than I could honor in a year. But the reason above all others is that in practically all cases such criticism would be pointless. Right or wrong, I think I can identify the badness of most of the poems submitted to us, and that I can, within reasonable limits, point out the sources of that badness. But the bad writers will not see the badness of their own writing even if it is pointed out. There are, heaven knows, understandable human reasons for that blindness. Even bad writing is likely to be powered by intense emotion. Feeling himself so moved, the bad writer is easily self-persuaded to take the power of his starting emotion as the measure of his writing. Consequently he sees only what he intended to write, what he was moved to write. *He never sees what he has actually written.*

Such a one is the entirely hopeless writer, and he is usually given to assaults upon the largest possible subjects. In mildest moments he is satisfied with stating the ultimate truth about childhood, grandma, the flag, the bomb, and nature's inner meaning. In full flight he settles for nothing less than hortatory statements about the universe and its intentions. He feels hugely (and grossly) about these subjects, and secure in those feelings, he is sure that he has written hugely—and grossly. As, alas, he has.

But all he ever has in sight is his starting *passion. He does not see the writing because, in plain fact, he cares nothing about it.* He is out for release, not for containment. He is a self-expresser, not a maker.

As such, he can probably find encouragement in the adult-kindergartens of what used to be called progressive education, but he is mistaken to look for it in the criticisms of a good teacher. For such a writer my starting maxim is always true: the badness of his writing is forever invisible to him. His blindness, to be sure, is only one of the symptoms of his fixed badness, but it is certainly the central symptom.

Usually such a writer will defend himself fiercely against all criticism. You might wonder why he even asks for it, except that you already know that it wasn't criticism but praise he came for. Whichever it is, you simply avoid giving it to him. You avoid it—and him.

But the case is no better with the gentle soul (the seemingly gentle soul?) who accepts all criticism in total meekness only to ignore it completely. The human race has available to it all sorts of ways of losing.

No good teacher will insist that his word is law. He knows he is a groper. He suggests, prods, points out, and hopes to make a contact that will count. His work is pointless if the writer comes to him in a defensive fury, and just as pointless if the writer comes too submissively.

If the would-be writer announces that he knows it is good writing because it is informed by Ultimate Truth, that has to end the discussion. And there is an end to it too, if the would-be writer says blandly, and over and over again, "Oh, yes! Oh, yes! How true! How true!"

The hopeful writer may beg off because he is already ashamed of what he passed in for criticism. If he does want the criticism, he will see the point of most of it at once. But the most hopeful response I know is that of the writer who says, "You're probably right, but let me take that away to think about. I need time to feel it out."

That is the most hopeful response because such a writer, even as a beginner, has learned how multiple the writing is, how many auras must be registered in arriving at his own sense of the light, and because no criticism is really to his purpose until he has registered it upon his own sense of the light—until he has felt it out for himself.

That man is going back to look at the writing and to think about it. And he is the one, I suspect, who will manage to see it. If it is bad he will see its badness (for him) and he will learn from it. He is not simply taking criticism, he is receiving it. And each perception so received is being built into him—wired into him, so to speak, as one more circuit of sensitivity in the infinite complex of his nervous system. The next time he writes he will have one more awareness going for him.

In time, that complex conditioning, those millions of awarenesses wired into his dendrites, will generate something almost separate from him. Critics call that something "aesthetic distance" or "detachment." Whatever it is called, it identifies a central possession of every good writer—the fact that he can be passionately committed to what he is writing at the same time that one part of his awareness is detached, calculating, and technical.

That state is neither easily achieved nor easily defined, but it comes close to being a first condition of all good writing, with an exception to be made only for those rare impassioned moments when a genius —which is to say a writer who has disciplined himself without losing the wildness of his talents—pours out, say, a "Kubla Khan" in a moment of what seems to be blind rapture. Is it necessary to argue that even a Coleridge must have the disciplined and essential duplicities of a lifetime to draw upon and to give form to his moment of rapture? I must believe that this world's writing will be put on its page by men who have developed their talents in passionate discipline to that point of doubleness that lets them be passionately in the writing at the same time that their monitoring awarenesses as artists are out of it.

Those awarenesses begin exactly in the writer's ability to see what he has written, in his ability to get outside the writing, to become its reader as well as its writer, and to learn from what he sees; to learn with every outside assistance he can get from others, but finally to learn from inside himself by learning to see himself.

HOW TO READ DANTE

In the opening allegory of *The Divine Comedy*, Dante finds himself lost and in darkness:

> Midway in our life's journey, I went astray
> from the straight road and woke to find myself
> alone in a dark wood.

These are familiar allegorical devices and no sensitive reader will fail to understand that "the straight road" has something to do with rectitude ("the straight and narrow"), that "the dark wood" has something to do with error/sinfulness/loss of purpose, and—by extension—that the proper course must lie in finding the light.

Having "something to do with" is not close enough, however. Dante demands more careful reading. Because of that demand, because of the immense and minute scholarship that has been expended upon Dante, and because too few English readers have been pointed in the right direction to him, Dante has acquired a reputation as an immensely difficult poet.

It is true that Dante writes in depth. Though his language is normally simple, his thought is normally complex. But if the gold of Dante runs deep, it also runs right up to the surface. A lifetime of devoted scholarship will not mine all that gold; yet enough lies on the surface—or just an inch below—to make a first reading a bonanza in itself. All one really needs is some first instruction in what to look for. Thereafter he need only follow the vein as it goes deeper and deeper into the core of things.

The instruction may properly begin with those opening lines. "Midway in our life's journey," writes Dante. The reader must understand that Dante is not tossing off a poetic generalization. "Our life's journey" means specifically the "three score years and ten" of the Biblically allotted life span. "Midway," therefore, means that Dante was thirty-five years old at the time of which he writes. Since he was born in 1265, it follows that the poem opens in the year 1300. And from a number of statements that can be culled from the poem, the careful reader can learn that the exact time is just before dawn of Good Friday.

By culling certain other statements, most of which are made at once, the reader may further learn that the sun is at the vernal equinox, that it is in the sign of Aries (the zodiacal sign in which God placed it at the Creation), and that the moon is full. These elements, added to the fact that it is the hour of the dawn and the season of Easter, clearly compound a massive symbol of rebirth. All things are at their regenerative peak when the lost soul realizes it has gone astray, for that realization is itself the beginning of the soul's rebirth.

Scholars have since shown that there was no Friday in the year 1300 on which all these conditions obtained. Dante, moreover, was a close student of astronomy and astrology. He knew that no such conjunction of sun, moon, zodiacal sign, and Easter season had taken place. He invented that conjunction as a full-swelling introductory theme in what amounts to a symphonic structure. The poem sounds its first chords with first light striking through darkness. In what follows, the darkness must grow more and more absolute to the very depth of dark (Hell); the light must then begin to overcome the darkness (Purgatory); and finally the "music" must mount from light to light to the ultimate indescribable glory of the all-blazing presence of God at the peak of Heaven.

As soon as Dante recognizes that he is lost and in darkness, he looks up and sees the first light of the new day glowing on the shoulders of a little hill. Throughout *The Divine Comedy*, the sun ("that planet/whose virtue leads men straight on every road") is a symbol for God, for Divine Illumination. In "Purgatorio," for example, souls may climb only in the light of the sun; once it has set, it is possible for them to descend, but they lack the power to move upward even so much as an inch. Only in the light of God may one ascend that road, for that is the light to which the soul must win.

Another allegorical theme begins immediately. Dante, in his passion to reach the light (God), races straight up the hill to it. He uses a grand and typical synecdoche to describe his speed, saying that he raced up that slope at such a pace "that the fixed foot was ever the lower."

Synecdoche is that figure of speech in which a part is taken to represent the whole. A less certain writer might have reached for all sorts of great metaphors to describe the speed of his climb. Dante focuses on a single detail that does for all. If the feet of a man climbing a steep slope move in such a way that the moving foot is forever above the one that is pausing, it follows that the climb must be taking place at a blurring speed—in fact, at an impossible rate, whereby hyperbole must be added to synecdoche as a reinforcement of the poetic effect. The point for the reader to remember is that it will not do to slide over Dante's details. They will take thinking about because they took thought to find.

There is perhaps nothing so entirely impressive about *The Divine Comedy* as its power of mind. The true mark of any writer is in the choices he makes. Having written three words, he must choose a fourth. Having written four, he must choose a fifth. Nothing happens into a good poem; everything must be chosen into it. A poem may be thought of as a construction for making choices, and it is in the quality of his choices that Dante makes his greatness known. His language and his prosody can be rough and awkward. Anyone who reads the original will wonder at times if this is really "poetry." Very well, then, let it be prose, if one insists on folly. But if it is prose, it is prose of a previously unknown order, for the depth and multiplicity of mind that seem to function at every choice have not been matched in any piece of Western writing.

Meanwhile, back at the narrative, Dante is racing up the slope to what would be immediate salvation, could he manage to reach that light. The sinner has realized he is in darkness, he has seen the light, he ardently desires it, and he races to be received by it. But salvation is not to be had that easily: Dante finds his way blocked by three beasts. There is a She-wolf that represents the sins of Incontinence, a

Lion that represents the sins of Violence and Bestiality, and a Leopard that represents Fraud. The beasts themselves are derived from
Jeremiah; the three categories of sin are derived from Aristotle. Into
these three categories fall all the sins of the world. The Three Beasts,
therefore, represent the total blindness of which the world is capable.
Symphonically, they also foreshadow the three divisions of Hell
through which Dante must journey. In the Hell of the She-wolf are
punished the sins of excessive animal appetite. In the lower Hell, the
Hell of the Lion, are punished the sins of bestial violence. In the lowest
Hell of the Leopard, are punished the sins of fraud, worse than the sins
of bestiality because they involve the perversion of the higher gift of
intellect—a beast, that is to say, can murder; but only a rational being,
by perverting the gift of rationality, can commit a fraudulent act.

These three beasts drive Dante back into the darkness, blocking
the direct and easy way to that light. In that darkness, when all seems
to have been lost, and when Dante can find no way around those
beasts of worldliness, there appears to him the figure of Virgil.

Virgil is a complex figure, combining within himself, among other
things, the classical heritage, genius, magic powers, and Dante's personal devotion. On the first level, however, it will do to take him as
representing Human Reason in its best development. More subtly, he
may be taken as Aesthetic Wisdom, the knowledge of the true poet.
For present purposes let him be taken simply as representing Human
Reason. In that role, he points out that there is no such express road
to God as Dante had imagined in racing up the hill: "He must go by
another way who would escape / this wilderness."

The other way—the long way round—is the total journey into ultimate darkness and out again to ultimate light. Such is the arduous
road of *The Divine Comedy*. It is the painful descent into Hell—to
the recognition of sin. It is the difficult ascent of Purgatory—to the
renunciation of sin. Then only may Dante begin the soaring flight
into Paradise, to the rapturous presence of God. God, that is to say,
may be found only on the other side of the total self-searching experience of a zealous life. There are no short cuts to that totally encompassing experience. Salvation must grow out of understanding, total
understanding can follow only from total experience, and experience
must be won by the laborious discipline of shaping one's absolute

attention. The object is to achieve God, and Dante's God exists in no state of childlike innocence: He is total knowledge and only those who have truly experienced knowledge can begin to approach Him.

Virgil, as Human Reason, is the first guide to that ultimate knowledge, but Virgil cannot guide Dante all the way. Reason is finite and God is infinite. The greater guide, in the medieval concept, was Faith. Reason was merely the handmaiden of Faith. Virgil can guide Dante to the recognition of sin and to its renunciation, which is to say, through Hell and to the top of Purgatory. But once at that summit, the soul has achieved purity. It has risen beyond Reason. It is ready to enter the Divine Mysteries. And there Beatrice (call her Divine Love) must take over.

It was in her infinite compassion as Divine Love that Beatrice sent Reason to the man's soul in his hour of darkness, that Reason might serve as his guide to bring him into her higher presence. One may not simply wish himself into that higher presence. That presence must be won to by devout labor.

That devout labor is what might be called the basic plot and the basic journey of *The Divine Comedy*. All that follows, once the journey has begun, is an amplification of themes that have already been established. That much understood, the writing itself will best explain itself as it unfolds—always, of course, with the help of those indispensable footnotes.

When, however, one has read all the way through the poem and has returned to reread these first Cantos, he will find many other themes rooted in them. There are four such themes that any beginning reader will do well to grasp as being particularly able to enrich his first experience.

The first has to do with Dante's sinfulness. What sin was it that had brought him into the dark wood of Error? Dante was expelled from Florence on charges of having been a grafter, and some commentators have tried to identify his guilt in that charge. In "Purgatorio" Dante himself recognizes that he is guilty of Pride, and to some extent of Wrath. He has both those offenses to pay for when he returns to Purgatory after his death. But the charges against Dante were certainly trumped up by his political enemies, and no specific act of Pride or Wrath can be cited to account for Dante's opening mood. His offense was, rather, Acedia. Let it serve to label this first theme.

The Seven Deadly Sins for which souls suffer in Purgatory are—in ascending order—Pride, Envy, Wrath, Acedia, Avarice, Gluttony, and Lust. Acedia is the central one, and it may well be the sin the twentieth century lost track of. Acedia is generally translated as Sloth. But that term in English tends to connote not much more than laziness and physical slovenliness. For Dante, Acedia was a central spiritual failure. It was the failure to be sufficiently active in the pursuit of the recognized Good. It was to acknowledge Good, but without fervor.

The spiritual awakening to which Dante comes in the Dark Wood —the enormous rebirth—is the awareness of the fact that he has not been sufficiently zealous in his pursuit of the Good. *The Divine Comedy* is the zealous journey from the man's recognized spiritual torpor (neglect of God) to the active pursuit of his soul's good (love of God). Every step of that journey may simultaneously be understood as the man's active embrace of his Godly experience, as the soul's active pursuit of the love of Good, and as the artist's active pursuit of form.

The second theme—perhaps it is not so much a theme as a method —is inseparable from the others. Call it the Five Levels. In a letter to his patron, Can Grande della Scala, Dante explicitly names four levels of meaning that he intends all the way through *The Divine Comedy—narrative, allegorical, moral,* and *anagogical.* That letter may, as many scholars contend, be a forgery. Whether it is genuine or not, what it states explicitly is clearly implicit in the writing. And to those four stated levels may be added a fifth: the journey seen as a *progress of the soul.*

Dante was a parochial man. He was persuaded that the One Truth had been revealed to him, and he was intolerant of all non-Catholic views. He refused, for example, to think of Mohammed as a religious leader but dismissed him as a schismatic and heretic and assigned to him a particularly grotesque punishment in Hell.

But if the man was parochial, the artist was universal as only art can be. *The Divine Comedy* is a triumph of art over creed. And that triumph—to paraphrase terms that Dante himself might have used —arises from the force of the Aesthetic Mysteries, which is to say, the power of form in the interplay of its structures and its levels of meaning.

The first obvious level, for example, is narrative: a travelogue. But that journey is through a country populated by second meanings. On one level Dante writes of Hell as a literal place of sin and punishment. The damned are there because they offended a theological system that enforces certain consequences of suffering. But part of that theological system has also decreed that salvation was available to all men. Christ in his ransom had procured endless mercy. One need only wish to be saved, need only surrender his soul to God in a last gasp of contrition, and he will be saved. He may have to suffer at length in Purgatory, but, once there, his place is reserved in Heaven and he will in time arrive there. Purgatory is like our modern colleges; no one can flunk out of them.

It follows, then, that the only way to get into Hell is to insist upon it. One must deliberately exclude himself from grace by hardening his heart against it. Hell is what the damned have actively and insistently wished for.

Thus, allegorically, Hell is the true goal of the damned. On the surface the state of the sinners is described in terms of sin. The wonder and the universality of it is that a reader who does not care for those terms may restate them in terms of behavior, and the "Inferno" remains entirely coherent as a dramatic treatise on self-destructive behavior. Like addicts, the damned both hate and love their self-destruction. "They yearn for what they fear," says Dante.

Thus Hell is not only a specific place but a moral and anagogical allegory of the guilty conscience of the damned. It is the projection into a physical reality of the inner state of the damned. As Purgatory is such a projection of the inner state of those who suffer toward grace. As Heaven is such another projection of the inner state of those who have achieved grace. Each environment is an allegory and a moral and anagogical commentary on the essential nature of the souls one finds in each. Hell exists from within.

In a detailed discussion in the "Purgatorio," Dante reinforces these levels of meaning by pointing out that though mortal man may deceive by hiding his true nature under false semblances, the dead, by the very nature of their aerial bodies, can only appear to be exactly what they are. The dead cannot dissemble. *What* they appear to be and *where* they appear, they are.

The third theme—let it be called the Moral Universe or the Sentient Universe—is the vast, overriding concept of the total universe that makes *The Divine Comedy* the massive vehicle it is. Every artist seeks the vehicle that will best engage all his possibilities, just as every actor seeks the perfect role for himself. So, any actor would rather play Hamlet than Uncle Tom. Hamlet gives him more chances to act.

Dante's vehicle is nothing less than the total universe. Where in all poetry is there an equivalent subject-structure? Dante not only draws a map of his universe; he walks it from end to end. But his map is both of a physical geography and of a structure of values. That universe exists on all five levels of meaning.

For Dante, as for classical man, there was no real distinction between moral and physical law; between, say, the moral law against incest and the physical law of gravity. All of matter was a projection of God's will, and what we call physical law and what we call moral law derived equally from that will. When Oedipus, though unknowingly, transgressed moral law by killing his father and marrying his mother, a plague descended upon Thebes. It would not have occurred to the Greeks that to think of a flight of locusts as a consequence of what happened in the king's bedroom was to cross categories.

Dante's physical universe is Ptolemaic. It consists of nine concentric circles (spheres) with the earth as the center. In ascending order those spheres are: the Moon, Mercury, Venus, the Sun, Mars, Jupiter, Saturn, the Fixed Stars, and the Primum Mobile. Beyond the Primum Mobile lies the Empyrean, which is the dwelling and presence of God. God is an essence that entirely surrounds and contains creation.

If God is the circumference of this nine-layered sphere, the center is the greatest distance one can travel from God. That center is the earth, and the center of that center is the bottom of Hell. Inevitably, it is there, at the Ultimate bottom of the universe, that Dante places Satan.

Satan is a powerful symbol. He is described as an unholy reverse-Trinity with three foul heads and three pairs of wings. He has been flung from Heaven to the farthest distance one can go from God. To his dark center drain all the waters of the earth, bearing the filthy sediment of all sin and uncleanliness. Satan's six wings beat madly in his efforts to escape from that foul lake but they succeed only in whipping up a freezing gale that turns all to ice, fixing him ever more securely in the bottom ice tray. From the top of Purgatory, moreover, there flow down to him the waters of Lethe, in which the finally purified souls bathe and are washed clean of every memory of sin. That memory, too, is frozen into the filthy ice about Satan.

Thus that center is the center of all weight, of all sin, of all darkness, and of all cold. And to it flows all the filth of time. Weight, sin, dark, cold, and filth are, of course, the five things farthest from God. And thus the universe becomes a scale of precise values: the closer a thing is to the center, the lower it is on that scale; the closer a thing is to the circumference, the higher it is.

The existence of that scale makes possible an enormous economy in Dante's writing. Dante need only place his finger on that map and say what he saw there. The very act of placement becomes the value judgment.

That economy is further assisted by the firm laws of the other world. As one sins, so is he punished; as he strove for grace, so is he rewarded. In Hell, then, each punishment is a symbolic analysis of the nature of the sin and of the state of the sinner's soul. The reader need only be told, for example, that the punishment of the Lustful is highest in the Infernal scale, and that it consists of being buffeted eternally round and round by a dark whirlwind. The reader knows at once that this sin, though sufficient for damnation, is the least weighty of all the sins of Hell proper, and that the nature of the sin is to allow one's soul to be buffeted round and round by the dark winds of immoderate passion. Love is a sweet human state, but by excessive physical love these sinners shut their souls from God, surrendering "reason to their appetites."

Dante's Cantos average about 140 lines. As a general thing he requires no more than twenty or thirty lines to identify the sinner and to describe the punishment. Since the value judgment is already established by the map, and since the punishment is a symbolic analysis of the sin, these essential matters are settled in short order, and Dante has the rest of his Canto available for all sorts of matters that attract his ranging mind.

Dante had once set out to be an encyclopedist. His *Il Convivio*—never finished—was an effort to set down in Italian all human "science." There is nothing that does not interest him. As a poet, moreover, he would naturally look for chances to use his dramatic, lyric, and didactic powers. So, with his structure firmly determined by its basic economy, Dante is free to range at will, packing every rift with those fascinating details that add so much to his poem. He has time for gossip, for prophecies, for marvelous dramatic interplays, for treatises on history, for analyzing the French monarchy, the corruption of the Church, the decay of Italian politics. He has time for all sorts of metaphysical treatises on such matters as the nature of the generative principle, literary criticism, meteorology—in short, for his whole unfinished encyclopedia. And he still has time to invent a death for Ulysses, to engage in a metamorphic contest with Ovid, to make side remarks to his friends. He can give full rein to his powers because he has found the inexhaustible vehicle.

The fourth principal theme will inevitably reveal itself to the careful reader, but he will lose nothing by having it in mind from the start. Call it the Architectonics. *The Divine Comedy* has often been compared to a cathedral, and, whether or not the comparison is finally apt, it is certainly true that Dante's details keep acquiring significance as one goes on and learns to look back at them from some corresponding point in the later structure. The structure, that is to say, produces a *back-illumination*.

Charon, for example, is the boatman of the damned, ferrying them across Acheron into Hell proper. He is a memorable figure. Later, one meets the Angel-Pilot who ferries souls to Purgatory. He, too, is a memorable figure. But no reasonably careful reader can fail to see that one ferryman stands in meaningful relation to the other. Thus, the Angel is not only himself, but an opposite figure to Charon, and

Charon seen backwards from the figure of the Angel acquires a dimension he did not have as an isolated figure. The development of these structural correspondences—of an endless number of them— is an everlasting and ever-enlarging source of the power of *The Divine Comedy*.

The supreme art of poetry is not to *assert* meaning but to *release* it by the juxtaposition of poetic elements. Form, in its interrelations, is the most speaking element. Because in any extended poetic structure these juxtapositions will fall into different perspectives when looked at from different points of vantage, that release of meaning is subject to endless meaningful reinterpretation. The inexhaustibility of *The Divine Comedy* is a consequence of this structural quality. It is for that reason that no one can ever finish reading it. There will always be a new way of viewing the elements. But if no man can finish the poem, any man may begin it and be the richer for having begun. The present imperfect gloss—skimming though it be—is really about all one needs to start with. And, having started, all he needs is to pay attention. The poem itself is the rest of the way, and the way is marked.

TRANSLATION

THE ART OF FAILURE

A translator's explanation of his method has no choice but to be an apology for failure. Frost may have been right when he said that "poetry is what disappears in translation." For a translator to dream of success would be overweening: what he tries for is no more than the best possible failure.

"Translation" is, in any case, the wrong word for the process of rendering a piece of writing from one language to another. The idea contained in "translation" smacks too much of that contained in "transliteration"—it seems to assume that there exists in Language A some word that will equal any given word in Language B, and that the translator need only find the equivalent word and put it in place, allowing of course for something called idiom.

But such an assumption ignores the nature of words. Semanticists claim, as a basic tenet, that no word ever means exactly the same thing twice—and that tenet takes no thought of crossing a language boundary. A look at a few of the ways in which words refuse to be exactly equivalent to other words is much to the point in identifying the translator's real work, and, by the way, in identifying one element of the poetic process. Words are complex things. We tend, in general usage, to consider only the top slice of a given word. Poets, on the other hand, are likely to use words in depth: they are interested, among other things, in the images locked inside a word, in its muscularity, in its history, in its connotations, and in its levels of usage. As soon as one begins to hunt the American-English language for words that are equivalent *in depth* to Italian words, he learns that whatever he does manage to get across the language boundary will not be got across by any simple one-for-one transliteration.

The American word "daisy," for example, labels the same flower the French intend by *la marguerite* and the Italians by *la margherita*, or at least approximately so (a botanist might be quick to say that the varieties of the European daisy are distinct from those of the American daisy). Nevertheless, those are the words one would naturally use in these three tongues for labeling any particular daisy. Semantically, that is to say, the denotations are reasonably firm.

But words consist of much more than denotation. Every word has a certain muscularity. That is to say, it involves certain speech muscles. Certainly any man who is word-sensitive is likely to linger over the difference between the long-drawn Italian *carina* and the common, though imprecise, American usage "cute" when applied to an attractive child. The physical gestures the two words invite are at least as different as the Italian child's goodbye wave (*"Fa ciao, carina"*) with the palm of the hand up, and the American child's (*"Wave bye-bye"*) with the back of the hand up. The very difference in ethnic concept between two peoples moves the words about in their mouths. As I once wrote in a poem I am not moved to cherish particularly but whose point remains:

> My mother facing a day in Avellino
> Tasted it: *una dolce giornata*.
>
> My wife's mother in Protestant Missouri
> Judges it: *it is a good day*.

There are two distinct kinds of muscularity. Other kinds could certainly be adduced. And all must function in the effort one must make to find truly equivalent language.

Every word, moreover, has a history. Sometimes the history changes out from under the word very rapidly. English "broadcast" once meant specifically "a way of sowing" and was borrowed by radio as an analogy. Meanwhile, new machines all but eliminated the old methods of broadcast-sowing, and the word has just about lost all farm connotation. What to do then when, to shift examples, one language uses a word denoting anxiety whose essential meaning is based on the history of medieval torture, when the only word in another language that will render that denotation is based on the history of, say, the internal-combustion engine? Pure hypotheticals, to be sure, but how does one find equivalents in any language for such English words as "billingsgate," or "to burke," or "boycott"—words whose meanings are inseparable from the local scene and local history in which the English language evolved?

Every word has an image locked into its roots. The English word "daisy" is a contraction of the earlier "day's eye," which is to say "the eye of day"—a lovely root image. *Marguerite* and *margherita* release a root connotation of all girls named Margaret/Marguerite/Margherita—and bless them all as lovely images. Behind that first suggestion, too, lies the true root of the Greek *margaron*, meaning "pearl"—another fine image. But what happened to "day's eye"? Not that there is any point here in arguing which is the more attractive root image. The point is simply that they are different. What then does one do for equivalent words?

And to point out only one more of many possibilities within the nature of words, every word connotes a certain level of usage. Italian *antipatico*, for example, is so common a usage that it falls readily from the lips of even very small children, whereas English "antipathetic" is a relatively learned word, and certainly not one for the normal nursery. What weight does one give this element of word usage in seeking equivalents?

Normally, we use words as simple things, paying attention to one, or at most two, levels of their meaning. But once the other levels of a word are allowed into consideration, no word is a simple thing. It becomes a complex. But if a single word is a complex, then a phrase is a complex of complexes, and a line is a complex of complexes of complexes, and a stanza, and a poem are . . . and so forth and so on.

I have now translated (or, rather, "rendered in English") two-thirds of *The Divine Comedy*. I don't honestly know how to make a theory of translation out of such musings and bewilderments as these. All I can truthfully say is that such equivalence as I have managed has happened by feel, and that I am more comfortable within specifications than I am in trying to defend theories that distort under every effort to state them.

I began to peck away at Dante because I could find no translation that satisfied my sense of the original. Let nothing in that statement imply that I have now satisfied my sense. When I read the original with my rendering in mind I have no choice but to feel sad. When I read any other translation with my rendering in mind, I feel relatively happy. No one, of course, should trust my sense of it, but I must. Who else's sense can I trust?

In looking at other translations I was distressed by the fact that none of them seemed to be using what I understood to be Dante's vulgate. They seemed rather to fall into literary language, the very sort of thing Dante took such pains to avoid. And none of them, above all else, gave me a satisfying sense of Dante's pace, which is to say, the rate at which the writing reveals itself to the reader.

I began to experiment out of curiosity. I rendered a number of Cantos in *terza rima* and satisfied myself that it could not do. English is a rhyme-poor language. It was obvious to me that the price of forcing that third rhyme into place in English was ruinous to the language. There are approximately 4,500 lines in each third of *The Divine Comedy*. One must find 1,500 triple rhymes to render each third into *terza rima*, and English has no such resources. Mechanically, it can be done, but not in anything approximating spoken American-English. I could see what wrestling agonies I had put into my own efforts in order to force the language around to that third rhyme, and the same agonies are immediately visible in every extant version in *terza rima*.

Abandoning all thought of *terza rima*, I tried blank verse. But there the language and its movement went askew on another characteristic of English verse. The blank-verse paragraph in English, as nearly as I can determine, runs to an average of about fourteen lines. (Interestingly, the paragraph of Pope's couplets runs to about the same average.) If one thinks of the structure of pauses in a poem as subtotaling points, I take that fact of English poetry to mean that blank verse pauses to complete its subthoughts about once every fourteen lines. But Dante sets his pauses (which is to say, his periods, or more usually his semicolons, or sometimes his commas) every three lines, and I take that fact to be, above all else, what determines the pace and sparseness of Dante's writing. If the fundamental unit runs from ten to twenty lines, there is room for all sorts of digression or even self-indulgence. An extra line or two, an extra image or two, an extra flourish or two, are easily possible. But if one is forcing his lines to some sort of summary every three lines, that fact must work to squeeze out all flab. Dante does, to be sure, write any number of run-on tercets, but the three-line unit remains firm as the rigorous basic measure of his way of writing. This writing is of bone and sinew.

I went on to experiment at all sorts of other possibilities. In another effort at *terza rima* I tried assonantal rhyming. Assonance may yet be a possibility for someone else. I can only report that I do not favor it as an English rhyme method. For a time I tried English couplets, thinking they might be made to render an Italian tercet: they cannot, at least not as a sustained measure. I tried various sorts of ballad stanzas: they had no hope of being for anything but the wastebasket. Then I hit on what I may as well call "dummy *terza rima*," which is to say, I kept the three-line unit but rhymed only the first and third lines. And with that it began to happen, at least for me. I could persuade myself that what came was reasonably English, reasonably poetry, and reasonably faithful to Dante's pace and to his special way of using language. What is reasonable can, of course, include an awareness of failure, but I could begin to believe this was a good enough failure to be worth investing in.

I had no theory at that point—only a feeling. And I still have no theory I can securely defend. The rest was trial and error, something like learning to walk a tightrope: if one can only manage to grab the rope when he falls, and if he can then manage to get back up, and if he falls only forward, there is always the possibility that he will make it to the other side. To let a single example do for all, the process can be illustrated from Canto viii of the "Purgatorio," which reads, in the original:

> Ben discerneva in lor la testa bionda;
>   Ma nella faccia l'occhio si smarria
>   Come virtù ch'a troppo si confonda.

The passage is part of the description of two angels that descend to Dante and his companions in the Valley of the Negligent Rulers. It is a simple enough passage as Dante goes, and almost any man with a sense of Latin roots can puzzle out most of the meaning. *Virtù* (virtue) in the Latin sense of "faculty/power/ability/generative force" (cf. "by virtue of the power invested in me") is perhaps the one word that might trip the unwary. How is one to render such a passage? In Pidgin-Literal it might read:

> Well was I discerning in them the head blond
>> but in their faces my eye was dazed
>> like a faculty which is overcome by excess.

But though such a rendering is approximately idiomatic, phrase by phrase, the sequence of phrases is not really intelligible as a communication in English. The passage is still in no spoken tongue, but, rather, in an unspeakable hodgepodge neither Italian nor English. So one might work toward a more speakable, which is to say, communicable, equivalent:

> I saw clearly that their heads were blond,
>> but looking into the faces my eyes grew dazed
>> like an overstimulated faculty of the senses.

That begins to be closer, but now one runs into a peculiarity of the way Dante describes the workings of his senses. If one has been reading from the beginning of *The Divine Comedy* he is used to this way Dante has of describing such matters. Dante often describes the workings of his eyes as if he could focus on, say, the forehead of a distant figure, seeing nothing else, and as if he then had deliberately to move his eyes downward in order to focus on the figure's nose. It is some such thing he is saying here: staring at the angels he can see that their hair is blond, but when he looks down from their hair to their faces, his eyes grow dazzled, overstimulated by the light that shines from them. Obviously, it would be impossible, at any distance, not to be entirely blinded by such light, and the literalist has firm grounds for arguing that Dante could not have seen either the hair or the faces of the angels. Such a device must be accepted by the reader as a well-established mannerism.

With that much understood, then, the passage may be simplified. Were one simply communicating Dante's thought in an English prose paraphrase it might be stated: "I could make out clearly that their hair was blond, but when I focused on their faces, my eyes were dazzled by the excess of light they gave forth."

Let the rendering remain ragged: it contains the essential intent. But the passage is written as poetry and it must be rendered within meter, rhyme, and in a language sufficient to its emotional intent. After much scratching and scrambling for a rhyme (and it sometimes happens that the very rhyme you want has been used in the preceding tercet and may not, therefore, be repeated so soon) I came up with the following:

> I could distinctly see their golden hair,
>> but my eyes drew back defeated from their faces
>> like a sense perceiving more than it can bear.

Such a rendering covers the law perhaps, and at times I have been forced to leave some of Dante in no better state than that, but certainly it is nothing to be satisfied with. I especially do not like the feel of that last line in English. As nearly as I can say it, the English word choice is being forced from Dante's Italian rather than being developed in sequence by the normal flow of English.

Whereupon, after more floundering I came to rest on:

> I could see clearly that their hair was gold,
>> but my eyes drew back bedazzled from their faces,
>> defeated by more light than they could hold.

It is simple enough to see that there are all sorts of things literally wrong with such a passage. The original says "the head" and the passage says "hair." There is nothing, at least explicitly, in the original that says the eye "drew back." *Virtù* his disappeared, and "defeated" is certainly not the same thing as "confounded."

When the charge is put in those terms, I have no defense and very little, if any, theory on which to base a defense. Nor any hope of arguing that I have achieved a perfect rendering. All I can really argue, as lamely as need be, is that within the essential failure, this final version *feels* enough like the original, and *feels* enough like English poetry (or at least verse) to allow me to conclude that I have probably caught it as well as I shall be able to. There must be some theory of translation implicit in these feelings, but in practice I suspect any translation turns out to be a long series of such individual cases, each met on its own grounds, and that each is finally settled by *feel*. What has any poet to trust more than the *feel* of the thing? Theory concerns him only until he picks up his pen, and it begins to concern him again as soon as he lays it down. But when the pen is in his hand he has to write by itch and twitch, though certainly his itch and twitch are intimately conditioned by all his past itching and twitching, and by all his past theorizing about them.

THE SITUATION
OF POETRY

The pieces here grouped together—two essays, an editorial, and an interview with Salvatore Quasimodo—were written without conscious reference to one another over a period of nearly four years. But though they are only imperfectly related, it is my impression that they can be read together as notes on the situation of poetry in our time. They are least coherent, perhaps, in tone. All of them do, however, enter into the question of the poet's relation to society and of his function within it.

"Poverty on Parnassus" appeared in SR as part of a series by many hands on the economic situation of the arts and of the artist in our time. Since most of our poets are in some way connected with a college or university, the article's concern is with the influence of the academies on our poetry.

But the academies are only one influence. With the loud emergence of the Beat Generation, the ever-present anti-intellectuals in the arts were given a label, a banner, and a credo of a sort. Some critics have been fond of referring to these two groups as the "Made" and the "Unmade" poets, trying thereby to distinguish between the formalities of the academic poets and the unrevised outpourings of the Beats. All such simplifications are unreliable, but to the extent that such labels may serve, "Poverty on Parnassus" discusses the situation of the "Made" poets and "Epitaph for the Dead Beats" the situation of the "Unmade," or as they are sometimes called the "Rumpled" poets (by obvious analogy to a bed). "Epitaph" was written some four years after the first article.

Because I must believe that the true course of poetry is set by no school but by the continuity of the civilization of the arts and by the power of that civilization on mankind, I find "Literature Undefended" (published as an editorial in SR but originally prepared as part of a talk to the National College English Association) relevant, and necessary as an effort to set the question in larger terms.

And because Salvatore Quasimodo discussed the question again in something like the largest possible terms, I cannot resist adding my interview with him as it appeared in SR. The merit of such an order is that the tone—and therefore the discussion—deepens, raising the great questions after the lesser ones have been touched upon.

POVERTY ON PARNASSUS
THE ECONOMICS OF POETRY

No good poet writing today in America is permitted the illusion that he might make his living from the sale of his poems. If he means to eat, therefore, and if the good fairy has failed to provide him with a private income, he must do something else. Overwhelmingly that something else has turned out to be university (including, of course, college) teaching, and that identification of the poets with the universities must certainly be counted as a ponderable influence on the directions our more recent poetry has taken.

By now at least 85 per cent of our serious poets under sixty are working, or have recently worked, at some sort of university career. There is even, as Charles Fenton of Yale pointed out a year or so ago,* a fairly definite progression by decades among the teacher-poets: the first generation of them, now fiftyish, tends to own a simple bachelor's degree; the middle generation, now fortyish, seems to have dawdled about in graduate school long enough to have acquired a master's degree; and the most recent generation, now thirtyish, tends to come armed with the full union-card doctorate. The relationship, one can see, is becoming increasingly formal.

Nor does it end there. The universities not only provide the poets with jobs but have become the principal sponsors of the publication of poetry. As the larger-circulation magazines have settled into their policy of paying less and less attention to poetry (and none at all to literary criticism as distinct from book reviewing) the universities have obligingly put up the subsidies on which dozens of literary quar-

* As of July 28, 1956. Charles Fenton has since died.

terlies continue to publish poetry and criticism at a loss. Every one in Academe seems happy with the arrangement: the poets can now find themselves in print almost as often as if they were critics (which most of them are, or try to be, between whiles); and the trustees— hard-headed and far-sighted good men and true in the Madison Avenue tradition of Western Man—have been persuaded that their insolvent quarterlies are good public relations, and that they attract to the faculty good men who, the prospect of family-publication before them, will be too dazzled to check their salaries against the latest cost-of-living index.

These quarterlies, moreover, are invariably edited by faculty members and are primarily distributed to other universities. The universities, that is to say, have taken over not only the function of the patron and of the arbiter but have bid to be the audience as well— to be at least a very articulate and persuasive segment of the audience, and one endowed with a considerable number of influential journals through which to express its tastes and requirements.

Thus, the arriving poet, university trained to begin with, joins a university faculty, publishes primarily on university subsidy under university editorship, reads primarily the poetry and criticism that the universities sanction or have themselves developed, and when he publishes his own slim volume (quite possibly on a university press imprint) finds it reviewed for praise or damnation very largely by university men in university magazines. And when, finally, he has achieved some sort of reputation he will find his principal added income in stumping the lecture platform—from university to university.

Such a near-total absorption of our poets into the universities has persuaded many commentators that there is serious danger of a kind of poetic inbreeding. Certainly the arguments against a university-poetry, to the extent that such a poetry does in fact exist, are not hard to marshal.

The first argument is from history. The fact of English literature seems to be that none of our master poets and few of our great minor poets were teachers. One might cite Housman and possibly Matthew Arnold (though Arnold was not properly speaking a teacher) and I would not willingly ignore Lewis Carroll, but beyond these one would have to leap back to Gray and to a number of very minor eighteenth-century poets, and beyond them to no poets of any consequence at all who could properly be classified as school or university teachers. The argument follows, then, that, since good poets of the past have almost entirely avoided teaching, teaching is an evil that all good poets, now and to come, should shun. Such reasoning may seem persuasive at first, but the argument is in fact merely verbal. The obvious fact is that the present-day university bears so little resemblance to the past university that it is pointless to assume that university-then equals university-now simply because one word pretends to describe both of them. The modern university may be better or worse than the past university but it is not the same thing.

The second of these arguments is from passion. It assumes that the university is an "ivory tower" and that life "must be gone out to." Thus, exhorters of the spirit will be heard crying: "Go out and swing a pick! Or go sell groceries! Or go drive a truck! But get out where life is!" The argument is not only silly but is itself academic, and it confuses the difference between experience and simple activity. What poem of any consequence has ever been brought about because the poet was a ditch digger, a grocer, or a truck driver? Even Whitman talked about the broadaxe a sight more than he ever swung one. The subject of poetry is human experience, and experience is not a physical occupation. I am tempted to argue that experience—the only kind of experience that counts—is an inner scale on which one balances his life against his death. A man either has that scale or he hasn't, and he either is able to find poetic forms that respond to it or he isn't, but the scale itself is independent of surface environment. Emily Dickinson stayed home and Florence Nightingale went to the Crimea, but it was Emily Dickinson who wrote the poems. The planet is large enough to be visible from any window, even one in an "ivory tower."

As a matter of fact, I am not at all sure what "ivory tower" means when applied to today's university. The term may have had some quaint appositeness when used to describe the mental habitat of an Oxford don of fifty or a hundred years ago, but certainly if today's university is to be labeled an "ivory tower" it is at least worth remembering that the faculty suites are preponderantly occupied by men, now fortyish, who grew up in a very un-ivoried Depression, who served from two to five years in the armed services, and who have since returned to some sort of heavily earthbound mortgage and the statistical 2.7 children. Such vital statistics are hardly the stuff that Romance or William Shakespeares are made of, but they certainly do seem reasonable evidence that this generation of college teachers is living somewhere within the area of life-and-death as it happens in the practical experience of American man at the mid-century.

But once these false arguments have been answered there is still the more pertinent objection that the poet turned academician may tend to become overspecialized. Not overspecialized in his techniques, one must add, but in his human concern, which runs a danger of becoming specifically literary. Every curriculum, it must be recognized, is based on rationality. I suspect that there lurks in every academy some ghostly form of the idea that everything is explainable. Poetry is a fiercely intellectual art at its best, but its fundamental concern is with those irrationalities we call the emotions. The universities are analytical and critical in intent. They are not creative. The poet in a university is in about the position of a pole vaulter at a convention of anatomists. He and they are both concerned with muscles, but not in the same way. Let the pole vaulter get the notion that the way to train is by cutting up corpses rather than by running and jumping, and all will be lost.

A poet working in a university, moreover, has to do a lot of talking, and certainly it will help his prospects if he can seem to talk brilliantly. It is impossible to doubt that much of the disproportion of recent poetic attitudes has started from the fact that certain kinds of poems give a lecturer an easy shot at brilliance. I do not hate Eliot's "Waste Land." Neither do I love it. I believe it to be a very considerable venture, and I do not believe it to be a fraction of the poem that, say, Frost's "Home Burial" is. But Frost by the very crystalline quality of his success robs the lecturer of easy remarks. Eliot, on the other hand, is the lecturer's dream; any teaching fellow who has read a few of the compilations of footnotes and explanations to "The Waste Land" can milk that poem for at least a dozen lectures guaranteed to stun any group of undergraduates. And, car-

ried away by his own borrowed brilliance, that teaching fellow may
have a hard time remembering that he has not been talking about
poetry at all but only about allusion and quotation. Even more seriously, he may come to assume that Frost is not a good poet because
he lacks footnotes. It is in this way that Ezra Pound, at his best a
good poet, is often presented as if he were a great one; while Robert
Burns, for example, a great poet, tends not to be presented at all.

As good an example as any of the kind of academic stupidity I mean
is Randall Jarrell's belated discovery that Robert Frost really is a
poet. Professor Jarrell (Woman's College of the University of North
Carolina) was splashing in a swimming hole in Bloomington, In-
diana, when the lightning struck. Typically enough, his swim was
between sessions of the Summer School for Critics. Splashing about
in the hot summer, Professor Jarrell found himself remembering
lines, passages, and whole poems of Robert Frost, and suddenly realized that he had never memorized them. They had just stuck. There
must have been an oversized splash at the moment the thought
came: "Frost is really a poet! Footnotes or no footnotes, he is a
poet!" Whereupon, I gather from the tone of Professor Jarrell's prose,
he beat his way up from his own surf, a bit like a damp butterfly,
and fluttered off to deliver the great news to *The Partisan Review*
in two momentous instalments—the same *Partisan*, though not the
same issue, in which Leslie Fiedler (also on the School for Critics
staff) had closed a monumentally stupid review of one of Frost's
books with a pained cry to the faithful: "Don't read this book!" The
danger, I gathered, was that the faithful might be tempted to write
like Frost, and that to do so they would first have to renounce the
academic credo.

Nor will it serve to dismiss Jarrell and Fiedler simply as fritillaries.
Once they correct for a certain natural tendency to flutter, they can
swoop like hawks when it comes to scooping up a reference on the
run, and they eat their weight in symbols every day. The disease they
suffer from is a fear of simplicity. Nor do they stand alone; they have
simply been more successful than thousands of other monographers
in the universities, and it is certainly chargeable to the universities
that such critics have been permitted their influence by the union
ground rules of academic advancement. "Publish or perish" is still the

law in the academies. "Write. Write something. Build that bibliog-raphy!" and so under the pressure to be brilliant the intellect of poetry tends to become merely intellectualoid.

What the universities and the new criticism they have bred seem to have lost sight of in the course of achieving other and admirable insights is the simple fact that once the poet has achieved technical competence the badness of a bad poem is always a failure of char-acter. I once sat for two hours to hear a panel of university critics prove that Joyce Kilmer's "Trees" is a bad poem. They subjected it to every sort of technical dissection without identifying a single device that could not be found in poems they all would agree were good poems. And they finally gave it up without having once sug-gested that it is a bad poem because it is a silly poem—silly because the author's attitude toward himself and toward his subject matter was both jejune and grandiose.

And if driving the young into being technically brilliant about poetry at the expense of more basic concerns were not enough, the universities have sinned again by tending to become bogs of re-spectable conformity. When a "professor" from one of the trade schools in agriculture or education or business administration talks like a pompous and overfed fool, that is bad enough, but when the faculties in what-should-be-the-humanities begin to make the same set of noises, then the universities must stand accused of their fearful timidity, their terrified don't-scare-away-the-businessmen-who-support-us conformity, and their incipient betrayal of all intellectual ven-turesomeness. When Shelley left Oxford he announced that all he brought away with him was a valuable disgust. To the rather alarm-ing extent that our faculties are made up of intellectual sheep our universities are profoundly worth being disgusted with, and woe to the poet who marries them in love and for better or worse.

At the same time, I would be ungrateful to my own good luck were I to fail to acknowledge that many of the larger, richer, and thereby more independent universities have been not only consist-ently venturesome but generous as well. I taught at Harvard for seven years right after the war and when I was working full-time it was a two-afternoon-a-week job. It was no way to get rich, but it kept the family bills paid and it left me large chunks of time in which to

write. Moreover, of my last three years at Harvard one was spent on
a sabbatical in Europe and one in happily doing as I pleased on a
Ford Grant. Since then I have taught for three years at Rutgers, and
I am now scheduled to spend my fourth year in Rome on an American Academy of Arts and Letters Grant. I call it princely. And
though I realize that I have been lucky I have not been uniquely so.
The universities (in combination with the foundations), if one can
resist being swallowed into their orthodoxies, can be generous with
the one gift above all others—time.

That is the supreme gift because, finally, a man is defined by what
he does with his human attention. The poet must keep his attention
ready to receive the poem when it comes. He cannot keep office
hours, and he cannot sit down and will himself to write a poem. He
has to wait for it, and he has to let the world go hang when the poem
comes. As Frost once put it: "If you want to be a poet you either
have to farm or cheat your employer."

I see no reason for the poets to stay out of the universities if they
will insist on being irregulars, and if they will have the moral assurance to cheat with a clear conscience. The danger is that too many of
them will cheat the poetry in favor of the employment. Too many
of them have joined the universities rather than lived off them. For a
piddling salary they have set themselves to be brilliant instead of
real. They are even in danger of becoming socially respectable. Even
their poems, in too many cases, are beginning to look as proper as
Nixon's dog. It is from that sort of empty-brightness and from the
manufactured passion that the good poet-teachers will have to rescue
their writing. Certainly the work of the best of them seems to indicate
that they have learned their own rescue.

EPITAPH FOR THE
DEAD BEATS

It wasn't much fun as rebellions go. Heaven knows the young need their rebellions. And let it be said of the Beats that there was a time when they might almost have been taken as an intellectual uprising. By now, however, it seems clear enough that the rebellion has gone for kicks, that what offered itself as intellectual refreshment has turned out to be little more than unwashed eccentricity, and that one more Parnassus has turned out to be a grimy dive not much different from the speakeasy or the back room of the Communist cell meeting.

The fact is that the Beat Generation is not only juvenile but certainly related to juvenile delinquency through a common ancestor whose best name is Disgust. The street-gang rebellion has gone for blood and violence. The Beats have found their kicks in an intellectual pose, in drugs (primarily marihuana, but also benzedrine, mescaline, peyote, assorted goofballs, and occasionally heroin), and in wine, Zen, jazz, sex, and a carefully mannered jargon.

There is in all of them an innate fidget. As high priest Kerouac tried to dramatize—at least to the extent that monotony can be drama—the Beats talk endlessly about serenity, detachment, and mangled Zen, but the last thing they know how to do is sit still. Were it not for the fact that the narcotics squad drives them to secrecy, and that few of them can afford fast cars, they would be off racing from roadhouse to roadhouse in an excellent imitation of their once-flapper and once-flaming parents. The impulse to run away from convention (while remaining close enough to it to flaunt it) is the same as it ever was. Nor is the search for "kicks" finally distinguishable from "making whoopee" back in the super-melogorgeous days of the cat's pajamas.

And like every essentially adolescent rebellion, that of the Beat Generation is marked by an orthodoxy as rigid as the blue laws. The Beats wear identical uniforms. They raise nearly identical beards (now beginning to disappear in reaction to the crop of beards being raised on campus by would-be beatnikoids). They practice an identical aversion to soap and water. They live in the same dingy alleys. They sit around in the same drab dives listening to the same blaring jazz with identical blanked-out expressions on their identical faces. And any one of them would sooner cut his throat than be caught doing anything "square."

It is clearly in the nature of all our rebel youth movements to need a touch of the illicit. The flappers and their plastic-age boy friends made a ritual of drinking rotgut, less because the human nervous system is naturally attracted to bad alcohol than because drinking it was against the law. The Young Communists plotted in secret meetings with dramatic precautions against undercover agents and dramatic fears of being raided, or they distributed pamphlets and howled from soap boxes in ecstatic defiance of "the Cossacks." The G.I. generation had its potential rebellion largely blurred by army restrictions and could do little more than grumble or go AWOL on a binge, but that much at least they did manage regularly enough. The Beat Generation has marihuana and the ritual of dodging the "narcos"—the narcotics squad.

The need to be illegal in some way is a simple enough need to thumb one's nose at society. The need to make a ritual of the illegality is as juvenile as the basic gesture itself. Let four Beats gather in a desert to fire up some marihuana and at least two of them will mention the narcos and look carefully in all directions before they bring the stuff out of hiding. It is exactly the ritual of four high school pals about to sneak a smoke in the boys' room.

The Beats have carried their little drama a step further by adding to it their special argot. The marihuana is "tea." The rolled cigarette, looking very much like a paper-wrapped toothpick, is a "joint." The butt is a "roach." You light up, take a deep drag, and pass it on, holding the smoke in your lungs as long as possible. You save the roachers when they get too small to hold, wad them up, pick the tobacco from the end of a "straight" (a regular cigarette), put in the wadded roach, crimp in the end of the straight, and fire it up for one last drag. Meanwhile, the chicks stare off glassy-eyed into the Ultimate-All and keep saying, "Yeh! . . . hyeh! . . . hyeh!"—long drawn out, ecstastic, and aspirate. I mean like real cosmic, man.

Ideally, the Beat plays it cool, talking a great deal about a serene detachment from the materialism of the square and the corniness of the hot hipster. But put him on wheels and he instantly becomes a raging hot-rodder, distinguishable from the leather-jacket boys only by his volubility in discoursing on "the magnitude of the risk" as he spins his way around a tricky curve.

Speed is, of course, another drug, the illusion of one more escape. In the kind of Beat who most resembles the late Jimmy Dean (who was most nearly a middle ground between the Beats and the leather-jacket hoods, and who finally found the big crack-up he had long been looking for) speed is some sort of death wish.

It is, simply enough, a child's game without the easy freshness of the child's imagination. To the Beat, anyone over thirty is "The Enemy." One trouble, of course, is that by now most of the boys and girls Father Kerouac celebrated in *The Subterraneans* are over the line into enemy territory.

But whatever its foibles, and whether "Beat" is taken to mean "done in," as most people seem to understand it, or "beatific," as Kerouac has been insisting, the separation of the Beat Generation from "square" society was conceived as an intellectual and spiritual revolution. The Beat is a Krazy Kat longing to be stoned by the Mouse he loves, who, in his turn, always manages to fling his brick despite the worst Officer Pup can do. He is Charlie Chaplin ridiculously in love and being chased by cops. He is the jazz-man blowing his soul out in a dive, or wailing through the jail bars. He lives in skid-row-under-the-stars in the company of other "personal madmen poets"—the phrase is Kerouac's. He is a soul rescuing its identity from square conformity. His object is to escape the blindness of the square not only by disassociation, but by a systematic flouting of all square values. The rationale of this disassociation, or so he insists, is Zen.

Zen is an ancient way of life whose ends can be achieved only through a lifetime of rigorous spiritual discipline, and I certainly have no notion of posing as an expert on it. Yet, though its method and discipline are profoundly complicated, Zen is profoundly simple in its basic Buddhist goal of achieving absorption into the All. Zen has been called a religion without a creed; yet it has a priesthood and its candidates must undergo a training as demanding as that imposed by any religion. Its rituals are basically rituals of purification from the dross of matter and of identification with the ultimate life force.

But though the Beats have cried loud the name of Zen, the boys and girls have never been close to adopting Zen discipline. The last thing they want on earth is a discipline. They have, rather, raided from Zen whatever offered them an easy rationale for what they wanted to do in the first place. What they seem to have found most attractive in Zen is the idea of the holiness of the personal impulse, and the dramatic role of the Zen lunatic.

By ritual detachment from materiality, and by ritual meditation on the All, the Zen disciple prepares to achieve that point at which all trace of the world's dross will be purged from his mind. At that point there is left only the pure, the spiritual, the holy, and the eternal. The self will have been absorbed into the All. And at that point, whatever speaks to the consciousness is ultimate and true. That goal achieved, every impulse of the soul is an impulse of holiness.

The idea is not, of course, uniquely Zen. It is, in fact, common to all religions whose goal is the surrender of reason to faith after proper purification. At the top of the Mount of Purgatory, Dante achieves an identical state of purification wherein he is free to act entirely on impulse, since his every impulse has become holy.

To the Beats, however, Zen purification has been reduced to little more than "get high and let it spill." Drugs, alcohol, long hours of voodoo sessions with jazz or bongo drums, plus a very eager self-hypnosis, make up the way to a "flip," which may be anything from an epileptic seizure to an inner illumination.

Most Beats are careful not to flip too far out. The really cool ones do not want to flip at all, nor even to get too high. What they want is a "low-high," a kind of serene marihuana-float that will induce a heightened awareness of sounds, smells, colors, and time. They are, that is to say, sensation seekers on the trail of a mildly "mystical" experience. I am surprised, in fact, that they have systematically overlooked the possibilities of laughing gas as a stimulus to semimystical hallucination, and I recommend that they look into William James's *The Varieties of Religious Experience* for some interesting details on this point. With the narcos sending in bearded, poetry-writing undercover men to make the scene and raid the tea parties—as they did recently in New York—it might be useful to know that there is, or so I am advised, no law against the inhalation of nitrous oxide.

On this level, Beat ritual is no more than sensation-seeking, which is itself the mark of an overcomfortable and sterile generation. The Beats like to claim the obsessive violence of Rimbaud as theirs, but too much of what they do is much closer to the raveled nerve ends of a Huysmans. For the Beats are sprung of a generation that had it easy. When someone accused Kenneth Rexroth (an *hombre*, may I say) of being Beat, he answered "Beat, Hell!—I've been beaten." And certainly the Beats would not be out on their particular limb of the nervous system had they had to face a tougher problem of basic subsistence or of basic survival. Had the Beats reached their early twenties in time for the Depression bread lines or for the army's dreary combination of foxholes and boredom, they would certainly have found other business than the elaborate cultivation of their sensations and of their purified sacred impulses.

The second aspect of Zen upon which the Beats have seized most avidly is the Zen-lunatic. The holy madman is a figure to be found in many religions. In Zen, as nearly as I understand it, the lunacy is cultivated as part of the long discipline of detaching oneself from the material appearances of reality and from the conventions of material rationality. As with Rimbaud, the goal is the deliberate derangement of all the senses in order to open oneself to the larger reality to which convention is blind. One plays the fool for God.

There is an innate nobility in the idea of playing the fool for God. David, as an example of humility, put by his majesty and danced before the Ark (II Samuel vi, 14). But these boys and girls come closer to playing the fool for the fun of it, drawing upon the Zen-lunatic as a sanction for their antics. Shedding one's clothes in public, for example, is a well-established Beat prank (the point of which is probably to prove one's purity of all traces of soap and water). Allen Ginsberg has even made the point by stripping naked in the course of a public lecture. Another kind of antic was demonstrated by three Beat poets at the end of a long radio interview in Chicago last year. Closing out the program, the announcer (Studs Terkel) asked if they had anything more they wanted to say. They replied that, yes, they had a message for the world, and they were, of course, invited to give it. Their three messages were, in order: "Fried shoes." "Meow." And "Chicago is a wose" (i.e., a "rose" with a lisp).

So much for the intellectual revolution. To the extent that the Beat Generation can be thought of as a literary movement, it has been systematically vitiated by this insistence on the holiness of the impromptu and by the urge to play the lunatic. Whether or not Jack Kerouac has traces of a talent, he remains basically a high school athlete who went from Lowell, Massachusetts, to Skid Row, losing his eraser en route. His method of composition, as he himself has described it, is to put a roll of paper in the typewriter and to bang out eight or ten feet a day. Nothing must be changed because "whatever you try to delete . . . that's what's most interesting to a doctor."

I take Kerouac's particular phrasing of that point as symptomatic of a narcissistic sickliness in all Beat writing. "This is important," it says, "because it happened to sacred me." The object seems to be to document one's own psyche on the assumption that every reader will find it as interesting as your psychiatrist does. Sorry, boys: I find it zany without illumination, precious rather than personal, and just plain dull.

For the Zen-spill turns out to be simply a license to write without revision. "It's a new method of composition," Allen Ginsberg told me over the phone a while back. He was assuring me that the first part of "Howl" was written entirely without revision. He had, he confessed, tinkered a bit with the second part.

Ginsberg, for all his carefully cultivated (and natural) zaniness, is a writer far above Kerouac in my estimation. I find that first part of "Howl" a compelling piece of writing. I also find it impossible to believe (though I may be confessing my own square blindness in saying so) that any man could put together without revision as tight a catalogue as I find there. By a "tight catalogue" I mean a piling up of specific details that are intimately related, that maintain interest despite lengthy enumeration, that move at a reader-compelling pace, and that mount to a unified effect that is somehow greater than the sum of its parts. Perhaps it was written exactly as Ginsberg says it was. Or perhaps he had prepared a great deal of it in his mind before committing it to paper. Perhaps he is simply making a claim for effect. All I can do here is record my need to doubt Ginsberg's insistence that the catalogue was entirely, or even substantially, impromptu.

But whatever the truth of the matter, and ready as I am to admire that first part of "Howl," I cannot find that Ginsberg has written anything worth reading since "Howl." Nor can I find any vein of poetic gold in Ferlinghetti, in Corso, or in the odds and ends of the less-well-known Beats. As the literary heritage of the Beat Generation, I conclude, we are left the unreadable un-novels of Kerouac and the first part of "Howl." Add the Beat influence on a few writers such as Norman Mailer who were on their way before the Beats, but took some of their later direction from behind the beard. It still seems a thin enough achievement for what has been the most-talked-of "literary" movement of the last decade. Its very paucity serves to underline the fact that even the literary leaders of the Beats have made their careers primarily in personal eccentricity rather than in writing.

There remains William S. Burroughs, whose *Naked Lunch* is a powerful empathetic descent into the Hell of dope addiction. But though Burroughs has been claimed by the Beats and has been featured in collections of Beat writing, he is, in simple fact, his own kind of madman, a lost soul who has skidded through every mud at the bottom of the world in his journey from one addiction to another. A writer of careful horrors, Burroughs certainly has admitted revision as part of his craft. His literary ancestry may perhaps be best described as a combination of surrealism and Henry Miller. The point is that he would have written exactly as he does write had there never been a Beat Generation. And though many readers will find Burroughs's writing revolting, the revulsion is from reality. Its passion has been suffered rather than theorized.

Aside from the frivolity of depending upon improvisation as a method of composition, it is exactly in its tendency to be theorized rather than suffered that Beat writing seems thinnest. It tends too readily to become not intellect but exhibitionism posing as intellect. It talks endlessly about itself (like those endless dull movies about making movies). And it claims even to be a revolution in human values, but the fact is that the Beat Generation is basically the product of a false dilemma.

There is always reason enough for the young to rebel from the patterns of American complacency. Up at 6:30 to punch an eight o'clock time card, and home at five to watch TV on the installment plan can hardly be expected to recommend itself to the young as a romance with the universe. Nor are the patterns of two-car and swimming-pool success much more attractive when it all comes down to sitting around on the patio and small-talking the world from martini to martini.

The young may be blatant, but their rebellions are always essentially noble. At the core of the Beat rebellion there lies a single, simple, all-embracing distinction between what is "square" and what is "hip." It is, in fact, all but impossible for a Beat to speak ten consecutive words without using one or both of those terms. They define the center of his world. By "square" the Beat means "complacent, stodgy, sterile, spiritually dead." By "hip" he means "aware"—aware of the life force, of reality, of the universe.

And were it a simple choice between going Madison Avenue and going Beat, I should certainly insist that the Beat has all the merit on his side.

The Beats have permitted themselves the ignorant assumption that they have stumbled on ultimate answers. What they have ignored in their youth and insolence is the simple fact that the human position has always been a middle term between good and evil, and that the simple continuity of man and woman born of man and woman, and seeking to transmit through every confusion a sense of the value of that continuity, is the one human position there is. It is an imperfect position, but it is the enduring one, and it will survive every doctrinaire fad.

What the surviving Beats have yet to learn is that they, too, must in time peter out into a random Bohemianism (as they have, by and large, already done) or take their own places within that continuity, to be accused in time, and with reason enough, by the confusions and rejections of their own young.

Bless their fling. May every child in his mad adolescence find parents who can remember their own madness. Perhaps the Beat Generation's dabble in Zen will even teach that detachment that leads to mercy and compassion. Even had the rebellion of the Beats lacked all theory, the very fact that the young will yet find their re-bellion is itself a cause for hope, the point of which seems to become remarkably clear when we lost souls on the faculty wander into a fraternity house for an evening session with our pink-scrubbed future corporation idiots.

And still, as rebellions go, this Beat jazz wasn't really much fun. As a literary movement it began and ended just about nowhere. As a set of antics, it still has a bit of mileage in it. They are still playing at it in the Village, out there at North Beach, and at Venice West. Certainly there is no problem in coming by marihuana in Chicago.* In Denver, I noted recently, a joint that bills itself as a Beat dive runs night after night with a fifty-foot line of high school and college kids waiting to get in. But if the Beats had any sort of rebellion going once, there seems to be little enough left of it now beyond a fad for hip-talk and blare-jazz in crumby dives. That's dead enough, as the man said waving away the buzzards; let's bury it.

˙I hope the next time the young go out for an intellectual rebellion, they will think to try the library. It's still the most subversive build-ing in town, and it's still human headquarters. And even rebels can find it useful to know something, if only to learn to sit still with a book in hand.

* And so it was in early 1960. I have not looked for it since.

LITERATURE UNDEFENDED

THE RESONANCE OF THE
CIVILIZING TONGUE

Ours must be a literary age, because the instant a person mentions
literature everyone in sight begins to defend it. Helen of Troy had
fewer heroes between her and the Greeks than literature has between
it and whatever besiegers are at the gates.

It may be that some sort of attacking force does, in fact, exist. If
it does, I am not worried by it. It is the defenders I am wary of, and
foremost among them are those apologists who begin by asserting that
"Literature Is Useful," and who thereupon proceed to praise the
study of literature in the name of communication skills. Reduced to
its basic absurdity, their argument is that the study of literature is
important because it prepares a man to write a better business letter
and thus to become more employable within the corporate structure
of American society. One may as well argue that surgical training is
important because it prepares a man to do a better job of carving his
Christmas goose. It does, but who cares?

It is a debasement to make the study of literature a substitute for
the minimum course in literacy. The fact that a certain amount of
what goes on in educational theory argues for just such a substitution
is no justification, but a cause for concern. The study of literature is
self-justifying. No apology is required. None is in order.

Literature is one of the central continuing experiences of the race.
It is no cultural ornament. It is as discreet a method of knowledge as
is science, and the kind of knowledge literature makes available is
not approachable by scientific method. Through literature, the voices
of mankind's most searching imaginations remain alive to all time.
No man is half-civilized until those voices have sounded within him.

A savage, after all, is simply a human organism that has not received enough news from the human race. Literature is one most fundamental part of that news. One needs to hear Job lift his question into the wind; it is, after all, every man's question at some time. One needs to stand by Oedipus and to hold the knife of his own most terrible resolution. One needs to come out of his own Hell with Dante and to hear that voice of joy hailing the sight of his own stars returned to. One needs to run with Falstaff, roaring in his own appetites and weeping into his own pathos. What one learns from those voices is his own humanity. He learns what it is to carry about within mortal meat a bulb of brain wired to a bush of dendrites. Until he has heard those voices deeply within himself, what man can have any sizable idea of himself?

Literature, however, is never about ideas, but always and only about *the experience of ideas*. Scientists and philosophers discuss ideas. The reader of a good poem does not discuss ideas with the poet; he *becomes* the poet and relives the experience of the poet's imagination.

That experience is a subtle and far-reaching thing. In the act of a good poem or of a play or novel or short story, the good reader lives a life, or a part of a life, which otherwise could not have occurred to him. And he is detached from that experience at the same time that he knows his own life is very much involved. That experience, moreover, is heightened by being shaped into form; the accidental is eliminated. If the form is good, everything works toward perception. There are no distractions. And because form is indestructible, the experience is always there to be returned to. Should life distract him, the reader can always return to the purity of experience within form, to find once more, and ever green, the center of value uncluttered by peripheral confusions.

The experience of great literature, above all, is inseparable from the experience of great language, and language is forever one of the profoundest activities of the human race. Language greatly used has all the sanction of a sacrament; the race is as incapable of forgetting a great poem as it is of losing its last wish under the stars. The resonance of great language taking place within the forms of great imagination is the civilizing force. To dismiss that resonance as merely useful is to strip society of its culture and to offer it only a technology in return. That resonance is to the life of man what breath is to his body. Art is the way the mind breathes.

As a practicing pessimist, I can locate most of my fears for the future of the United States in the disappearance of that fundamental resonance from the language of official pronouncement. Certainly a nation so lacking in resonance that it can accept federal prose as a language capable of legislating human destinies is a nation part way to the door of darkness. Does any man seriously believe he can hope to discover who we are by reading the day's prose from Washington?

Let him try it, and then let him return to the Declaration of Independence to hear again the resonance of what we were in the beginning. "We hold these truths to be self evident, that all men are created equal, that they are endowed by their Creator with certain unalienable Rights, that among these are Life, Liberty and the pursuit of Happiness."

Who can imagine a statement of such force and resonance except as the product of minds shaped and informed by a life-giving contact with all that continuity of experience we call the humanities? There is no education and there is no civilization except as it keeps alive and transmits that resonance. There is no society worth preserving except as that resonance echoes in the voices of its laws, its legislators, and its citizens. There is no question of defending literature. It defends us. Without its voices in us, we are all indefensible.

INTERNAL MAN AND
EXTERNAL WORLD

AN INTERVIEW WITH
SALVATORE QUASIMODO

Salvatore Quasimodo (the family name is accented on the second syllable) was in New York recently and I called on him at the Hotel Gotham, accompanied by Professor Sergio Pacifici of Yale, who had come to town to escort the poet to a lecture in New Haven.

Signor Quasimodo met us at the door, waved us to chairs, and himself sat on the edge of the bed, leaning across it on one arm, very much at ease. He spoke rapidly, without rhetorical flourishes, but with the self-assurance of a man who has taken the time to think his way into himself. Signor Quasimodo, as his poems have dramatized and as his prose writings have explicated, has a firm conception of the role of the poet as the guardian of the culture of his people. By "culture" he understands "the internal organization of man." The never-ending conflict is between man's internal needs and the external forces upon him.

Having so defined his position, Signor Quasimodo developed it in an easy but precise flow of Italian that ranged over many subjects, and that—subject to all the perils of both translation and abridgment—ran about so:

Signor Quasimodo: No matter what the velocity of change in modern living, culture is the indestructible. "Culture" is, of course, an inclusive term. It contains within itself everything from artisanship to art, to poetry. But always it seeks to give form to the internal needs of man. Every society depends on its cultural development for its progress from the caves.

Change cannot destroy culture, nor the need for it. Even when the culture is given form by only a few men who become cultural islands, it will be reborn from those islands again and again. It is culture that wins, not armies.

During World War II Germany had won: there was a certain point at which the victory of Germany was a fact. But the next day it was no longer a fact. And not for military reasons. The man of culture had dug in his heels for the last time—in an extreme act of decision— and Germany had lost. It is always intelligence that wins; else we should still be back in the caves.

Question: Do you think it significant that the entire Nazi movement produced no artist of any real consequence?

Signor Quasimodo: How could it? When politics is pre-eminent, man disappears. He becomes but a number.

Question (by Professor Pacifici): Can the same thing be said of the Russians?

Signor Quasimodo: The same. Because what the artist does there is restricted by ideology: he cannot shape the culture in a true and absolute sense.

For ideology creates a philosophy, and philosophy is never the sum of a culture, but only one part. Under an ideology, this one part tries to impose itself as the total. And therein lies the central conflict: between the internal man and the forces that try to determine him from the outside.

What the Russians have cannot, of course, be measured by what we have in our democracies, but by what the Russians had under the Czar. That difference exists. And there *is* a force of cultural awareness there: one may see the housewives out shopping with a copy of the literary gazette under their arms. And there are many foreign students now in Russia. Many young Italians, for example, are studying in Moscow.

One fact remains: man keeps striving to realize his internal needs, and the external organization imposed by an ideology will never be enough for his purposes. But this external force and this internal need

—this conflict—exist also in the popular republics. In the West—in America, let us say—the question to be asked is: what sort of civil courage must a man of culture possess? How much must he resist? For the man of culture must always assume before the world the responsibility of his resistance. It is the literati who use poetry simply as play. For without this commitment no poet is more than a dilettante.

The history of man is a slow progress from his savagery. And the battle of the true man of culture in this progress has become a terrible one. For, increasingly, as he works for civilization, society refuses to recognize him. He ends by being trampled under the very forces he creates.

The middle class is guilty of grave wrongs in this conflict. At the end of the nineteenth century it was the middle class that fought for cultural liberty. At that time the middle class contained within itself all the men of culture—artists, poets, mathematicians—all the intelligentsia. But when it had achieved its freedom it began to think it could do without the intelligentsia. This is the decadence of the European middle class.

Question: What is the function of the poet in this conflict?

Signor Quasimodo: It is always important. As I have said, the true poet is no dilettante. His role is moral. Not that he determines the morality of his people. His morality—and this is the real point—is in finding the forms that will express anew for his generation the reality of human dignity. That is why the poet does not deal in the worn-out forms of past ages. The image of man is no eternal thing. We must remake it generation by generation.

Question: The poet creates a sort of "moral mirror" for his people?

Signor Quasimodo: Just so: a moral mirror. He is no pedantic moralizer. He does not write tracts. He writes his poems. And the poems do not dogmatize. The poet's morality is to recognize the eternal worth of humanity through every change. He studies himself and his fellows, and he forms within himself what might be called a genetic sentiment. He makes concrete images for the condition of man in every new age. All else is merely mental play, and barren.

Question: Does this function of the poet involve him in politics?

Signor Quasimodo: Politics does not enter into this. The poet *engagé* is finished. Such a poet climbs barricades to incite one part of his people against another. There is no such divisive sentiment in my poetry. What is needed, rather, is the historical recognition of the moment of mankind in terms of the total culture of one's people.

Question: The Swedish Academy, in awarding you the Nobel Prize, cited your interpretation of Italian culture as "a daily anonymous grief and the incessant contemplation of death." Do you accept that description of Italian culture?

Signor Quasimodo: Latins have—let us say—a cult of death; not so much in a philosophical sense but as a conditioning of their religious history. The church has been there a long time, we must recognize. And its influence has been profound, even upon those who no longer cling to the faith.

But that familiar preoccupation with death is only one part of the cultural motivation. More important is the need to find a common body of aesthetic values. And here we have a grave problem in Italian cultural history. Especially since the war. For with the end of the war factionalism returned to Italy.

The Italian, we must note, is always directed toward civil conflict. The Greeks invented civil war; the Latins perfected it. But the need of a true culture is to express values of an aesthetic order for all of a people, not for one faction and another.

Question: In your *Discourse on Poetry* you state that philosophers are the enemies of poetry. Does that conflict relate to the cultural conflict?

Signor Quasimodo: In an absolute sense this enmity has always been there. Philosophers—and critics too—have always sought to create *a priori* categoric systems. They try to prescribe what the poet should write, to determine the course of poetry. But the true criticism has always been after the fact of creation: descriptive, not prescriptive.

Question: In the same *Discourse* you stated that a poet must be valued for his content, not for his voice and cadence. Do you . . . ?

Signor Quasimodo: The intrinsic value of all poetry is recognizable as soon as one begins to read. But what is it one reads? That is the question. The poet is important for what he has to say.

Question: But is it possible to be a poet without developing a voice and a cadence? Without, that is to say, aesthetic form?

Signor Quasimodo: No. No. There must always be the formal content. Nothing can happen outside form. Form itself is what one says. Else we should all be philosophers. No. No. But we value poets for what they have to say to other men, for their communication.

As I have said, the good poet does not seek to communicate by repeating the worn-out forms of the past. Kafka, Proust, Joyce—these are great writers. But it will not do to rewrite them. The poet must make his forms anew, generation by generation. There are poets to-day who simply want to do over again what has already been done. But how can they? How, for example, can such a poet as Leopardi be born again? He was of a period that is now finished. Or Sappho— how could her poems have been written before or after her times?

Poetry will always be important to man. Whatever the form of society, there will always be poets. Should we come to a time when all books are published as movies, or as tapes to be played into your pillow as you sleep—still there will endure the man who thinks and who speaks and who writes.

And that man will still be concerned with man's changing image of himself. For there is no final type of man. And yet man's internal problems are always the same. Who can resolve those internal problems for him? He must resolve them himself—over and over again— however much the world may change around him.

Question: But, still, may not the philosopher have this same concern? What distinguishes the poet as poet?

Signor Quasimodo: The poet is born with a capacity for harmonies. That is why the ancients called poetry *canto*—not because it was accompanied by music. The dilettantes, the cerebral literati, seek these harmonies externally. They construct sequences of vowels and consonants; they prepare rules in advance for creating harmonies. But the true poet has them within himself. They are his way of speaking himself.

They are, that is to say, born in him. The merely cerebral poet can write endlessly—even ten poems a day. The poet refuses this sort of cerebration. He writes at unpredictable moments, in moments of rage.

Question (by Professor Pacifici): Or of serenity?

Signor Quasimodo: Perhaps. But, no, really of rage. "Why should I sit and write?" the poet says to himself. "Why should I not leave this desk and go out and live?" But his creative rage holds him. There is this voice that *must* say something. *That* is the poet. He cannot write at will. At times he can write nothing.

He does, to be sure, take on aesthetic difficulties. These are his formal elements. Rhyme, for example, is a difficulty. But it is also a help. It firms his poem for him.

But the technical passion alone is nothing. Had Dante stopped with the *Vita Nuova*, he would have remained a poet inferior to Guido Cavalcanti. But he passed on to reality—from the genteel lady to (if you will forgive the expression) the dungy fingernails.

Question: But what if Dante had never studied Virgil?

Signor Quasimodo: Ah, but one must study the techniques of the great poets. The poet's capacity for harmonies is born in him, but what is born must also grow.

For myself, what I seek is directness and concreteness of utterance; to find the purest and most immediate tongue, the tongue that makes true communication possible. All the great ancients wrote in this language. And it is this language that is enormously difficult to achieve —the language that will truly express the inner spiritual need of one's people in their conflict with the external forces of their times.